specters of marx

specters of marx

the state of the debt,
the work of mourning,
and the new international

Jacques Derrida

translated by
Peggy Kamuf

with an introduction by
Bernd Magnus
and Stephen Cullenberg

Routledge > New York and London

Published in 1994 by
Routledge
29 West 35 Street
New York, NY 10001

Published in Great Britain in 1994 by
Routledge
11 New Fetter Lane
London EC4P 4EE

English translation © 1994 by Routledge.
Originally published in French as *Spectres de Marx*, © Editions Galileé, 1993.

Copyright © 1994 by Routledge

Printed in the United States of America.

Library of Congress Cataloging-in-Publication Data
Derrida, Jacques
    [Spectres de Marx. English]
    Specters of Marx: the state of the debt, the work of mourning, and the New International / by Jacques Derrida; translated by Peggy Kamuf.
    p.   cm.
    Translation of Spectres de Marx..
    Includes index.
    ISBN 0-415-91044-7 — ISBN 0-415-91045-5 (pbk.)
    1. Marx, Karl, 1818–1883. 2. Communism. 3. Post-communism.
    I. Title
HX39.5.D4613   1994
335.4—dc20
                          94-20564
                          CIP

British Library Cataloguing-in-Publication Data also available

contents

editors' introduction

In the wake of the orgy of self-congratulations which followed the 1989 crumbling of the Berlin Wall, the subsequent dissolution of the Soviet Union, and a series of confrontations perhaps forever to be captured best in Tiananmen Square in the image of a single individual blocking the path of an onrushing military tank, a wave of optimism engulfed the Western democratic States. This contagious optimism was best exemplified by the confidence and popularity of Francis Fukuyama's claim that the end of history was at hand, that the future—if that word could still be said to have the same meaning—was to become the global triumph of free market economies.

At the same time many of us felt a vague sense of foreboding, a haunted sense that international changes of such magnitude were as likely to result, at least initially, and perhaps for a long time to come, in transformations as malign as they are benign. Some of us grew tired more quickly than others of the many hasty postmortems of Marxism, as if the virtually global collapse of communism and Marxism referred to the very same thing, especially in different times and places as well as to different thinkers.

And yet, it seemed to many that the collapse of communism in Eastern Europe and the Soviet Union, as well as democratic insurgencies in China, had created a new world order. Politicians from George Bush to Václav Havel had proclaimed that the ideological and political alliances which structured the global community prior to 1989 must now be rethought and restructured. Less dramatically, but just as significantly, the economic integration of Europe beginning in 1992, and the continued economic growth of Japan and the emergence of South Korea, Taiwan, and Singapore as economic forces have all profoundly changed the international economic, social, and political land-scapes. The meaning and consequences of these changes are of vital importance to us all; no discipline or sector of culture has a monopoly on potential analyses, much less a monopoly on answers.

In response to the changing social, political, philosophical, and economic dimensions of the global community, scholars and intellectuals throughout the world are rethinking the meaning of past verities and developing new theoretical approaches. Among the central contested issues: What remains of the socialist vision(s) after the "collapse" in 1989? Has the collapse of communism also spelled the death of Marxism, and of Marx as an important philosopher and political thinker? Have we indeed reached "the end of history" as Fukuyama has argued, where pluralistic democracies and capitalist economies reign supreme? Is the future now to be simply a choice between Scandinavian-style social democracy on the one hand, and unrestrained free market capitalism on the other? Given the difficulties some democratic, free market economies are experiencing—including the plight of the homeless, the lack of adequate health care, environmental degradation, and enormous national debt burdens—what sort of model for the future do we have? And what is one to make of the destructive, even violent "nationalisms" which have followed in the wake of the collapse of communism, not to mention virulent forms of ethnocentrism and xenophobia perhaps not seen since Hitler's Germany? What does this imply, then, about the future structure and func-tioning of the global economy and life throughout our shared world? What new international tensions will emerge and what will be the nature of theoretical and political discourse as we approach the twenty-first century? Who must ask such questions and to whom must they be addressed?

In particular, how will intellectuals in the Marxist tradition respond, theoretically and politically, to the global transformations now occurring? How has the crisis in Eastern Europe and the former Soviet Union affected the way intellectuals, scholars, and government officials in those countries and around the world reconceive their intellectual and political projects? What is to be the status of Marxist social goals that informed so many Marxist thinkers and social revolutionaries throughout the world—the egalitarian distribution of income, increased workplace democracy, the end of economic exploitation and the eradication of class differences—given the current rush to various forms of capitalism in Eastern Europe, Russia, and China? Does the "end of history" also portend the end of Marxist theory? What is living and what is dead in Marxism?

In October 1991, in an environment charged by such questions, several of us began a conversation at the University of California, at Riverside's Center for Ideas and Society, about what it might be like to have a conference which would *not* consist of yet another autopsy administered mostly by Anglophone economists and policy analysts who typically were and are very far from the sites of struggle and transformation. We wondered how our colleagues on location, so to speak, understand their circumstances, both historically and philosophically.

We decided to convene a multinational, multidisciplinary conference—"Whither Marxism? Global Crises in International Perspective"—which would include distinguished thinkers and participants from China, Russia, Armenia, Poland, Romania, Mexico, Germany, France, the United States and elsewhere. Equally important, it seemed to us significant to provide a forum within which one of the most famous and influential contemporary philosophers—Jacques Derrida—could reflect on the conference's topic, something he had not yet been able to do in a sustained and systematic way in print. We thought that such a sustained reflection on Marx by Derrida would be of intrinsic as well as historical importance.

The conference itself was organized and managed by the Center for Ideas and Society at the University of California, Riverside. It began on Thursday, April 22, 1993 with Jacques Derrida's plenary address and ended on Saturday,

April 24, 1993. His plenary address was delivered in two parts, on the evenings of April 22nd and 23rd. That lecture, "Specters of Marx: The State of the Debt, the Work of Mourning, and the New International," is the basis of the text now before you, a text which bears the same name; and this longer version—"augmented, clarified..." as Derrida says—is no less marked by that occasion, setting, and interlocutors than is the original plenary address.

It would be inappropriate, indeed, impossible, to convey in summary the many specters that haunt the texts of Marx, and, through him, of Derrida. Here we would merely wish to note that in this text Derrida takes his position for a certain spirit of Marxism, that "deconstruction," if there is such a thing, always already moves within a certain spirit of Marx. It should also be noted that, for Derrida, in speaking of a certain spirit of Marx

> it is not in the first place in order to propose a scholarly, philosophical discourse. It is first of all so as not to flee from a responsibility. More precisely, it is in order to submit for your discussion several hypotheses on the nature of such a responsibility. What is ours? In what way is it historical? And what does it have to do with so many specters?

Jacques Derrida's *Specters of Marx: The State of the Debt, the Work of Mourning, and the New International* is intended to be in conversation with and supplemented by its companion volume of conference essays, *Whither Marxism? Global Crises in International Perspective.* This second volume contains selected conference essays by Ashot K. Galoian, Keith Griffin and Azizur Rahman Khan, Abdul JanMohamed, Douglas Kellner, Andrei Marga, Stephen Resnick and Richard Wolff, Gayatri Chakravorty Spivak, Su Shaozhi, Carlos M. Villas, and Zhang Longxi.

While some of the essays are in direct conversation with the text of Derrida, others illustrate the force of his argument, whether they intend to do so or not. Specifically and telegraphically, at least four points of contact emerge from Derrida's *Specters of Marx* and its companion volume *Whither Marxism?* (1) The proper names "Marx" and/or Marxism have always already been plural nouns, despite their grammatical form, and despite the fact that they have been understood as if they were rigid designators; (2) "communism" (in its own pluralities) is not the same as "Marxism"; (3) both communism and Marxism are historically sited, situated, inflected, mediated by particular traditions and histories; (4) the proper name "Marx" is—in a certain sense—

entirely uncircumventable.

The purpose of these two volumes, *Specters of Marx* and *Whither Marxism?* is to begin to address questions about the connection between the death of communism and the fate of Marxism. The volumes raise these questions in an international and interdisciplinary context. Their goal is not simply to produce another postmortem on Marxism, nor is it simply to defend Marxism against its critics. Rather, these volumes, each in its own way, explore the effects that the global crises engendered by the collapse of communism has had on avant-garde scholars, many of whom have lived through and often participated in these transitions themselves.

—Bernd Magnus and Stephen Cullenberg

note on the text

At the origin of this work was a lecture given in two sessions, April 22 and 23, 1993, at the University of California, Riverside. That lecture opened an international colloquium organized by Bernd Magnus and Stephen Cullenberg under the ambiguous title "Whither Marxism?" in which one may hear beneath the question "Where is Marxism going?" another question: "Is Marxism dying?"

Augmented, clarified, the present text nevertheless retains the argumentative structure, the rhythm, and the oral form of the lecture. Notes were added later, of course. A few new developments appear in square brackets.

dedication

O*ne name for another, a part for the whole: the historic violence of Apartheid can always be treated as a metonymy. In its past as well as in its present. By diverse paths (condensation, displacement, expression, or representation), one can always decipher through its singularity so many other kinds of violence going on in the world. At once part, cause, effect, example, what is happening there translates what* takes place *here, always here, wherever one is and wherever one looks, closest to home. Infinite responsibility, therefore, no rest allowed for any form of good conscience.*

But one should never speak of the assassination of a man as a figure, not even an exemplary figure in the logic of an emblem, a rhetoric of the flag or of martyrdom. A man's life, as unique as his death, will always be more than a paradigm and something other than a symbol. And this is precisely what a proper name should always name.

address, the one that goes most often from father to son, master to disciple, or master to slave ("I'm going to teach you to live"). Such an address hesitates, therefore: between address as *experience* (is not learning to live experience itself?), address as *education*, and address as *taming* or *training* [dressage].

But to learn to live, to learn it *from oneself and by oneself*, all alone, to teach *oneself* to live ("I would like to learn to live finally"), is that not impossible for a living being? Is it not what logic itself forbids? To live, by definition, is not something one learns. Not from oneself, it is not learned from life, taught by life. Only from the other and by death. In any case from the other at the edge of life. At the internal border or the external border, it is a heterodidactics between life and death.

And yet nothing is more necessary than this wisdom. It is ethics itself: to learn to live—alone, from oneself, by oneself. Life does not know how to live otherwise. And does one ever do anything else but learn to live, alone, from oneself, by oneself? This is, therefore, a strange commitment, both impossible and necessary, for a living being supposed to be alive: "I would like to learn to live." It has no sense and cannot be *just* unless it comes to terms with death.[2] Mine as (well as) that of the other. Between life and death, then, this is indeed the place of a sententious injunction that always feigns to speak like the just.

What follows advances like an essay in the night—into the unknown of that which must remain to come—a simple attempt, therefore, to analyze with some consistency such an exordium: "I would like to learn to live. Finally." Finally what.

If it—learning to live—remains to be done, it can happen only between life and death. Neither in life nor in death *alone*. What happens between two, and between all the "two's" one likes, such as between life and death, can only *maintain itself* with some ghost, can only *talk with or about* some ghost [s'entretenir *de quelque fantôme*]. So it would be necessary to learn spirits. Even and especially if this, the spectral, *is not*. Even and especially if this, which is neither substance, nor essence, nor existence, *is never present as such*. The time of the "learning to live," a time without tutelary present, would amount to this, to which the exordium is leading us: to learn to live *with* ghosts, in the upkeep, the conversation, the company, or the companionship, in the commerce without commerce of ghosts. To live otherwise, and better. No, not better, but more justly. But *with them*. No *being-with* the other, no *socius* without this *with* that makes *being-with* in general more enigmatic than ever for us. And

specter, that is how Marx, along with Engels, will have also thought, described, or diagnosed a certain dramaturgy of modern Europe, notably that of its great unifying projects. One would even have to say that he represented it or staged it. In the shadow of a filial memory, Shakespeare will have often inspired this Marxian theatricalization. Later, closer to us but according to the same genealogy, in the nocturnal noise of its concatenation, the rumbling sound of ghosts chained to ghosts, another descendant would be Valéry. *Shakespeare qui genuit Marx qui genuit Valéry* (and a few others).

But what goes on *between* these generations? An omission, a strange lapsus. *Da*, then *fort*, exit Marx. In "La crise de l'esprit" ("The Crisis of Spirit," 1919: "As for us, civilizations, we know now we are mortal…"), the name of Marx appears just once. It inscribes itself, here is the name of a skull to come into Hamlet's hands:

> Now, on an immense terrace of Elsinore, which stretches from Basel to Cologne, that touches on the sands of Nieuport, the lowlands of the Somme, the chalky earth of Champagne, the granite earth of Alsace— the European Hamlet looks at thousands of specters. But he is an intellectual Hamlet. He meditates on the life and death of truths. His ghosts are all the objects of our controversies; his remorse is all the titles of our glory…. If he seizes a skull, it is an illustrious skull—"Whose was it?"—This one was *Lionardo*…. And this other skull is that of *Leibniz* who dreamed of universal peace. And this one was *Kant qui genuit Hegel, qui genuit Marx, qui genuit*…. Hamlet does not know what to do with all these skulls. But if he abandons them!… Will he cease to be himself?[3]

Later, in "La politique de l'esprit," Valéry has just defined man and politics. Man: "an attempt to create what I will venture to call *the spirit of spirit*."[4] As for politics, it always "implies some idea of man." At this point, Valéry quotes himself. He reproduces the page of "the European Hamlet," the one we have just cited. Curiously, with the errant but infallible assurance of a sleepwalker, he then omits from it only *one* sentence, *just one*, without even signalling the omission by an ellipsis: the one that names Marx, in the very skull of Kant ("And this one was *Kant qui genuit Hegel, qui genuit Marx, qui genuit*…").[5] Why this omission, the only one? The name of Marx has disappeared. Where did it go? *Exeunt Ghost and Marx*, Shakespeare might have noted. The name of the one who disappeared must have gotten inscribed someplace else.

In what he says, as well as in what he forgets to say about the skulls and generations of spirits, Valéry reminds us of at least *three things*. These three things concern precisely this *thing* that is called spirit. As soon as one no longer distinguishes spirit from specter, the former assumes a body, it incarnates itself, as spirit, in the specter. Or rather, as Marx himself spells out, and we will get to this, the specter is a paradoxical incorporation, the becoming-body, a certain phenomenal and carnal form of the spirit. It becomes, rather, some "thing" that remains difficult to name: neither soul nor body, and both one and the other. For it is flesh and phenomenality that give to the spirit its spectral apparition, but which disappear right away in the apparition, in the very coming of the *revenant* or the return of the specter. There is something disappeared, departed in the apparition itself as reapparition of the departed. The spirit, the specter are not the same thing, and we will have to sharpen this difference; but as for what they have in common, one does not know what it *is*, what it is presently. *It is* something that one does not know, precisely, and one does not know if precisely it *is*, if it exists, if it responds to a name and corresponds to an essence. One does not know: not out of ignorance, but because this non-object, this non-present present, this being-there of an absent or departed one no longer belongs to knowledge. At least no longer to that which one thinks one knows by the name of knowledge. One does not know if it is living or if it is dead. Here is—or rather there is, over there, an unnameable or almost unnameable thing: something, between something and someone, anyone or anything, some thing, "this thing," but this thing and not any other, this thing that looks at us, that concerns us [*qui nous regarde*], comes to defy semantics as much as ontology, psychoanalysis as much as philosophy ("*Marcellus*: What, ha's this thing appear'd againe tonight? *Barnardo*: I haue seene nothing"). The Thing is still invisible, it is *nothing* visible ("I haue seene nothing") at the moment one speaks of it and in order to ask oneself if it has reappeared. It is still nothing that can be seen when one speaks of it. It is no longer anything that can be seen when Marcellus speaks of it, but it has been seen twice. And it is in order to adjust speech to sight that Horatio the skeptic has been convoked. He will serve as third party and witness (*terstis*): "...if againe this Apparition come, He may approue our eyes and speake to it" (I, i).

Nor does one see in flesh and blood this Thing that is not a thing, this thing that is invisible between its apparitions, when it reappears. This Thing meanwhile looks at us and sees us not see it even when it is there. A spectral asymmetry interrupts here all specularity. It de-synchronizes, it recalls us to anachrony. We will call this the *visor effect*: we do not see who looks at us. Even though in his ghost the King looks like himself ("As thou art to thy selfe," says Horatio), that does not prevent him from looking without being seen: his apparition makes him appear still invisible beneath his armor ("Such was the very Armour he had on…"). We will probably not speak of this *visor effect* any more, at least not by that name, but it will be presupposed by everything we advance on the subject of the specter in general, in Marx and elsewhere. As will be spelled out later on the basis of *The German Ideology* and the argument with Stirner, what distinguishes the specter or the *revenant* from the *spirit*, including the spirit in the sense of the ghost in general, is doubtless a supernatural and paradoxical phenomenality, the furtive and ungraspable visibility of the invisible, or an invisibility of a visible X, that *non-senuous sensuous* of which *Capital* speaks (we will come to this) with regard to a certain exchange-value; it is also, no doubt, the tangible intangibility of a proper body without flesh, but still the body of some*one* as some*one other*. And of some*one other* that we will not hasten to determine as self, subject, person, consciousness, spirit, and so forth. This already suffices to distinguish the specter not only from the icon or the idol but also from the image of the image, from the Platonic *phantasma*, as well as from the simple *simulacrum* of something in general to which it is nevertheless so close and with which it shares, in other respects, more than one feature. But that is not all, and that is not the most irreducible. Another suggestion: This spectral *someone other looks at us,*[6] we feel ourselves being looked at by it, outside of any synchrony, even before and beyond any look on our part, according to an absolute anteriority (which may be on the order of generation, of more than one generation) and asymmetry, according to an absolutely unmasterable disproportion. Here anachony makes the law. To feel ourselves seen by a look which it will always be impossible to cross, that is the *visor effect* on the basis of which we inherit from the law. Since we do not see the one who sees us, and who makes the law, who delivers the injunction (which is, moreover, a contradictory injunction), since we do not see the one who orders "swear," we cannot identify it in all certainty, we must fall back on its voice. The one who says "I am thy Fathers Spirit" can only be taken at his word. An essentially blind submission to his secret, to the secret of his origin: this is a first obedience to the injunction. It will condition all the others. It may always be a case of still someone else. Another can always lie, he can disguise himself as a ghost, another ghost may also be passing himself off for this one. It's always possible. Later we will talk about the *society* or the *commerce* of specters among themselves, for there is always *more than one* of them. The armor, this "costume" which no stage production will ever be able to leave out, we see it cover from head to foot, in Hamlet's eyes, the supposed body of the father. We do not know whether it is or is not part of the spectral apparition. This protection is rigorously *problematic* (*problema* is also a shield) for it prevents perception from deciding on the identity that it wraps so solidly in its carapace. The armor may be but the body of a real artifact, a kind of technical prosthesis, a body foreign to the spectral body that it dresses, dissimulates, and protects, masking even its identity. The armor lets one see nothing of the spectral body, but at the level of the head and *beneath the visor*, it permits the so-called father to see and to speak. Some slits are cut into it and adjusted so as to permit him to see without being seen, but to speak in order to be heard. The *helmet*, like the visor, did not merely offer protection: it topped off the coat of arms and indicated the chief's authority, like the blazon of his nobility.

For the helmet effect, it suffices that a visor be *possible* and that one play with it. Even when it is raised, *in fact*, its possibility continues to signify that someone, beneath the armor, can safely see without being seen or without being identified. Even when it is raised, the visor remains, an available resource and structure, solid and stable as armor, the armor that covers the body from head to foot, the armor of which it is a part and to which it is attached. This is what distinguishes a visor from the mask with which, nevertheless, it shares this incomparable power, perhaps the supreme insignia of power: the power to see without being seen. The helmet effect is not suspended when the visor is raised. Its power, namely its possibility, is in that case recalled merely in a more intensely dramatic fashion. When Horatio reports to Hamlet that a figure like his father's appeared "Arm'd at all points exactly, *Cap a Pe*..."), the son is worried and questions. He first insists on the armor and the "Cap a Pe" ("*Hamlet:* Arm'd, say you? *Barnardo and Marcellus:* Arm'd, my Lord. *Hamlet:* From top to toe? *Both:* My Lord, from head to foote"). Then Hamlet gets to the head, to the face, and especially the look beneath the visor. As if he had been hoping that, beneath an armor that hides and protects from head to foot, the ghost would have shown neither his face, nor his look, nor therefore his identity ("*Hamlet:* Then saw you not his face? *Horatio:* Oh yes, my Lord, he wore his Beaver up" [I, ii]).

Three things, then, would decompose in analysis this single *thing*, spirit, or specter—or king, for the king occupies this place, here the place of the father, whether he keeps it, takes it, or usurps it, and beyond the return of the rhyme (for example "The Play's the thing,/ Wherein Ile catch the Conscience of the King"). King is a thing, Thing is the King, precisely where he separates from his body which, however, does not leave him (contract of secession, necessary pact in order to have *more than one body*, that is, in order to reign, and, first of all, to inherit royal dignity, whether by crime or election: "The body is with the King, but the King is not with the body. The King, is a thing").

What, then, are these *three things of the thing*?

1. First of all, mourning. We will be speaking of nothing else. It consists always in attempting to ontologize remains, to make them present, in the first place by *identifying* the bodily remains and by *localizing* the dead (all ontologization, all semanticization—philosophical, hermeneutical, or psychoanalytical—finds itself caught up in this work of mourning but, as such, it does not yet think it; we are posing here the question of the specter, to the specter, whether it be Hamlet's or Marx's, on this near side of such thinking). One has to know. *One has to know it. One has to have knowledge* [Il faut le savoir]. Now, to know is to know *who* and *where*, to know whose body it really is and what place it occupies—for it must stay in its place. In a safe place. Hamlet does not ask merely to whom the skull belonged ("Whose was it?" the question that Valéry quotes). He demands to know to whom the grave belongs ("Whose grave's this, sir?"). Nothing could be worse, for the work of mourning, than confusion or doubt: one *has to know* who is buried where—and *it is necessary* (to know—to make certain) that, in what remains of him, *he remain there*. Let him stay there and move no more!

2. Next, one cannot speak of generations of skulls or spirits (*Kant qui genuit Hegel qui genuit Marx*) except on the condition of language—and the voice, in any case of that which *marks* the name or takes its place ("*Hamlet*: That Scull had a tongue in it, and could sing once").

3. Finally (*Marx qui genuit Valéry...*), the thing *works*, whether it transforms or transforms itself, poses or decomposes itself: the spirit, the "spirit of the spirit" is *work*. But what is work? What is its concept if it supposes the spirit of the spirit? Valéry underscores it: "By 'Spirit' here I mean a certain *power of transformation...the spirit...works*."[7]

So "Whither Marxism?" That is the question the title of this colloquium would ask us. In what way would it be signaling toward Hamlet and Denmark and England? Why does it whisper to us to *follow* a ghost? Where? Whither? What does it mean to follow a ghost? And what if this came down to being followed by it, always, persecuted perhaps by the very chase we are leading? Here again what seems to be out front, the future, comes back in advance: from the past, from the back. "Something is rotten in the state of Denmark," declares Marcellus at the point at which Hamlet is preparing, precisely, to *follow* the ghost ("I'll follow thee" [I, iv]). And he too will soon ask him "Whither?": "Where wilt thou lead me? speak; I'll go no further. *Ghost*: Mark me…I am thy Fathers Spirit."]

Repetition *and* first time: this is perhaps the question of the event as question of the ghost. *What is* a ghost? What is the *effectivity* or the *presence* of a specter, that is, of what seems to remain as ineffective, virtual, insubstantial as a simulacrum? Is there *there*, between the thing itself and its simulacrum, an opposition that holds up? Repetition *and* first time, but also repetition *and* last time, since the singularity of any *first time* makes of it also a *last time.* Each time it is the event itself, a first time is a last time. Altogether other. Staging for the end of history. Let us call it a *hauntology.* This logic of haunting would not be merely larger and more powerful than an ontology or a thinking of Being (of the "to be," assuming that it is a matter of Being in the "to be or not to be," but nothing is less certain). It would harbor within itself, but like circumscribed places or particular effects, eschatology and teleology themselves. It would *comprehend* them, but incomprehensibly. How to *comprehend* in fact the discourse of the end or the discourse about the end? Can the extremity of the extreme ever be comprehended? And the opposition between "to be" and "not to be"? *Hamlet* already began with the expected return of the dead King. After the end of history, the spirit comes by *coming back* [revenant], it figures *both* a dead man who comes back and a ghost whose expected return repeats itself, again and again.

Oh, Marx's love for Shakespeare! It is well known. Chris Hani shared the same passion. I have just learned this and I like the idea. Even though Marx more often quotes *Timon of Athens*, the *Manifesto* seems to evoke or convoke, right from the start, the first coming of the silent ghost, the apparition of the spirit that does not answer, on those ramparts of Elsinore which is then the old Europe. For if this first theatrical apparition already marked a repetition, it implicated political power in the folds of this iteration ("In the same figure, like the King that's dead," says Barnardo as soon as he thinks he recognizes the "Thing," in his irrepressible desire for identification). From what could be called the other time, from the other scene, from the eve of the play, the witnesses of history fear and hope for a return, then, "again" and "again," a coming and going. (*Marcellus:* "What, ha's this thing appear'd againe tonight?" Then: *Enter the Ghost, Exit the Ghost, Enter the Ghost, as before*). A question of repetition: a specter is always a *revenant*. One cannot control its comings and goings because it *begins by coming back*. Think as well of Macbeth, and remember the specter of Caesar. After having expired, he returns. Brutus also says "*again*—": "Well; then I shall see thee again?" *Ghost:* "Ay, at Philippi" (IV, ii).

Now, one may very well wish to take a breath. Or let out a sigh: after the expiration itself, for it is a matter of the spirit. What seems almost impossible is to speak always *of the* specter, to speak *to the* specter, to speak with it, therefore especially *to make or to let* a spirit *speak*. And the thing seems even more difficult for a reader, an expert, a professor, an interpreter, in short, for what Marcellus calls a "scholar." Perhaps for a spectator in general. Finally, the last one to whom a specter can appear, address itself, or pay attention is a spectator as such. At the theater or at school. The reasons for this are essential. As theoreticians or witnesses, spectators, observers, and intellectuals, scholars believe that looking is sufficient. Therefore, they are not always in the most competent position to do what is necessary: speak to the specter. Herein lies perhaps, among so many others, an indelible lesson of Marxism. There is no longer, there has never been a scholar capable of speaking of anything and everything while addressing himself to everyone and anyone, and especially to ghosts. There has never been a scholar who really, and as scholar, deals with ghosts. A traditional scholar does not believe in ghosts—nor in all that could be called the virtual space of spectrality. There has never been a scholar who, as such, does not believe in the sharp distinction between the real and the unreal, the actual and the inactual, the living and the non-living, being and non-being ("to be or not to be," in the conventional reading), in the opposition between what is present and what is not, for example in the form of objectivity. Beyond this opposition, there is, for the scholar, only the hypothesis of a school of thought, theatrical fiction, literature, and speculation. If we were to refer uniquely to this traditional figure of the "scholar," we would therefore have to be wary here of what we could define as the illusion, the mystification, or the *complex of Marcellus*. The latter was perhaps not in a situation to understand that a classical scholar would not be able to speak to the ghost. Marcellus did not know what the singularity of a position is, let's not call it a class position as one used to say long ago, but the singularity of a place of speech, of a place of experience, and of a link of filiation, places and links from which alone one may address oneself to the ghost. "Thou art a Scholler— speake to it, Horatio," he says naively, as if he were taking part in a colloquium. He appeals to the scholar or to the learned intellectual, to the man of culture as a spectator who better understands how to establish the necessary distance or how to find the appropriate words for observing, better yet, for apostrophizing the ghost, which is to say also for speaking the language of kings or of the dead. For Barnardo has just spied the face of the dead king, he thinks he has identified it through its likeness ("*Barnardo:* In the same figure, like the King that's dead. *Marcellus:* Thou art a Scholler—speake to it, Horatio"). He does not ask him merely to speak to the ghost, but to call it, interpellate it, interrogate it, more precisely, to question the Thing that it still is: "Question it Horatio." And Horatio enjoins the Thing to speak, he orders it to do so twice in a gesture that is at once imperious and accusing. He orders, he summons at the same time as he conjures ("By heaven I Charge thee speake! ...speake, speake! I Charge thee, speake!"). And in French, in fact, "I charge thee" is often translated by "je t'en conjure," which indicates a path where later we will see injunction crossing with conjuration. By charging or conjuring him to speak, Horatio wants to inspect, stabilize, *arrest* the specter in its speech: "(For which, they say, you Spirits oft walke in death) —Speake of it. Stay and speake. — Stop it Marcellus."

Inversely, Marcellus was perhaps anticipating the coming, one day, one night, several centuries later, of another "scholar." The latter would finally be capable, beyond the opposition between presence and non-presence, actuality and inactuality, life and non-life, of thinking the possibility of the specter, the specter as possibility. Better (or worse) he would know how to address himself to spirits. He would know that such an address is not only already possible, but that it will have at all times conditioned, as such, address in general. In any case, here is someone mad enough to hope to *unlock* the possibility of such an address.

It was thus a fault on my part to have put so far out of memory what was the most manifest thing about the *Manifesto*. What manifests itself in the first place is a specter, this first paternal character, as powerful as it is unreal, a hallucination or simulacrum that is virtually more actual than what is so blithely called a living presence. Upon rereading the *Manifesto* and a few other great works of Marx, I said to myself that I know of few texts in the philosophical tradition, perhaps none, whose lesson seemed more urgent *today*, provided that one take into account what Marx and Engels themselves say (for example, in Engels' "Preface" to the 1888 re-edition) about their own possible "aging" and their intrinsically irreducible historicity. What other thinker has ever issued a similar warning in such an explicit fashion? Who has ever called for the *transformation* to come of his own theses? Not only in view of some progressive enrichment of knowledge, which would change nothing in the order of a system, but so as to take into account there, another account, the effects of rupture and restructuration? And so as to incorporate in advance, beyond any possible programming, the unpredictability of new knowledge, new techniques, and new political givens? No text in the tradition seems as lucid concerning the way in which the political is becoming worldwide, concerning the irreducibility of the technical and the media in the current of the most thinking thought—and this goes beyond the railroad and the newspapers of the time whose powers were analyzed in such an incomparable way in the *Manifesto*. And few texts have shed so much light on law, international law, and nationalism.

It will always be a fault not to read and reread and discuss Marx—which is to say also a few others—and to go beyond scholarly "reading" or "discussion." It will be more and more a fault, a failing of theoretical, philosophical, political responsibility. When the dogma machine and the "Marxist" ideological apparatuses (States, parties, cells, unions, and other places of doctrinal production) are in the process of disappearing, we no longer have any excuse, only alibis, for turning away from this responsibility. There will be no future without this. Not without Marx, no future without Marx, without the memory and the inheritance of Marx: in any case of a certain Marx, of his genius, of at least one of his spirits. For this will be our hypothesis or rather our bias: *there is more than one of them, there must be more than one of them.*

Nevertheless, among all the temptations I will have to resist today, there would be the temptation of memory: to recount what was for me, and for those of my *generation* who shared it during a whole lifetime, the experience of Marxism, the quasi-paternal figure of Marx, the way it fought in us with other filiations, the reading of texts and the interpretation of a world in which the Marxist inheritance was—and still remains, and so it will remain—absolutely and thoroughly determinate. One need not be a Marxist or a communist in order to accept this obvious fact. We all live in a world, some would say a culture, that still bears, at an incalculable depth, the mark of this inheritance, whether in a directly visible fashion or not.

Among the traits that characterize a certain experience that belongs to my generation, that is, an experience that will have lasted at least forty years, and which is not over, I will isolate first of all a troubling paradox. I am speaking of a troubling effect of "déjà vu," and even of a certain "toujours déjà vu." I recall this malaise of perception, hallucination, and time because of the theme that brings us together this evening: "whither Marxism?" For many of us the question has the same age as we do. In particular for those who, and this was also my case, opposed, to be sure, *de facto* "Marxism" or "communism" (the Soviet Union, the International of Communist Parties, and everything that resulted from them, which is to say so very many things…), but intended at least never to do so out of conservative or reactionary motivations or even moderate right-wing or republican positions. For many of us, a certain (and I emphasize *certain*) end of communist Marxism did not await the recent collapse of the USSR and everything that depends on it throughout the world. All that started—all that was even *déjà vu*, indubitably—at the beginning of the '50s. Therefore, the question that brings us together this evening—"whither Marxism?"—resonates like an old repetition. It was already, but in an altogether different way, the question that imposed itself on the many young people who we were at the time. The same question had already *sounded.* The same, to be sure, but in an altogether different way. And the difference in the sound, that is what is echoing this evening. It is still evening, it is always night-fall along the "ramparts," on the battlements of an old Europe at war. With the other and with itself.

Why? It was the same question, already, as final question. Many young people today (of the type "readers-consumers of Fukuyama" or of the type "Fukuyama" himself) probably no longer sufficiently realize it: the eschatological themes of the "end of history," of the "end of Marxism," of the "end of philosophy," of the "ends of man," of the "last man" and so forth were, in the '50s, that is, forty years ago, our daily bread. We had this bread of apocalypse in our mouths naturally, already, just as naturally as that which I nicknamed after the fact, in 1980, the "apocalyptic tone in philosophy."

What was its consistency? What did it taste like? It was, *on the one hand*, the reading or analysis of those whom we could nickname the *classics of the end*. They formed the canon of the modern apocalypse (end of History, end of Man, end of Philosophy, Hegel, Marx, Nietzsche, Heidegger, with their Kojevian codicil and the codicils of Kojève himself). It was, *on the other hand and indissociably*, what we had known or what some of us for quite some time no longer hid from concerning totalitarian terror in all the Eastern countries, all the socio-economic disasters of Soviet bureaucracy, the Stalinism of the past and the neo-Stalinism in process (roughly speaking, from the Moscow trials to the repression in Hungary, to take only these minimal indices). Such was no doubt the element in which what is called deconstruction developed— and one can understand nothing of this period of deconstruction, notably in France, unless one takes this historical entanglement into account. Thus, for those with whom I shared this singular period, this double and unique experience (both philosophical and political), for us, I venture to say, the media parade of current discourse on the end of history and the last man looks most often like a tiresome anachronism. At least up to a certain point that will have to be specified later on. Something of this tiresomeness, moreover, comes across in the body of today's most *phenomenal culture*: what one hears, reads, and sees, what is most *mediatized* in Western capitals. As for those who abandon themselves to that discourse with the jubilation of youthful enthusiasm, they look like latecomers, a little as if it were possible to take still the last train after the last train—and yet be late to an end of history.

How can one be late to the end of history? A question for today. It is serious because it obliges one to reflect again, as we have been doing since Hegel, on what happens and deserves the name of *event*, after history; it obliges one to wonder if the end of history is but the end of a *certain* concept of history. Here is perhaps one of the questions that should be asked of those who are not content just to arrive late to the apocalypse and to the last train of the end, if I can put it like that, without being out of breath, but who find the means to puff out their chests with the good conscience of capitalism, liberalism, and the virtues of parliamentary democracy—a term with which we designate not parliamentarism and political representation *in general*, but the *present*, which is to say in fact, *past* forms of the electoral and parliamentary apparatus.

We are going to have to complicate this outline in a moment. We will have to put forward another reading of the media's anachronism and of good conscience. But so that one might better appreciate the discouraging impression of *déjà vu*, which risks causing us to drop all this literature on the end of history and other similar diagnoses, I will quote only (from among so many other possible examples) an essay from 1959 whose author *also* published a fiction *already* entitled, in 1957, *The Last Man*. About thirty-five years ago, then, Maurice Blanchot devoted an article, "The End of Philosophy," to a good half-dozen books from the '50s.[8] They were all testimonies from former Marxists or communists, and just in France. Blanchot would later write "On an Approach to Communism" and "Marx's Three Voices."[9]

[I would have liked to quote here, so as to subscribe to them without reservation, the three admirable pages that bear the title "Marx's Three Voices" ["Les trois paroles de Marx"]. With the sober brilliance of an incomparable density, in a manner that is at once discreet and dazzling, their utterances are less the full response to a question than the measure of that to which we must respond today, inheritors that we are of *more than one* form of speech, as well as of an injunction that is itself *disjointed*.

Let us consider first of all, the radical and necessary *heterogeneity* of an inheritance, the difference without opposition that has to mark it, a "disparate" and a quasi-juxtaposition without dialectic (the very plural of what we will later call Marx's spirit*s*). An inheritance is never gathered together, it is never one with itself. Its presumed unity, if there is one, can consist only in the *injunction* to *reaffirm by choosing*. "One must" means one *must* filter, sift, criticize, one must sort out several different possibles that inhabit the same injunction. And inhabit it in a contradictory fashion around a secret. If the readability of a legacy were given, natural, transparent, univocal, if it did not call for and at the same time defy interpretation, we would never have anything to inherit from it. We would be affected by it as by a cause—natural or genetic. One always inherits from a secret—which says "read me, will you ever be able to do so?" The critical choice called for by any reaffirmation of the inheritance is also, like memory itself, the condition of finitude. The infinite does not inherit, it does not inherit (from) itself. The injunction itself (it always says "choose and decide from among what you inherit") can only be one by dividing itself, tearing itself apart, differing/deferring itself, by speaking at the same time several times—and in several voices. For example:

In Marx, and always coming from Marx, we see three kinds of voices gathering force and taking form, all three of which are necessary, but separated and more than opposed, as if they were juxtaposed. The disparate that holds them together designates a plurality of demands to which, *since Marx*, everyone who speaks or writes can not fail to feel himself subjected, *unless he is to feel himself failing in everything*. (P. 18; my emphasis)

"Unless he is to feel himself failing in everything": What does that mean? And "since Marx"?

To fail in everything, it is true, will always remain possible. Nothing will ever give us any insurance against this risk, still less against this feeling. And a "since Marx" continues to designate the place of assignation from which we are *pledged*. But if there is pledge or assignation, injunction or promise, if there has been this appeal beginning with a word that resounds before us, the "since" marks a place and a time that doubtless precedes us, but so as to be as much *in front of us* as *before us*. Since the future, then, since the past as absolute future, since the non-knowledge and the non-advent of an event, of what remains to be: to do and to decide (which is first of all, no doubt, the sense of the "to be or not to be" of Hamlet—and of any inheritor who, let us say, comes to swear before a ghost). If "since Marx" names a future-to-come as much as a past, the past of a proper name, it is because the proper of a proper name will always remain to come. And secret. It will remain to come not like the future now [*maintenant*] of that which "holds together" the "disparate" (and Blanchot says the impossible of a "disparate" that itself "holds together"; it remains to be thought how a disparate could still, itself, hold together, and if one can ever speak of the *disparate itself*, selfsame, of a sameness without property). What has been uttered "since Marx" can only promise or remind one to maintain together, in a speech that defers, deferring not what it affirms but deferring just *so as to* affirm, to affirm *justly*, so as to have the power (a power without power) to affirm the coming of the event, its future-to-come itself.

Blanchot does not name Shakespeare here, but I cannot hear "since Marx," since Marx, without hearing, like Marx, "since Shakespeare." To maintain together that which does not hold together, and the disparate itself, the same disparate, all of this can be thought (we will come back to this incessantly as well as to the spectrality of the specter) only in a dis-located time of the present, at the joining of a radically dis-jointed time, without certain conjunction.

Not a time whose joinings are negated, broken, mistreated, dysfunctional, dis-adjusted, according to a *dys-* of negative opposition and dialectical disjunction, but a time without *certain* joining or determinable conjunction. What is said here about time is also valid, consequently and by the same token, for history, even if the latter can consist in repairing, with effects of conjuncture (and that is the world), the temporal disjoining. "The time is out of joint": time is *disarticulated*, dislocated, dislodged, time is run down, on the run and run down [*traqué et détraqué*], *deranged*, both out of order and mad. Time is off its hinges, time is off course, beside itself, disadjusted. Says Hamlet. Who thereby opened one of those breaches, often they are poetic and thinking peepholes [*meurtrières*], through which Shakespeare will have kept watch over the English language; at the same time he signed its body, with the same unprecedented stroke of some arrow. Now, when does Hamlet name in this way the dis-joining of time, but also of history and of the world, the disjoining of things as they are nowadays, the disadjustment of *our* time, each time ours? And how is one to translate "The time is out of joint"? A striking diversity disperses across the centuries the translation of a masterpiece, a work of genius, a *thing* of the *spirit* which precisely seems to *engineer itself* [s'ingénier]. Whether evil or not, a genius *operates*, it always resists and defies after the fashion of a spectral thing. The animated work becomes that thing, the Thing that, like an elusive specter, *engineers* [s'ingénie] a habitation without proper inhabiting, call it a *haunting*, of both memory and translation. A masterpiece always moves, by definition, in the manner of a ghost. The Thing [*Chose*] haunts, for example, it causes, it inhabits without residing, without ever confining itself to the numerous versions of this passage, "The time is out of joint." In their plurality, the words of translation organize themselves, they are not dispersed at random. They disorganize themselves as well through the very effect of the specter, because of the Cause that is called the original and that, like all ghosts, addresses same-ly disparate demands, which are more than contradictory. In the French translations, the demands are distributed here, it seems, around several major possibilities. These are types. In "The time is out of joint," time is either *le temps* itself, the temporality of time, or else what temporality makes possible (time as *histoire*, the way things are at a certain time, the time that we are living, nowadays, the period), or else, consequently, the *monde*, the world as it turns, our world today, our today, currentness itself, current affairs: there where it's going okay (whither) and there where it's not going so well, where it

justice? And what if this double register condensed its enigma, precisely [*juste-ment*], and potentialized its superpower in that which gives its unheard-of force to Hamlet's words: "The time is out of joint"? Let us not be surprised when we read that the OED gives Hamlet's phrase as example of the ethico-political inflection. With this example one grasps the necessity of what Austin used to say: a dictionary of words can never give a definition, it only gives examples. The perversion of that which, out of joint, does not work well, does not walk straight, or goes askew (*de travers*, then, rather than *à l'envers*) can easily be seen to oppose itself as does the oblique, twisted, wrong, and crooked to the good direction of that which goes right, straight, to the spirit of that which orients or founds the law [*le droit*]—and sets off directly, without detour, toward the right address, and so forth.[15] Hamlet moreover clearly opposes the being "out of joint" of time to its *being-right*, in the right or the straight path of that which walks upright. He even curses the fate that would have caused him to be born to set right a time that walks crooked. He curses the destiny that would precisely have destined him, Hamlet, to do justice, to put things back in order, to put history, the world, the age, the time *upright*, on the right path, so that, in conformity with the rule of its correct functioning, it advances straight ahead [*tout droit*]—and following the law [*le droit*]. This plaintive malediction itself appears to be affected by the torsion or the tort that it denounces. According to a paradox that poses itself and gets carried away by itself, Hamlet does not curse so much the corruption of the age. He curses first of all and instead this unjust effect of the disorder, namely, the fate that would have destined him, Hamlet, to put a dislocated time back on its hinges—and to put it back right, to turn it back over to the law. He curses his mission: to do justice to a de-mission of time. He swears against a destiny that leads him to do justice for a fault, a fault of time and of the times, by rectifying an *address*, by making of rectitude and right ("to set it right") a movement of *correction*, reparation, restitution, vengeance, revenge, punishment. He swears against this misfortune, and this misfortune is unending because it is nothing other than himself, Hamlet. Hamlet is "out of joint" because he curses his own mission, the punishment that consists in having to punish, avenge, exercise justice and right in the form of reprisals; and what he curses in his mission is this expiation of expiation itself; it is first of all that it is *inborn* in him, given *by* his birth as much as *at* his birth. Thus, it is assigned by who (what) came before him. Like Job (3,1), he curses the day that saw him born: "The time is out of joint.

O cursèd spite, / That ever I was born to set it right!" ("to set it right" is translated as "rejointer" [Bonnefoy], "rentrer dans l'ordre" [Gide], "remettre droit"
[Derocquigny], "remettre en place" [Malaplate]).[16] The fatal blow, the *tragic
wrong* that would have been done at his very birth, the hypothesis of an intolerable perversion in the very order of his destination, is to have made him,
Hamlet, *to be* and *to be born*, for the right, *in view of the right*, calling him thus to
put time on the right path, to do right, to render justice, and to redress history, the *wrong* [tort] of history. There is tragedy, there is essence of the tragic
only on the condition of this originarity, more precisely of this pre-originary
and properly spectral anteriority of the crime—the crime of the other, a mis-
deed whose event and reality, whose truth can never *present themselves* in flesh
and blood, but can only allow themselves to be presumed, reconstructed, fan-
tasized. One does not, for all that, bear any less of a responsibility, beginning at
birth, even if it is only the responsibility to repair an evil at the very moment
in which no one can admit it except in a self-confession that *confesses the other*,
as if that amounted to the same. Hamlet curses the destiny that would have
destined him to be the man of right, precisely [*justement*], as if he were cursing
the right or the law itself that has made of him a righter of wrongs, the one
who, like the right, can only come after the crime, or simply *after*: that is, in a
necessarily second generation, originarily late and therefore destined to *inherit*. One never inherits without coming to terms with [*s'expliquer avec*] some
specter, and therefore with more than one specter. With the fault but also the
injunction of *more than one*. That is the originary wrong, the birth wound from
which he suffers, a bottomless wound, an irreparable tragedy, the indefinite
malediction that marks the history of the law or history as law: that time is
"out of joint" is what is also attested by birth itself when it dooms someone
to be the man of right and law only by becoming an inheritor, redresser of
wrongs, that is, only by castigating, punishing, killing. The malediction would
be inscribed in the law itself: in its murderous, bruising origin.

   If right or law stems from vengeance, as Hamlet seems to complain that it
does—before Nietzsche, before Heidegger, before Benjamin—can one not
yearn for a justice that one day, a day belonging no longer to history, a quasi-
messianic day, would finally be removed from the fatality of vengeance?
Better than removed: infinitely foreign, heterogeneous at its source? And is
this day before us, to come, or more ancient than memory itself? If it is difficult, in truth impossible, *today*, to decide between these two hypotheses, it is

precisely because "The time is out of joint": such would be the originary corruption of the day of today, or such would be, as well, the malediction of the
dispenser of justice, of the day I saw the light of day. Is it impossible to gather
under a single roof the apparently disordered plurivocity (which is itself "out
of joint") of these interpretations? Is it possible to find a rule of cohabitation
under such a roof, it being understood that this house will always be haunted rather than inhabited by the meaning of the original? This is the stroke of
genius, the insignia trait of spirit, the signature of the Thing "Shakespeare":
to authorize each one of the translations, to make them possible and intelligible without ever being reducible to them. Their adjoining would lead back
to what—in honor, dignity, good aspect, high renown, title or name, titling
legitimacy, the estimable in general, even the just, if not the right—is always
supposed by adjoining, by the articulated gathering up of oneself, coherence,
responsibility.[17] But if adjoining in general, if the joining of the "joint" supposes first of all the adjoining, the correctness [*justesse*], or the justice of time,
the being-with-oneself or the concord of time, what happens when *time itself*
gets "out of joint," dis-jointed, disadjusted, disharmonic, discorded, or unjust?
Ana-chronique?

What does *not* happen in this anachrony! Perhaps "the time," time itself,
precisely, always "our time," the epoch and the world shared among us, ours
every day, nowadays, the present as our present. Especially when "things are
not going well" among us, precisely [*justement*]: when "things are going badly,"
when it's not working, when things are bad. But with the other, is not this disjuncture, this dis-adjustment of the "it's going badly" necessary for the good, or
at least the just, to be announced? Is not disjuncture the very possibility of the
other? How to distinguish between two disadjustments, between the disjuncture of the unjust and the one that opens up the infinite asymmetry of the
relation to the other, that is to say, the place for justice? Not for calculable
and distributive justice. Not for law, for the calculation of restitution, the economy of vengeance or punishment (for if *Hamlet* is a tragedy of vengeance and
punishment in the triangle or circle of an Oedipus who would have taken an
additional step into repression—Freud, Jones, and so forth—one must still
think the possibility of a step beyond repression: there is a beyond the economy of repression whose law impels it to *exceed itself, of itself* in the course of a
history, be it the history of theater or of politics between *Oedipus Rex* and
Hamlet). Not for calculable equality, therefore, not for the symmetrizing and

synchronic accountability or imputability of subjects or objects, not for a *rendering justice* that would be limited to sanctioning, to restituting, and to *doing right*, but for justice as incalculability of the gift and singularity of the an-eco-nomic ex-position to others. "The relation to others—that is to say, justice," writes Lévinas.[18] Whether he knows it or not, Hamlet is speaking in the space opened up by this question—the appeal of the gift, singularity, the coming of the event, the excessive or exceeded relation to the other—when he declares "The time is out of joint." And this question is no longer dissociated from all those that Hamlet apprehends as such, that of the specter-Thing and of the King, that of the event, of present-being, and of what *there is to be, or not*, what there is *to do*, which means *to think*, to make do or to let do, to make or to let come, or to give, even if it be death. How does the concern with what *there is to be* intersect, in order perhaps to exceed it, with the logic of vengeance or right?

A trajectory that is necessarily without heading and without assurance. The trajectory of a *precipitation* toward which trembles, vibrates, at once orients and disorients itself the question that is here addressed to us under the name or in the name of *justice*, surely a problematic translation of *Dikē*. One of the most sensitive, though certainly not the only, places today for this singular topology would be perhaps *Der Spruch des Anaximander*. Heidegger there interprets *Dikē* as joining, adjoining, adjustment, articulation of accord or harmony, *Fug, Fuge* (*Die Fuge ist der Fug*). Insofar as it is thought on the basis of presence (*als Anwesen gedacht*), *Dikē* harmoniously conjoins, in some way, the joining and the accord. *Adikia* to the contrary: it is at once what is disjointed, undone, twisted and out of line, in the wrong of the injust, or even in the error of stupidity.[19]

Let us note in passing that *mit Fug und Recht* commonly means "within rights," "rightfully," "rightly" versus "wrongly." The German equivalent of "out of joint," in the sense of disarticulated, dislocated, undone, beside itself, deranged, off its hinges, disjointed, disadjusted, is *aus den Fugen, aus den Fugen gehen*. Now, when Heidegger insists on the necessity of thinking *Dikē* on this side of, before, or at a distance from the juridical-moral determinations of justice, he finds in his language, with the expression "aus den Fugen," the multiple, collected, and suspended virtualities of "The time is out of joint": something in the present is not going well, it is not going as it *ought to go*.

> The word *a-dikia* immediately suggests that *dikē* is absent [*wegbleibt*]. We are accustomed to translate *dikē* as right [*Recht*]. The translations of the

fragment [*des Spruches*, i.e. of Anaximander] even use "penalties" to translate "right." If we resist our own juridical-moral notions, [*juristich-moralischen Vorstellungen*], if we restrict ourselves to what comes to language, then we hear that wherever *adikia* rules all is not right with things [*dass es, wo sie waltet, nicht mit rechten Dingen zugeht*]. That means something is out of joint [*etwas ist aus den Fugen*]. But of what are we speaking? Of what is present, lingering awhile [*Vom je-weilig Anwesenden*].[20]

It is important to recall here, regarding the translation of "je-weilig" ("lingering awhile") that Heidegger's meditative writing no doubt passes through this determination of the present (*Anwesend*) as *je-weilig* (of the moment, of the epoch, each time, and so forth), as well as through this indispensable attribution as *Weile* (moment, passing moment, lapse of time) or *weilen* (to stay, linger, remain). But still more important here appears to be the interpretation of *weilen*: a passage, to be sure, and thus by definition a transitory moment, but whose transition comes, if one can say that, from the future. It has its provenance in what, by essence, has not yet come-from [*provenu*], still less come about, and which therefore remains to come. The passage of this time of the present comes from the future to go toward the past, toward the going of the gone [*l'en allé*] (*Das Weilen ist der Übergang aus Kunft zu Gang. Das Anwesende ist das Je-weilige*).[21] Heidegger continues: "But where are there jointures in what is present? Or where is there even one jointure [*nur eine Fuge*]? How can what is present [*das Anwesende*] without jointure be *adikon*, out of joint [*aus der Fuge*]"? One may, as the translator did here, translate Heidegger, the reader of Anaximander, into the language of Hamlet: how is it possible, that which is? Namely, how is it possible that the present, and therefore time, be out of joint? The rest of the interpretation cannot be reconstituted here. It would deserve long and minute approaches. Let us indicate merely a reading hypothesis and the principle of a question. Would the *Spruch* of Anaximander signify that to the presence of the present, to the *eon* of the *eonta* belongs the *adikia*, the disjointure, which is most often translated, as Nietzsche did in this case, by injustice (*Ungerechtigkeit*)? Can one conclude from this that there was a "pessimism" or "nihilism" in the Greek experience of Being? Heidegger doubts it. To nihilistic pessimism, as well as to optimism, he opposes the "trace" of the "tragic," of an essence of the tragic (we are never far from Oedipus and Hamlet) that cannot be explained in an "esthetic" or "psychological" fashion,[22] which also means, for Heidegger, in a psychoanalytic fashion. Beyond the esthetico-psychoanalytic, this trace of the tragic calls us to thinking, on the basis of the interpretation of the Being of being, the *didonai diken...tes adikias*.[23] What is this gift of the *Dikē*? What is this justice beyond right? Does it come along simply to compensate a wrong, restitute something due, to do right or do justice? Does it come along simply to render justice or, on the contrary, to give *beyond* the due, the debt, the crime, or the fault? Does it come simply to repair injustice (*adikia*) or more precisely to rearticulate *as must be* the disjointure of the present time ("to set it right" as Hamlet said)?

The disjointure in the very presence of the present, this sort of non-contemporaneity of present time with itself (this radical untimeliness or this anachrony on the basis of which we are trying here to *think the ghost*) is, according to Heidegger, "said and not said" by the fragment of Anaximander.[24]
A. To be sure, it says "without equivocation" (*eindeutig*) that the present (*das Anwesende*), as present, is in *adikia*, that is, as Heidegger translates,[25] deranged, off its hinges, out of joint (*aus der Fuge*). The present is what passes, the present comes to pass [*se passe*], it lingers in this transitory passage (*Weile*), in the coming-and-going, *between* what *goes* and what *comes*, in the middle of what leaves and what arrives, at the articulation between what absents itself and what presents itself. This in-between articulates conjointly the double articulation (*die Fuge*) according to which the two movements are adjoined (*gefügt*). Presence (*Anwesen*) is enjoined (*verfugt*), ordered, distributed in the two directions of absence, at the articulation of what is no longer and what is not yet. To join and enjoin. This thinking of the jointure is also a thinking of injunction.
B. And yet, declaring this "without equivocation," the *Spruch* also says something else—or it only says this on condition. It would name the disjointure (*adikia*) or the "injustice" of the present only in order to say that it is necessary *didonai diken*. (The duty or the debt of the "it is necessary" is perhaps excessive, even if Nietzsche translates: *Sie müssen Busze zahlen*, they must pay penalty.) In any case, it is clearly a matter of giving. Of giving *Dikē*. Not of *rendering justice*, to render it in return by means of punishment, payment, or expiation, as one most often translates (Nietzsche and Diels). There is first of all a gift without restitution, without calculation, without accountability. Heidegger thus removes such a gift from any horizon of culpability, of debt, of right, and even, perhaps, of duty. He would especially like to wrest it away from that experience of vengeance whose idea, he says, remains "the opinion of those who

equate the Just (*das Gerechte*) with the Avenged (*das Gerächte*)." (Which, let us say in passing, would surely not in the least disqualify, in this case or in others, a reading, for example in Hamlet, of the logic of vengeance, whether psycho-analytic or not, and wherever it remains so powerful. All the same, without depriving it of its pertinence, this other reading causes to appear precisely its economic closure, even its circular fatality, the very limit that makes possi-ble the pertinence or correctness of this interpretation; this latter limit prevents one in fact from understanding the very things which it wants to explain: tragedy, precisely [*justement*], the hestitation to take revenge, the delib-eration, the non-naturality or the non-automaticity of the calculation: neurosis, if you like.) The question of justice, the one that always carries beyond the law, is no longer separated, in its necessity or in its aporias, from that of the gift. Heidegger interrogates the paradox of this gift without debt and without guilt in a movement that I have evoked elsewhere.[26] He then wonders in fact, following the traces of Plotinus whom he does not name here, or hardly ever: is it possible to give what one does not have? "What does 'give' mean here? How should whatever lingers awhile, whatever comes to pres-ence in disjunction, be able to give jointure [*Wie soll das Je-weilige, das in der Un-Fuge west, Fuge geben können*]? Can it give what it doesn't have? [*Kann es geben, was es nicht hat?*] If it gives anything at all, doesn't it give jointure away?"[27] Heidegger's answer: giving rests here only in presence (*Anwesen*), it does not signify simply to give away (*weggeben*) but, more originarily, to accord, that is here, *zugeben* which most often indicates addition, even excess, in any case that which is offered in *supplement*, over and above the market, off trade, with-out exchange, and it is said sometimes of a musical or poetic work. This offering is supplementary, but without raising the stakes, although it is neces-sarily excessive with regard to the giving away or a privation that would separate one from what one might have. The offering consists in leaving: in leaving to the other what properly belongs to him or her (*Solches Geben lässt einem anderen das gehören, was als Gehöriges ihm eignet*). Now, Heidegger then specifies, what properly (*eignet*) belongs to a present, be it to the present of the other, to the present as the other, is the jointure of its lingering awhile, of its time, of its moment (*die Fuge seiner Weile*). What the one does not have, what the one therefore does not have to give away, but what the one gives to the other, over and above the market, above market, bargaining, thanking, com-merce, and commodity, is to leave to the other this accord with himself that is *proper* to him (*ihm eignet*) and gives him presence. If one still translates *Dikē* with this word "justice," and if, as Heidegger does, *Dikē* is thought on the basis of Being as presence, then it would turn out that "justice" is first of all, and finally, and especially *properly*, the jointure of the accord: the proper jointure to the other given by one who does not have it. Injustice would be the disjointure or disjoining (let us quote again: "*Dikē, aus dem Sein als Anwesen gedacht, ist der fugend-fügende Fug. Adikia, die Un-Fuge, ist der Un-Fug*").

This is where our question would come in. Has not Heidegger, as he always does, skewed the asymmetry *in favor* of what he in effect interprets as the pos-sibility of *favor* itself, of the accorded favor, namely, of the accord that gathers or collects while harmonizing (*Versammlung, Fug*), be it in the sameness of dif-ferents or of disagreements [*différends*], and before the synthesis of a sys-tem? Once one has recognized the force and the necessity of thinking justice on the basis of the gift, that is, beyond right, calculation, and commerce, once one has recognized therefore the necessity (*without force*, precisely [*justement*], without necessity, perhaps, and without law) of thinking the gift to the other as gift of that which one does not have and which thus, paradoxically, can only *come back* or belong to the other, is there not a risk of inscribing this whole movement of justice under the sign of presence, be it of the presence to mean-ing of the *Anwesen*, of the event as coming into presence, of Being as presence joined to itself, of the proper of the other as presence? As the presence of the received present, yes, but appropriable as the same and therefore gathered together? Beyond right, and still more beyond juridicism, beyond morality, and still more beyond moralism, does not justice as relation to the other sup-pose on the contrary the irreducible excess of a disjointure or an anachrony, some *Un-Fuge*, some "out of joint" dislocation in Being and in time itself, a disjointure that, in always risking the evil, expropriation, and injustice (*adikia*) against which there is no calculable insurance, would alone be able to *do justice* or to *render justice* to the other as other? A *doing* that would not amount only to action and a *rendering* that would not come down just to restitution? To put it too quickly and to formalize in the extreme the stakes: here, in this inter-pretation of the *Un-Fug* (whether or not it is on the basis of Being as presence and the property of the proper), would be played out the relation of decon-struction to the possibility of justice, the relation of deconstruction (insofar as it proceeds from the irreducible possiblity of the *Un-Fug* and the anachron-ic disjointure, insofar as it draws from there the very resource and injunction of its reaffirmed affirmation) to what must (without debt and without duty) be rendered to the singularity of the other, to his or her absolute *pre*cedence or to his or her absolute *prev*iousness,[28] to the heterogeneity of a *pre-*, which, to be sure, means what comes before me, before any present, thus before any past present, but also what, for that very reason, comes from the future or as future: as the very coming of the event. The necessary disjointure, the de-totalizing condition of justice, is indeed here that of the present—and by the same token the very condition of the present and of the presence of the present. This is where deconstruction would always begin to take shape as the thinking of the gift and of undeconstructible justice, the undeconstructible condition of any deconstruction, to be sure, but a condition that is itself *in deconstruction* and remains, and must remain (that is the injunction) in the disjointure of the *Un-Fug.* Otherwise it rests on the good conscience of having done one's duty, it loses the chance of the future, of the promise or the appeal, of the desire also (that is its "own" possibility), of this desert-like messianism (without content and without identifiable messiah), of this also *abyssal* desert, "desert in the desert," that we will talk about later (p. 167), one desert signaling toward the other, abyssal and *chaotic* desert, if chaos describes first of all the immensity, excessiveness, disproportion in the gaping hole of the open mouth—in the waiting or calling for what we have nicknamed here without knowing the messianic: the coming of the other, the absolute and unpredictable singularity of the *arrivant as justice.* We believe that this messianic remains an *ineffaceable* mark—a mark one neither can nor should efface—of Marx's legacy, and doubtless of *inheriting,* of the experience of inheritance in general. Otherwise, one would reduce the event-ness of the event, the singularity and the alterity of the other.

Otherwise justice risks being reduced once again to juridical-moral rules, norms, or representations, within an inevitable totalizing horizon (movement of adequate restitution, expiation, or reappropriation). Heidegger runs this risk, despite so many necessary precautions, when he gives priority, as he always does, to gathering and to the same (*Versammlung, Fuge, legein,* and so forth) over the disjunction implied by my address to the other, over the interruption commanded by respect which commands it in turn, over a difference whose uniqueness, disseminated in the innumerable charred fragments of the absolute mixed in with the cinders, will never be assured in the One. Which, moreover, never fails to happen also, but it happens only in the trace of what would *happen otherwise* and thus also happens, like a specter, in that which does not happen. Hamlet could never know the peace of a "good ending": in any case in the theater and in history. To be "out of joint," whether it be present Being or present time, can do harm and do evil, it is no doubt the very possibility of evil. But without the opening of this possibility, there remains, perhaps, beyond good and evil, only the necessity of the worst. A necessity that would not (even) be a fated one.

Injunctions and sworn faith: that is what we are trying to think here. We ought to try to understand together, to adjoin, if one prefers, two signs in one, a double sign. Hamlet declares "The time is out of joint" precisely at the moment of the oath, of the injunction to swear, to *swear together* [conjurer], at the moment in which the specter, who is always a sworn conspirator [*conjuré*], one more time, from beneath, from beneath the earth or beneath the stage, has just ordered: "Swear." And the sworn conspirators swear together ("*They swear*").

We are still in the process of reading, in a certain way, "Marx's Three Voices." Let us not forget them. Blanchot reminds us that we are asked by them, in the first place, to think the "holding together" of the *disparate* itself. Not to maintain together the disparate, but to put ourselves there where the disparate itself *holds together*, without wounding the dis-jointure, the dispersion, or the difference, without effacing the heterogeneity of the other. We are asked (enjoined, perhaps) to turn *ourselves* over to the future, to join ourselves in this *we*, there where the disparate is turned over to this singular *joining*, without concept or certainty of determination, without knowledge, without or before the synthetic junction of the conjunction and the disjunction. The alliance of a *rejoining* without conjoined mate, without organization, without party, without nation, without State, without property (the "communism" that we will later nickname the new International).

One question is *not yet* posed. Not as such. It is hidden rather by the *philosophical*, we will say more precisely *ontological response* of Marx himself. It responds to what we are naming here—Blanchot does not do so—the spirit or the specter. Hidden question, we said, for a time and to a certain degree, to be sure. But all these words are treacherous: perhaps it is no longer at all a matter of a question and we are aiming instead at another structure of "presentation," in a gesture of thinking or writing, not the measure of a certain time. The thing happens, it ought to happen there where Blanchot speaks of an "absence of question," the full measure that dispenses with the void, the too-full made to avoid the void:

> Giving a response—alienation, the primacy of need, history as process of material practice, the total man—it nevertheless leaves undetermined or undecided the questions to which it responds: depending on how today's or yesterday's readers formulate differently that which, according to them, should take place in such an absence of the question—thus filling in a void that ought rather to be increasingly emptied out—this form of Marx's speech is interpreted here as humanism, or even historicism, there as atheism, antihumanism, or even nihilism. (Pp. 18–19)

Let us translate into this language of Blanchot the hypothesis we are venturing to put forward here: opened with Marx's signature as a question, but also as a promise or an appeal, the spectrality whose "logic" we are going to analyze will have been covered over ("filling in a void," as Blanchot says, there where the void "ought rather to be increasingly emptied out") by Marx's *ontological* response. The response of Marx himself for whom the ghost must be nothing, nothing period (non-being, non-effectivity, non-life) or nothing imaginary, even if this nothing takes on a body, a certain body, that we will approach later. But also the response of his "Marxist" successors wherever they have drawn, practically, concretely, in a terribly effective, massive, and immediate fashion, its political consequences (at the cost of millions and millions of supplementary ghosts who will keep on protesting in us; Marx had his ghosts, we have ours, but memories no longer recognize such borders; by definition, they pass through walls, these *revenants*, day and night, they trick consciousness and skip generations).

Needless to spell it out here, therefore, still less to insist on it too heavily: it is not a taste for the void or for destruction that leads anyone to recognize the right of this necessity to "empty out" increasingly and to deconstruct the philosophical responses that consist in *totalizing*, in filling in the space of the question or in denying its possibility, in fleeing from the very thing it will have allowed one to glimpse. On the contrary, it is a matter there of an ethical and political imperative, an appeal as unconditional as the appeal of thinking from which it is not separated. It is a matter of the injunction itself—if there is one.

What also resonates in "Marx's three voices" is the *appeal* or the political injunction, the pledge or the promise (the oath, if one prefers: "swear!"), the originary performativity that does not conform to preexisting conventions, unlike all the performatives analyzed by the theoreticians of speech acts, but whose force of *rupture* produces the institution or the constitution, the law itself, which is to say also the meaning that appears to, that ought to, or that appears to have to guarantee it in return. *Violence* of the law before the law and before meaning, violence that interrupts time, disarticulates it, dislodges it, displaces it out of its natural lodging: "out of joint." It is there that differ*a*nce, if it remains irreducible, irreducibly required by the spacing of any promise and by the future-to-come that comes to open it, does not mean only (as some people have too often believed and so naively) deferral, lateness, delay, postponement. In the incoercible differ*a*nce the here-now unfurls. Without lateness, without delay, but without presence, it is the precipitation of an absolute singularity, singular because differing, precisely [*justement*], and always other, binding itself necessarily to the form of the instant, in *imminence and in urgency*: even if it moves toward what remains to come, there is the *pledge* [gage] (promise, engagement, injunction and response to the injunction, and so forth). The pledge is given here and now, even before, perhaps, a decision confirms it. It thus responds without delay to the demand of justice. The latter by definition is impatient, uncompromising, and unconditional.

No differ*a*nce without alterity, no alterity without singularity, no singularity without here-now.

(Why insist on imminence, on urgency and injunction, on all that which in them does not wait? In order to try to remove what we are going to say from what risks happening, if we judge by the many signs, to Marx's work today, which is to say also to his injunction. What risks happening is that one will try to play Marx off against Marxism so as to neutralize, or at any rate muffle the political imperative in the untroubled exegesis of a classified work. One can sense a coming fashion or stylishness in this regard in the culture and more precisely in the university. And what is there to worry about here? Why fear what may also become a cushioning operation? This recent stereotype would be destined, whether one wishes it or not, to depoliticize profoundly the *Marxist reference*, to do its best, by putting on a tolerant face, to neutralize a potential force, first of all by enervating a *corpus*, by silencing in it the revolt [the *return* is acceptable provided that the *revolt*, which initially inspired uprising, indignation, insurrection, revolutionary momentum, does not come back].

People would be ready to accept the return of Marx or the return to Marx, on the condition that a silence is maintained about Marx's injunction not just to decipher but to act and to make the deciphering [the interpretation] into a transformation that "changes the world." In the name of an old concept of reading, such an ongoing neutralization would attempt to conjure away a danger: now that Marx is dead, and especially now that Marxism seems to be in rapid decomposition, some people seem to say, we are going to be able to concern ourselves with Marx without being bothered—by the Marxists and, why not, by Marx himself, that is, by a ghost that goes on speaking. We'll treat him calmly, objectively, without bias: according to the academic rules, in the University, in the library, in colloquia! We'll do it systematically, by respecting the norms of hermeneutical, philological, philosophical exegesis. If one listens closely, one already hears whispered: "Marx, you see, was despite everything a philosopher like any other; what is more [and one can say this now that so many Marxists have fallen silent], he was a *great-philosopher* who deserves to figure on the list of those works we assign for study and from which he has been banned for too long.[29] He doesn't belong to the communists, to the Marxists, to the parties, he ought to figure within our great canon of Western political philosophy. Return to Marx, let's finally read him as a great philosopher." We have heard this and we will hear it again.

It is something altogether other that I wish to attempt here as I turn or return to Marx. It is "something other" to the point that I will have occasion instead, and this will not be only for lack of time and space, to insist even more on what commands us today, without delay, to do everything we can so as to avoid the neutralizing anesthesia of a new theoreticism, and to prevent a philosophico-philological return to Marx from prevailing. Let us spell things out, let us insist: to do everything we can so that it does not *prevail*, but not to avoid its taking place, because it remains just as necessary. This will cause me, for the moment, to give priority to the political gesture I am making here, at the opening of a colloquium, and to leave more or less in the state of a program and of schematic indications the work of philosophical exegesis, and all the "scholarship" that this "position-taking," today, still requires.)

But the here-now does not fold back into immediacy, or into the reappropriable identity of the present, even less that of self-presence. Although "appeal," "violence," "rupture," "imminence," and "urgency" are Blanchot's words in the following paragraph, the demand that he says is "always present" must implicitly, it seems to us, find itself affected by the same rupture or the same dislocation, the same "short circuit." It can never be always present, it *can be, only, if there is any*, it can be only possible, it must even remain a *can-be* or *maybe* in order to remain a demand. Otherwise it would become presence again, that is, substance, existence, essence, *permanence*, and not at all the *excessive* demand or urgency that Blanchot speaks of so correctly [*justement*]. The "permanent revolution" supposes the rupture of that which links permanence to substantial presence, and more generally to all onto-logy:

> The second voice is political: it is brief and direct, more than brief and more than direct, because it short-circuits every voice. It no longer carries a meaning, but a call, a violence, a decision of rupture. It says nothing strictly speaking, it is the urgency of what it announces, bound to an impatient and always excessive demand, since excess is its only measure: thus calling to the struggle and even (which is what we hasten to forget) postulating "revolutionary terror," recommending "permanent revolution," and always designating the revolution not as a final necessity, but as *imminence*, since it is the characteristic of the revolution, if it opens and traverses time, to offer no delay, giving itself to be lived as ever-present demand.[*]
>   [*]This was manifest, and in a striking manner, during May 68. (P. 19) [Blanchot's note]

Blanchot names finally the necessary *disjunction* of Marx's languages, their non-contemporaneity with themselves. That they are "disjoined," and first of all in Marx himself, must neither be denied, reduced, nor even deplored. What one must constantly come back to, here as elsewhere, concerning this text as well as any other (and we still assign here an unlimited scope to this value of text) is an irreducible heterogeneity, an internal untranslatability in some way. It does not necessarily signify theoretical weakness or inconsistency. The lack of a system is not a fault there. On the contrary, heterogeneity opens things up, it lets itself be opened up by the very effraction of that which unfurls, comes, and remains to come—singularly from the other. There would be neither injunction nor promise without this disjunction. Blanchot insisted upon this at the time (between 1968 and 1971, therefore) in order to issue a warning not against knowledge but against scientistic ideology that often, in the name of Science or Theory as Science, had attempted to unify or to purify the "good" text of Marx. If Blanchot seems to agree here with certain

Althusserian motifs, he is already warning against the risk that, according to him, was inherent in them:

> The third voice is the indirect one (thus the lengthiest), that of scientific discourse. On this account, Marx is honored and recognized by other representatives of knowledge. He is thus a man of science, responds to the ethics of the scholar, agrees to submit himself to any and all critical revision.... Still, *Capital* is an essentially subversive work. Not so much because it would lead, by means of scientific objectivity, to the necessary consequence of revolution; rather it is because it includes, without formulating it too much, a mode of theoretical thinking that overturns the very idea of science. Actually, neither science nor thinking emerges from Marx's work intact. This must be taken in the strongest sense, inasmuch as science is designated there as radical transformation of itself, as theory of a mutation always in play within practice, just as, in this practice, the mutation is always theoretical. (P. 19.)

This other *thinking of knowledge*, if I can put it that way, does not exclude science. But it overturns and overflows its received idea. Blanchot recognizes in this "the example of Marx." Why example? We will ask even before knowing why "the example of Marx." Before quoting again, let us insist on this point. An example always carries beyond itself: it thereby opens up a testamentary dimension. The example is first of all for others, and beyond the self. Sometimes, perhaps always, whoever gives the example is not equal to the example he gives, even if he does everything to follow it in advance, "to learn how to live," as we were saying, imperfect example of the example he gives—which he gives by giving then what he has not and even what he is not. For this reason, the example thus disjoined separates enough from itself or from whoever gives it so as to be no longer or not yet example *for itself*. We do not have to solicit the agreement of Marx—who died to this even before being dead—in order to inherit it: to inherit this or that, this rather than that which comes to us nevertheless by him, through him if not from him. And we do not have to suppose that Marx was in agreement with himself. ("What is certain is that I am not a Marxist," he is supposed to have confided to Engels. Must we still cite Marx as authority in order to say likewise?) For Blanchot does not hesitate to suggest that Marx *had difficulty living* with this disjunction of the injunctions within him and with the fact that they were *untranslatable* into each other. How is one to receive, how is one to understand a speech, how is one to inherit it when it does not let itself be *translated* from itself into itself? This may appear impossible. And, we have to acknowledge, it is probably impossible. But since this sums up perhaps the strange subject of this lecture devoted to the specters of Marx, as well as the avowed distortion of its axiom, permit me then to turn the objection around. Guaranteed translatability, given homogeneity, systematic coherence in their *absolute forms*, this is surely (certainly, *a priori* and not probably) what renders the injunction, the inheritance, and the future—in a word the other—*impossible*. *There must be* disjunction, interruption, the heterogeneous if at least *there must be*, *if there must be* a chance given to any "there must be" whatsoever, be it beyond duty.[30]

Once again, here as elsewhere, wherever deconstruction is at stake, it would be a matter of linking an *affirmation* (in particular a political one), *if there is any*, to the experience of the impossible, which can only be a radical experience of the *perhaps*.

So, once again, Blanchot; and in this very powerful ellipsis, in this almost tacit declaration, I take the liberty of underlining a few words there where Blanchot only underlines, but significantly, the words "multiple" and "at once," that is, at the sign of the contradiction without contradiction, of the non-dialectical (or "almost" non-dialectical) difference that runs through and is at work in every injunction:

> Let us not develop these remarks any further here. The example of Marx helps us to understand that the voice of writing, a voice of unceasing contestation, must constantly develop itself and *break itself* into *multiple* forms. The communist voice is always *at once* tacit and violent, political and scholarly, direct, indirect, total and fragmentary, lengthy and *almost* instantaneous. Marx does not live comfortably with this *plurality of languages* that are always colliding and *disjoining* with each other in him. Even if these languages seem to converge toward the same end, *they could not be retranslated into each other*, and their *heterogeneity*, the divergence or gap, the distance that decenters them, renders them non-contemporaneous. In producing an effect of irreducible distortion, they oblige those who have to withstand the reading (the practice) of them to submit themselves to an ceaseless recasting.
>
> The word "science" is becoming again a key word. Let's admit it. But let us remember that although there may be sciences, there is not yet science, because the scientificity of science always remains dependent on ideology, an ideology that no particular science, be it human science, is able to reduce today; and on the other hand, let us remember that no writer, even if he is a Marxist, can turn himself over to writing as to a kind of knowledge... (P. 19–20)]

So, more than thirty years ago, already, Blanchot wrote "The End of Philosophy." At that time, in 1959, a funerary note already echoed there—crepuscular, spectral, and therefore resurrectional. Re-insurrectional. It is indeed a question of the philosophical "spirit": its very process consists of visibly heading the march at the moment of its "disappearance" and its "putting in the ground," it consists of leading its own funeral procession and of *raising* itself in the course of this march, of hoping at least to right itself again so as to stand up ("resurrection," "exaltation"). This wake, this joyous death watch of philosophy is the double moment of a "promotion" and of a "death of philosophy," a promotion in death. Here is philosophy—and is this absolutely new?—becoming its own *revenant*; it itself haunts its own places more than it inhabits them. And philosophy, of course, is always more than philosophy:

> This promotion of philosophy, which has become the all-powerful force in our world and the shape of our destiny, can only coincide with its *disappearance*, announcing at least the beginning of its *putting in the ground*. This *death of philosophy* would belong, therefore, to our philosophical time. The death does not date from 1917, nor even from 1857, the year in which Marx, as if performing a carnival test of strength, would have overturned the system. For the last century and a half, with his name as with that of Hegel, Nietzsche, and Heidegger, it is philosophy itself that has been affirming or realizing its own end, whether it understands that end as the accomplishment of absolute knowledge, its theoretical suppression linked to its practical realization, the nihilist movement in which all values are engulfed, or finally by the culmination of metaphysics, precursor sign of another possibility that does not yet have a name. This then is the sunset that from now on accompanies every thinker, a strange *funereal* moment which the philosophical spirit celebrates in an exaltation that is, moreover, often joyful, leading its slow funeral procession during which it expects, in one way or another, to obtain its *resurrection*. And of course, such an expectation, crisis and feast of negativity, experience pushed as far as it will go to find out what resists, does not touch only on philosophy… (Pp. 292–93; my emphasis)

Imminence and desire of resurrection. Re-naissance or *revenance*? At nightfall, one does not know if imminence means that the expected one has already returned. Had he not already announced himself? To announce oneself, moreover, is that not already to be there in some way? *One does not know* if the expectation prepares the coming of the future-to-come or if it recalls the repetition of the same, of the same thing as ghost ("What, ha's this thing appear'd againe tonight?"). This not-knowing is not a lacuna. No progress of knowledge could saturate an opening that must have nothing to do with knowing. Nor therefore with ignorance. The opening must preserve this heterogeneity as the only chance of an affirmed or rather reaffirmed future. It is the future itself, it comes from there. The future is its memory. In the experience of the end, in its insistent, instant, always imminently eschatological coming, at the extremity of the extreme today, there would thus be announced the future of what comes. More than ever, for the future-to-come can announce itself as such and in its purity only on the basis of a *past end*: beyond, *if that's possible*, the last extremity. If that's possible, *if there is any* future, but how can one suspend such a question or deprive oneself of such a reserve without *concluding in advance*, without reducing in advance both the future and its chance? Without totalizing in advance? We must discern here between eschatology and teleology, even if the stakes of such a difference risk constantly being effaced in the most fragile and slight insubstantiality—and will be in a certain way always and necessarily deprived of any insurance against this risk. Is there not a messianic extremity, an *eskhaton* whose ultimate event (immediate rupture, unheard-of interruption, untimeliness of the infinite surprise, heterogeneity without accomplishment) can exceed, *at each moment*, the final term of a *phusis*, such as work, the production, and the *telos* of any history?

The question is indeed "whither?" Not only whence comes the ghost but first of all is it going to come back? Is it not already beginning to arrive and where is it going? What of the future? The future can only be for ghosts. And the past.

In proposing this title, *Specters of Marx*, I was initially thinking of all the forms of a certain haunting obsession that seems to me to organize the *dominant* influence on discourse today. At a time when a new world disorder is attempting to install its neo-capitalism and neo-liberalism, no disavowal has managed to rid itself of all of Marx's ghosts. Hegemony still organizes the repression and thus the confirmation of a haunting. Haunting belongs to the structure of every hegemony.[31] But I did not have in mind first of all the exordium of the *Manifesto*. In an apparently different sense, Marx-Engels spoke there already, in 1847–48, of a specter and more precisely of the "specter of communism" (*das Gespenst des Kommunismus*). A terrifying specter for all the powers of old Europe (*alle Mächte des alten Europa*), but specter of a communism then *to come*.

Of a communism, to be sure, already namable (and well before the League of the Just or the Communist League), but still to come beyond its name. Already promised but only promised. A specter all the more terrifying, some will say. Yes, on the condition that one can never distinguish between the future-to-come and the coming-back of a specter. Let us not forget that, around 1848, the First International had to remain quasi-secret. The specter was there (but what is the *being-there* of a specter? what is the mode of presence of a specter? that is the only question we would like to pose here). But that of which it was the specter, communism (*das Gespenst des Kommunismus*), was itself not there, by definition. It was dreaded as communism to come. It had already been announced, with this name, some time ago, but it was not yet *there*. It is only a specter, seemed to say these allies of old Europe so as to reassure themselves; let's hope that in the future it does not become an actual, effectively present, manifest, non-secret reality. The question old Europe was asking itself was already the question of the future, the question "whither?": "whither communism?" if not "whither Marxism?" Whether one takes it as asking about the future of communism or about communism in the future, this anguished question did not just seek to know how, in the future, communism would affect European history, but also, in a more muffled way, already whether there would still be any future and any history at all for Europe. In 1848, the Hegelian discourse on the end of history in absolute knowledge had already resounded throughout Europe and had rung a consonant note with many other knells [*glas*]. And communism was essentially distinguished from other labor movements by its *international* character. No organized political movement in the history of humanity had ever yet presented itself as *geo-political*, thereby inaugurating the space that is now ours and that today is reaching its limits, the limits of the earth and the limits of the political.

The representatives of these forces or all these powers (*alle Mächte*), namely the States, wanted to *reassure* themselves. They wanted to be sure. So they were sure, for there is no difference between "being sure" and "wanting to be sure." They were sure and certain that between a specter and an actually present reality, between a spirit and a *Wirklichkeit*, the dividing line was assured. It *had* to be safely drawn. It *ought* to be assured. No, it *ought to have been* assured. The sureness of this certainty is something they shared, moreover, with *Marx himself*. (This is the whole story, and we are coming to it: Marx thought, to be sure, on his side, from the other side, that the dividing line between the ghost and actuality ought to be crossed, like utopia itself, by a realization, that is, by a revolution; but *he too* will have continued to believe, to try to believe in the existence of this dividing line as real limit and conceptual distinction. He too? No, someone in him. Who? The "Marxist" who will engender what for a long time is going to prevail under the name of "Marxism." And which was also haunted by what it attempted to foreclose.)

Today, almost a century and a half later, there are many who, throughout the world, seem just as worried by the specter of communism, just as convinced that what one is dealing with there is only a specter without body, without present reality, without actuality or effectivity, but this time it is supposed to be a past specter. It was only a specter, an illusion, a phantasm, or a ghost: that is what one hears everywhere today ("Horatio saies, 'tis but our Fantasie,/ And will not let beleefe take hold of him"). A still worried sigh of relief: let us make sure that in the future it does not come back! At bottom, the specter is the future, it is always to come, it presents itself only as that which could come or come back; in the future, said the powers of old Europe in the last century, it must not incarnate itself, either publicly or in secret. In the future, we hear everywhere today, it must not re-incarnate itself; it must not be allowed to come back since it is past.

What exactly is the difference from one century to the next? Is it the difference between a past world—for which the specter represented a coming threat—and a present world, today, where the specter would represent a threat that some would like to believe is past and whose return it would be necessary again, once again in the future, to conjure away?

Why in both cases is the specter felt to be a threat? What is the time and what is the history of a specter? Is there a present of the specter? Are its comings and goings ordered according to the linear succession of a before and an after, between a present-past, a present-present, and a present-future, between a "real time" and a "deferred time"?

If there is something like spectrality, there are reasons to doubt this reassuring order of presents and, especially, the border between the present, the actual or present reality of the present, and everything that can be opposed to it: absence, non-presence, non-effectivity, inactuality, virtuality, or even the simulacrum in general, and so forth. There is first of all the doubtful contemporaneity of the present to itself. Before knowing whether one can differentiate between the specter of the past and the specter of the future, of the past present and the future present, one must perhaps ask oneself whether the *spectrality effect* does not consist in undoing this opposition, or even this dialectic, between actual, effective presence and its other. One must perhaps ask oneself whether this opposition, be it a dialectical opposition, has not always been a closed field and a common axiomatic for the antagonism between Marxism and the cohort or the alliance of its adversaries.

Pardon me for beginning with such an abstract formulation.

In the middle of the last century, an alliance was constituted against this specter, to drive off the evil. Marx did not call this coalition a Holy Alliance, an expression he plays with elsewhere. In the *Manifesto*, the alliance of the worried conspirators assembles, more or less secretly, a nobility and a clergy—in the old castle of Europe, for an unbelievable expedition against what will have been haunting the night of these masters. At twilight, before or after a night of bad dreams, at the presumed end of history, it is a "holy hunt against this specter": "All the powers of old Europe have joined [*verbündet*] into a holy hunt against this specter [*zu einer heiligen Hetzjagd gegen dies Gespenst*]."

It would thus be possible to form a secret alliance against the specter. If Marx had written his *Manifesto* in my language, and if he had had some help with it, as a Frenchman can always dream of doing, I am sure he would have played on the word *conjuration*. Then he would have diagnosed today the same *conjuration*, this time not only in old Europe but in the new Europe, the New World, which already interested him very much a century and a half ago, and throughout the world, in the new world order where the hegemony of this new world, I mean the United States, would still exercise a more or less critical hegemony, more and less assured than ever.

The word *conjuration* has the good fortune to put to work and to produce, without any possible reappropriation, a forever errant surplus value. It capitalizes first of all two orders of semantic value. What is a "conjuration"?

The French noun "conjuration" gathers up and articulates the meanings of two English words—and also two German words.

1. *Conjuration* signifies, *on the one hand*, "conjuration" (its English homonym) which itself designates two things at once:

a. *On the one hand*, the conspiracy (*Verschwörung* in German) of those who promise solemnly, sometimes secretly, by swearing together an oath (*Schwur*) to struggle against a superior power. It is to this conspiracy that Hamlet appeals, evoking the "Vision" they have just seen and the "honest ghost," when

he asks Horatio and Marcellus to swear ("swear't," "Consent to swear"). To
swear upon his sword, but to swear or to swear together *on the subject of the spec-*
tral apparition itself, and to promise secrecy on the subject of the apparition of
an honest ghost that, from beneath the stage, conspires with Hamlet to ask
the same thing from the sworn: (*"The Ghost cries from under the stage:* Sweare"). It
is the apparition that enjoins them to conspire to *silence the apparition*, and to
promise secrecy on the subject of the one who demands such an oath from
them: one must not know whence comes the injunction, the conspiracy, the
promised secret. A son and the "honest ghost" of the father, the supposedly
honest ghost, the spirit of the father, conspire together to bring about such an
event.

b. "Conjuration" signifies, *on the other hand*, the magical incantation destined
to *evoke*, to bring forth with the voice, to *convoke* a charm or a spirit.
Conjuration says in sum the appeal that causes to come forth *with the voice* and
thus it makes come, by definition, what *is not there* at the present moment of
the appeal. This voice does not describe, what it says certifies nothing; its
words cause something to happen. This is the usage encountered again in the
words of the Poet at the opening of *Timon of Athens*. After having asked "How
goes the world?" and after the Painter has told him "It wears, sir, as it grows,"
the Poet exclaims:

> Ay, that's well known;
> But what particular rarity, what strange,
> Which manifold record not matches? —See,
> Magic of bounty, all these spirits thy power
> Hath *conjur'd* to attend. I know the merchant. (I,i)

Marx evokes more than once *Timon of Athens*, as well as *The Merchant of*
Venice, in particular in *The German Ideology*. The chapter on "The Leipzig
Council—Saint Max," also supplies, and we will say more about this later, a
short treatise on the spirit or an interminable theatricalization of ghosts. A
certain "Communist Conclusion" appeals to *Timon of Athens*.[32] The same quotation will reappear in the first version of *A Contribution to the Critique of Political*
Economy. In question is a spectralizing disincarnation. Apparition of the bodiless body of money: not the lifeless body or the cadaver, but a life without
personal life or individual property. Not without identity (the ghost is a "who,"
it is not of the simulacrum in general, it has a kind of body, but without prop-

erty, without "real" or "personal" right of property). One must analyze the proper of property and how the general property (*Eigentum*) of money neutralizes, disincarnates, deprives of its difference all personal property (*Eigentümlichkeit*). The genius of Shakespeare will have understood this phantomalization of property centuries ago and said it better than anyone. The *ingenium* of his paternal geniality serves as reference, guarantee, or confirmation in the polemic, that is, in the ongoing war—on the subject, precisely, of the monetary specter, value, money or its fiduciary sign, gold: "It was known to Shakespeare better than to our theorizing petty bourgeois [*unser theoretisierender Kleinbürger*] ...[h]ow little connection there is between money, the most general form of property [*die allgemeinste Form des Eigentums*], and personal peculiarity [*mit der persönlichen Eigentümlichkeit*] ..."[33]

The quotation will also make apparent (as a supplementary benefit but in fact it is altogether necessary) a theologizing fetishization, the one that always links ideology irreducibly to religion (to the idol or the fetish) as its principal figure, a species of "invisible god" to which adoration, prayer, and invocation are addressed ("Thou visible god"). Religion, and we will come back to this, was never one ideology among others for Marx. What, Marx seems to say, the genius of a great poet—and the spirit of a great father—will have uttered in a poetic flash, with one blow going faster and farther than our little bourgeois colleagues in economic theory, is the becoming-god of gold, which is at once ghost and idol, a god apprehended by the senses. After having marked the heterogeneity between the property of money and personal property (there is "little connection" between them), Marx adds, and it is not a negligible clarification it seems to me, that in truth they are not only different but opposed (*entgegensetzt*). And it is then that, cutting into the body of the text and making choices that should be analyzed closely, he wrests a long passage from that prodigious scene in *Timon of Athens* (IV, iii). Marx loves the words of this imprecation. One must never keep silent about the imprecation of the just. One must never silence it in the most analytic text of Marx. An imprecation does not theorize, it is not content to say how things are, it cries out the truth, it promises, it provokes. As its name indicates, it is nothing other than a prayer. Marx appropriates the words of this imprecation with a kind of delight whose signs are unmistakable. Declaring his hatred of the human race ("I am Misanthropos and hate mankind"), with the anger of a Jewish prophet and sometimes the very words of Ezechiel, Timon curses corruption, he casts down anathema, he swears against prostitution—prostitution in the face of gold and the prositution of gold itself. But he takes the time to analyze, nevertheless, the transfiguring alchemy, he denounces the reversal of values, the falsification and especially the perjury of which it is the law. One imagines the impatient patience of Marx (rather than Engels) as he transcribes in his own hand, at length, in German, the rage of a prophetic imprecation:

> …Thus much of this will make
> Black white, foul fair, wrong right,
> Base noble, old young, coward valiant.

> This yellow slave
> Will…
> Make the hoar leprosy adored…

> This is it
> That makes the wappered widow wed again.
> She whom the spittle house and ulcerous sores
> Would cast the gorge at, this embalms and spices
> To th' April day again…

> Thou visible god,
> That sold'rest closest impossibilities
> And mak'st them kiss…

> *sichtbare Gottheit,*
> *Die du Unmöglichkeiten eng verbrüderst*
> *Zum Kusz sie zwingst!*

Among all the traits of this immense malediction of malediction, Marx will have had to efface, in the economy of a long citation, those that are most important for us here, for example the aporias and the double bind that carry the act of swearing and conjuring off into the history of venality itself. At the moment he goes to bury the gold, a shovel in his hand, the prophet-gravedigger, anything but a humanist, is not content to evoke the breaking of vows, the birth and death of religions ("This yellow slave/ Will knit and break religions; bless the accurs'd"); Timon also begs [*conjure*] the other, he pleads with him to promise, but he conjures thus by perjuring and by confessing his perjury in a same and single bifid gesture. In truth, he conjures *by feigning the truth*, by feigning at least to make the other promise. But if he feigns to make the other promise, it is in truth to make the other promise not to keep his promise, that is, not to promise, even as he pretends to promise: to perjure or to abjure in the very moment of the oath; then following from this same logic, he begs him to spare all oaths. As if he were saying in effect: I beg you [*je vous en conjure*], do not swear, abjure your right to swear, renounce your capacity to swear, moreover no one is asking you to swear, you are asked to be the non-oath-ables that you are ("you are not oathable"), you, the whores, you who are prostitution itself, you who give yourselves to gold, you who give yourselves for gold, you who are destined to general indifference, you who confuse in equivalency the proper and the improper, credit and discredit, faith and lie, the "true and the false," oath, perjury, and abjuration, and so forth. You the whores of money, you would go so far as to abjure ("forswear") your trade or your vocation (of perjured whore) for money. Like a madam who would give up even her whores for money.

The very essence of humanity is at stake. Absolute double bind on the subject of the *bind* or the *bond* themselves. Infinite misfortune and incalculable chance of the performative—here named literally ("perform," "perform none" are Timon's words when he asks [*conjure*] the other *to promise not to keep a promise*, calling therefore for perjury or abjuration). Force, as weakness, of an ahuman discourse on man. Timon to Alcibiades: "Promise me friendship, but perform none. If thou wilt promise, the gods plague thee, for thou art a man. If thou dost not perform, confound thee, for thou art a man" (IV, iii). Then to Phyrnia and Timandra who ask for gold—and whether Timon has any more:

> Enough to make a whore forswear her trade,
> And to make wholesomeness a bawd. Hold up, you sluts,
> Your aprons mountant. You are not oathable,
> Although I know you'll swear, terribly swear,
> Into strong shudders and to heavenly agues
> Th'immortal gods that hear you. Spare your oaths;
> I'll trust to your conditions. Be whores still…

Addressing himself to prostitution or to the cult of money, to fetishism or to idolatry itself, Timon trusts. He gives faith, he believes, he indeed wants to *credit* ("I'll trust") but only in the imprecation of a paradoxical hyperbole: he himself pretends to trust in that which, from the depths of abjuration, from the depths of that which is not even capable or worthy of an oath ("you are not oathable"), remains nevertheless faithful to a natural instinct, as if there were a pledge of instinct, a fidelity to itself of instinctual nature, an oath of living nature before the oath of convention, society, or law. And it is the fidelity to infidelity, the constancy in perjury. This life enslaves itself regularly, one can trust it to do so, it never fails to kneel to indifferent power, to that power of mortal indifference that is money. Diabolical, radically bad in that way, nature is prostitution, it enslaves itself faithfully, one can have confidence here in it, it enslaves itself to what is betrayal itself, perjury, abjuration, lie, and simulacrum.

Which are never very far from the specter. As is well known, Marx always described money, and more precisely the monetary sign, in the figure of appearance or simulacrum, more exactly of the ghost. He not only described them, he also defined them, but the figural presentation of the concept seemed to describe some spectral "thing," which is to say, "someone." What is the necessity of this figural presentation? What is its relation to the concept? Is it contingent? That is the classic form of our question. As we do not believe in any contingency here, we will even begin to worry about the classical (basically Kantian) form of this question which seems to marginalize or keep at a distance the figural schema even as it takes it seriously. *The Critique of Political Economy* explains to us how the existence (*Dasein*) of money, metallic *Dasein*, gold or silver, produces a *remainder*.[34] This remainder is—it remains, precisely—but the shadow of a great name: "*Was übrigbleibt ist* magni nominis umbra." "The body of money is but a shadow [*nur noch ein Schatten*]."[35] The whole movement of idealization (*Idealisierung*) that Marx then describes, whether it is a question of money or of ideologems, is a production of ghosts, illusions, simulacra, appearances, or apparitions (*Scheindasein* of the *Schein-Sovereign* and of the *Schein-gold*). Later he will compare this spectral virtue of money with that which, in the desire to hoard, speculates on the use of money *after death*, in the other world (*nach dem Tode in der andern Welt*).[36] *Geld, Geist, Geiz*: as if money (*Geld*) were the origin both of spirit (*Geist*) and of avarice (*Geiz*). "Im Geld liegt der Ursprung des Geizes," says Pliny as quoted by Marx right after this. Elsewhere, the equation between *Gaz* and *Geist* will be joined to the chain.[37] The metamorphosis of commodities (*die Metamorphose der Waren*) was already a process of transfiguring idealization that one may legitimately call spectropoetic. When the State emits paper money at a fixed rate, its intervention is compared to "magic" (Magie) that transmutes paper into gold. The State appears then, for it is an appearance, indeed an apparition; it "seems now to transform paper into gold by the magic of its imprint [*scheint jetzt durch die Magie seines Stempels Papier in Gold zu verwandeln*; Marx is referring to the imprint that stamps gold and prints paper money]."[38] This magic always busies itself with ghosts, it does business with them, it manipulates or busies *itself,* it becomes a business, the business it does in the very element of haunting. And this business attracts the undertakers, those who deal with cadavers but so as to steal them, to make the departed disappear, which remains the condition of their "apparition." Commerce and theater of gravediggers. In periods of social crisis, when the social "nervus rerum" is, says Marx, "buried [*bestattet*] along-side the body whose sinew it is" (131), the speculative burying of the treasure inters only a useless metal, deprived of its monetary soul (*Geldseele*). This bur-ial scene recalls not only the great scene of the cemetery and gravediggers in *Hamlet,* when one of them suggests that the work of the "grave-maker" lasts longer than any other: until Judgment Day. This scene of burying gold also evokes more than once, and still more exactly, *Timon of Athens.* In Marx's funer-ary rhetoric, the "useless metal" of the treasure once buried becomes like the burnt-out ashes (*ausgebrannte Asche*) of circulation, like its *caput mortuum,* its chemical residue. In his wild imaginings, in his nocturnal delirium (*Hirngespinst*), the miser, the hoarder, the speculator becomes a martyr to exchange-value. He now refrains from exchange because he dreams of a pure exchange. (And we will see later how the apparition of exchange-value, in *Capital,* is precisely an apparition, one might say a vision, a hallucination, a *properly* spectral apparition if this figure did not prevent us from speaking here properly of the proper.) The hoarder behaves then like an alchemist (*alchimistisch*), speculating on ghosts, the "elixir of life," the "philosophers' stone." Speculation is always fascinated, bewitched by the specter. That this alchemy remains devoted to the apparition of the specter, to the haunting or the return of *revenants* is brought out in the literality of a text that translations sometimes overlook. When, in this same passage, Marx describes the trans-mutation, there is haunting at stake. What operates in an alchemical fashion are the exchanges and mixtures of *revenants,* the *madly spectral* compositions or conversions. The lexicon of haunting and ghosts (*Spuk, spuken*) takes center stage. Whereas the English translation speaks of the "alchemist's apparitions" ("The liquid form of wealth and its petrification, the elixir of life and the philosophers' stone are wildly mixed together like an alchemist's apparitions"), the French translation drops the reference to ghosts (*spuken alchimistisch toll durcheinander*) with the phrase "fantasmagorie d'une folle achimie."[39]

In short, and we will return to this repeatedly, Marx does not like ghosts any more than his adversaries do. He does not want to believe in them. But he thinks of nothing else. He believes rather in what is supposed to distinguish them from actual reality, living effectivity. He believes he can oppose them, like life to death, like vain appearances of the simulacrum to real presence. He believes enough in the dividing line of this opposition to want to denounce, chase away, or exorcise the specters but by means of critical analysis and not by some counter-magic. But how to distinguish between the analysis that denounces magic and the counter-magic that it still risks being? We will ask ourselves this question again, for example, as regards *The German Ideology*. "The Leipzig Council—Saint Max" (Stirner) also organizes, let us recall once more before coming back to it later, an *irresistible* but *interminable* hunt for ghosts (*Gespenst*) and for *revenants* or spooks (*Spuk*). *Irresistible* like an effective critique, but also like a compulsion; *interminable* as one says of an analysis, and the comparison would not be at all fortuitous.

This hostility toward ghosts, a terrified hostility that sometimes fends off terror with a burst of laughter, is perhaps what Marx will always have had in common with his adversaries. He too will have tried to *conjure* (away) the ghosts, and everything that was neither life nor death, namely, the re-apparition of an apparition that will never be either the appearing or the disappeared, the phenomenon or its contrary. He will have tried to conjure (away) the ghosts *like* the conspirators [*conjurés*] of old Europe on whom the *Manifesto* declares war. However inexpiable this war remains, and however necessary this revolution, it conspires [*conjure*] *with them* in order to *exorc-analyze* the spectrality of the specter. And this is today, as perhaps it will be tomorrow, our problem.

2. For "conjuration" means, on the other hand, "conjurement" (*Beschwörung*), namely, the magical exorcism that, on the contrary, tends to expulse the evil spirit which would have been called up or convoked (OED: "the exorcising of spirits by invocation," "the exercise of magical or occult influence").

A conjuration, then, is first of all an alliance, to be sure, sometimes a political alliance, more or less secret, if not tacit, a plot or a conspiracy. It is a matter of neutralizing a hegemony or overturning some power. (During the Middle Ages, *conjuratio* also designated the sworn faith by means of which the bourgeois joined to together, sometimes against a prince, in order to establish free towns.) In the occult society of those who have sworn together [*des conjurés*], certain subjects, either individual or collective, represent forces and ally themselves together in the name of common interests to combat a dreaded political adversary, that is, also to conjure it away. For to conjure means *also* to exorcise: to attempt both to destroy and to disavow a malignant, demonized, diabolized force, most often an evil-doing spirit, a specter, a kind of ghost who comes back or who still risks coming back *post mortem*. Exorcism conjures away the evil in ways that are also irrational, using magical, mysterious, even mystifying practices. Without excluding, quite to the contrary, analytic procedure and argumentative ratiocination, exorcism consists in repeating in the mode of an incantation that the dead man is really dead. It proceeds by *formulae*, and sometimes theoretical formulae play this role with an efficacity that is all the greater because they mislead as to their magical nature, their authoritarian dogmatism, the occult power they share with what they claim to combat.

But effective exorcism pretends to declare the death only in order to put to death. As a coroner might do, it certifies the death but here it is in order to inflict it. This is a familiar tactic. The constative form tends to reassure. The certification is effective. It wants to be and it must be *in effect*. It is *effectively* a performative. But here effectivity phantomalizes itself. It is in fact [*en effet*] a matter of a performative that seeks to reassure but first of all to reassure itself by assuring itself, for nothing is less sure, that what one would like to see dead is indeed dead. It speaks in the name of life, it claims to know what that is. Who knows better than someone who is alive? it seems to say with a straight face. It seeks to convince (itself) there where it makes (itself) afraid:[40] now, it says (to itself), what used to be living is no longer alive, it does not remain effective in death itself, don't worry. (What is going on here is a way of not wanting to know what everyone alive knows without learning and without knowing, namely, that the dead can often be more powerful than the living; and that is why to interpret a philosophy as philosophy or ontology of life is never a simple matter, which means that it is always too simple, incontestable, like what goes without saying, but finally so unconvincing, as unconvincing as a tautology, a rather heterological tauto-ontology, that of Marx or whomever, which relates everything back to life only on the condition of including there death and the alterity of its other without which it would not be what it is.) In short, it is often a matter of pretending to certify death there where the death certificate is still the performative of an act of war or the impotent gesticulation, the restless dream, of an execution.

the verb to be, in the third person indicative, seems to offer a predestined hospitality to the return of any and all spirits, a word that one needs merely to write in the plural in order to extend a welcome there to specters. *To be*, and especially when one infers from the infinitive "to be *present*," is not a *mot d'esprit* but *le mot de l'esprit*, the word of the spirit, it *is* its first verbal body.

A time of the world, today, in these times, a new "world order" seeks to stabilize a new, necessarily new disturbance [*dérèglement*] by installing an unprecedented form of hegemony. It is a matter, then, but as always, of a novel form of war. It at least resembles a great "conjuration" against Marxism, a "conjurement" of Marxism: once again, another attempt, a new, always new mobilization to struggle against it, against that which and those whom it represents and will continue to represent (the idea of a new International), and to combat an International by exorcising it.

Very novel and so ancient, the conjuration appears both powerful and, as always, worried, fragile, anxious. The enemy to be conjured away, for those sworn to the conjuration, is, to be sure, called Marxism. But people are now afraid that they will no longer recognize it. They quake at the hypothesis that, by virtue of one of those metamorphoses that Marx talked about so much ("metamorphosis" was one of his favorite words throughout his life), a new "Marxism" will no longer have the face by which one was accustomed to identify it and put it down. Perhaps people are no longer afraid of Marxists, but they are still afraid of certain non-Marxists who have not renounced Marx's inheritance, crypto-Marxists, pseudo- or para-"Marxists" who would be standing by to change the guard, but behind features or quotation marks that the anxious experts of anti-communism are not trained to unmask.

Besides the reasons just given, we will privilege this figure of conjuration for still other reasons. They have already begun to make their appearance. In its two concepts (conjuration and conjurement, *Verschwörung* and *Beschwörung*), we must take into account another essential meaning: the act that consists in swearing, taking an oath, therefore promising, deciding, taking a *responsibility*, in short, committing oneself in a performative fashion—as well as in a more or less secret fashion, and thus more or less public, there where this frontier between the public and the private is constantly being displaced, remaining less assured than ever, as the limit that would permit one to identify the political. And if this important frontier is being displaced, it is because the medium in which it is instituted, namely, the medium of the media themselves (news, the press, tele-communications, techno-tele-discursivity, techno-tele-iconic-ity, that which in general assures and determines the *spacing* of public space, the very possibility of the *res publica* and the phenomenality of the political), this element itself is neither living nor dead, present nor absent: it spectral-izes. It does not belong to ontology, to the discourse on the Being of beings, or to the essence of life or death. It requires, then, what we call, to save time and space rather than just to make up a word, *hauntology*. We will take this cate-gory to be irreducible, and first of all to everything it makes possible: ontology, theology, positive or negative onto-theology.

This dimension of performative interpretation, that is, of an interpretation that transforms the very thing it interprets, will play an indispensable role in what I would like to say this evening. "An interpretation that transforms what it interprets" is a definition of the performative as unorthodox with regard to speech act theory as it is with regard to the 11th Thesis on Feuerbach ("The philosophers have only *interpreted* the world in various ways; the point, how-ever, is to *change* it [*Die Philosophen haben die Welt nur verschieden interpretiert; es kömmt aber drauf an, sie zu verändern*]").

If I take the floor at the opening of such an impressive, ambitious, neces-sary or risky, others might say historic colloquium; if, after hesitating for a long time and despite the obvious limits of my competence, I nevertheless accepted the invitation with which Bernd Magnus has honored me, it is not in the first place in order to propose a scholarly, philosophical discourse. It is first of all so as not to flee from a responsibility. More precisely, it is in order to submit for your discussion several hypotheses on the nature of such a respon-sibility. What is ours? In what way is it historical? And what does it have to do with so many specters?

No one, it seems to me, can *contest* the fact that a dogmatics is attempting to install its worldwide hegemony in paradoxical and suspect conditions. There is today in the world a *dominant* discourse, or rather one that is on the way to becoming dominant, on the subject of Marx's work and thought, on the subject of Marxism (which is perhaps not the same thing), on the subject of the social-ist International and the universal revolution, on the subject of the more or less slow destruction of the revolutionary model in its Marxist inspiration, on the subject of the rapid, precipitous, recent collapse of societies that attempt-ed to put it into effect at least in what we will call for the moment, citing once again the *Manifesto*, "old Europe," and so forth. This dominating discourse often has the manic, jubilatory, and incantatory form that Freud assigned to the so-called triumphant phase of mourning work. The incantation repeats and ritualizes itself, it holds forth and holds to formulas, like any animistic magic. To the rhythm of a cadenced march, it proclaims: Marx is dead, communism is dead, very dead, and along with it its hopes, its discourse, its theories, and its practices. It says: long live capitalism, long live the market, here's to the survival of economic and political liberalism!

If this hegemony is attempting to install its dogmatic orchestration in suspect and paradoxical conditions, it is first of all because this triumphant conjuration is striving in truth to disavow, and therefore to hide from, the fact that never, never in history, has the horizon of the thing whose survival is being celebrated (namely, all the old models of the capitalist and liberal world) been as dark, threatening, and threatened. And never more "historic," by which we mean inscribed in an absolutely novel moment of a process that is nonetheless subject to a law of iterability.

What are we doing by speaking, with these first words, of a *dominant* discourse and of an *incontestable* self-evidence regarding it?

At least *two things*. We are obviously having recourse to received concepts: (1) that of hegemony ("dominant discourse") and (2) that of testimony ("*incontestable* self-evidence"). We will have to account for these and justify them.

1. We have implicitly referred (particularly so as to speak of what no one, I presume, would dream of contesting) to that which everywhere organizes and commands public manifestation or testimony in the public space. In question here is a set constituted by *three* indissociable places or apparatuses of our culture:

a. There is first of all the culture called more or less properly political (the official discourses of parties and politicians in power in the world, virtually everywhere Western models prevail, the speech or the rhetoric of what in France is called the "classe politique").

b. There is also what is rather confusedly qualified as mass-media culture: "communications" and interpretations, selective and hierarchized production of "information" through channels whose power has grown in an absolutely unheard-of fashion at a rhythm that coincides precisely, no doubt not fortuitously, with that of the fall of regimes on the Marxist model, a fall to which it contributed mightily but—and this is not the least important point—in forms and modes of appropriation, and at a speed that also affect in an essential fash-

ion the very concept of public space in so-called liberal democracies; and at
the center of this colloquium the question of media tele-technology, economy,
and power, in their irreducibly spectral dimension, should cut across all our
discussions. What can one do with the Marxist schemas in order to deal with
this today—theoretically and practically—and thus in order to change it? To
put it in a word that would sum up the *position* I am going to defend (and what
I am putting forward here, pardon me for saying this again, corresponds more
to a *position-taking* than to the work such a position calls for, presupposes, or
prefigures), these schemas appear both indispensable and insufficient in their
present form. Marx is one of the rare thinkers of the past to have taken seriously, at least in its principle, the originary indissociability of technics and
language, and thus of tele-technics (for every language is a tele-technics). But
it is not at all to denigrate him, it is even to speak in what we will still dare to
call the *spirit of Marx*, it is almost to quote word for word his own predictions,
it is to *register* [prendre acte] and to *confirm* to say: as regards tele-technics,
and thus also as regards science, he could not accede to the experience and
to the anticipations on this subject that are ours today.

c. There is finally scholarly or academic culture, notably that of historians,
sociologists and politologists, theoreticians of literature, anthropologists,
philosophers, in particular political philosophers, whose discourse is itself
relayed by the academic and commercial press, but also by the media in general. For no one will have failed to notice that the three places, forms, and
powers of culture that I have just identified (the expressly political discourse
of the "political class," media discourse, and intellectual, scholarly, or academic discourse) are more than ever welded together by the same apparatuses or
by ones that are indissociable from them. These apparatuses are doubtless
complex, differential, conflictual, and overdetermined. But whatever may be
the conflicts, inequalities, or overdeterminations among them, they commu-
nicate and cooperate at every moment toward producing the greatest force
with which to assure the hegemony or the imperialism in question. They do so
thanks to the mediation of what is called precisely the media in the broadest,
most mobile, and, considering the acceleration of technical advances, most
technologically invasive sense of this term. As it has never done before, either
to such a degree or in these forms, the politico-economic hegemony, like the
intellectual or discursive domination, passes by way of techno-mediatic
power—that is, by a power that at the same time, in a differentiated and con-

tradictory fashion, *conditions and endangers* any democracy. Now, this power, this differentiated set of powers cannot be analyzed or potentially combatted, supported here, attacked there, without taking into account so many *spectral* effects, the new speed of *apparition* (we understand this word in its ghostly sense) of the simulacrum, the synthetic or prosthetic image, and the virtual event, cyberspace and surveillance, the control, appropriations, and speculations that today deploy unheard-of powers. Have Marx and his heirs helped us to think and to treat this phenomenon? If we say that the answer to this question is at once *yes* and *no, yes* in one respect, *no* in another, and that one must filter, select, differentiate, restructure the questions, it is only in order to announce, in too preliminary a fashion, the tone and the general form of our conclusions: namely, that one *must assume the inheritance* of Marxism, assume its most "living" part, which is to say, paradoxically, that which continues to put back on the drawing board the question of life, spirit, or the spectral, of life-death beyond the opposition between life and death. This inheritance must be reaffirmed by transforming it as radically as will be necessary. Such a reaffirmation would be both faithful to something that resonates in Marx's appeal—let us say once again in the spirit of his injunction—and in conformity with the concept of inheritance in general. Inheritance is never a *given*, it is always a task. It remains before us just as unquestionably as we are heirs of Marxism, even before wanting or refusing to be, and, like all inheritors, we are in mourning. In mourning in particular for what is called Marxism. *To be*, this word in which we earlier saw the word of the spirit, means, for the same reason, to inherit. All the questions on the subject of being or of what is to be (or not to be) are questions of inheritance. There is no backward-looking fervor in this reminder, no traditionalist flavor. Reaction, reactionary, or reactive are but interpretations of the structure of inheritance. That we *are* heirs does not mean that we *have* or that we *receive* this or that, some inheritance that enriches us one day with this or that, but that the *being* of what we are *is* first of all inheritance, whether we like it or know it or not. And that, as Hölderlin said so well, we can only *bear witness* to it. To bear witness would be to bear witness to what we *are* insofar as we *inherit*, and that—here is the circle, here is the chance, or the finitude—we inherit the very thing that allows us to bear witness to it. As for Hölderlin, he calls this language, "the most dangerous of goods," given to man "so that he bears witness to having inherited/ what he is [*damit er zeuge, was er sei/ geerbt zu haben*]."[1]

2. When we advance at least the hypothesis that the dogma on the subject of the end of Marxism and of Marxist societies is today, tendentially, a "dominant discourse," we are still speaking, of course, in the Marxist code. We must not deny or dissimulate the problematic character of this gesture. Those who would accuse it of being circular or begging the question would not be altogether wrong. At least provisionally, we are placing our trust, in fact, in this form of critical analysis we have inherited from Marxism: In a given situation, provided that it is determinable and determined as being that of a socio-political antagonism, a hegemonic force always seems to be represented by a dominant rhetoric and ideology, whatever may be the conflicts between forces, the principal contradiction or the secondary contradictions, the overdeterminations and the relays that may later complicate this schema—and therefore lead us to be suspicious of the simple opposition of *dominant* and *dominated*, or even of the final determination of the forces in conflict, or even, more radically, of the idea that force is always stronger than weakness (Nietzsche and Benjamin have encouraged us to have doubts on this score, each in his own way, and especially the latter when he associated "historical materialism" with the inheritance, precisely, of some "weak messianic force"[2]). Critical inheritance: one may thus, for example, speak of a dominant discourse or of dominant representations and ideas, and refer in this way to a hierarchized and conflictual field without necessarily subscribing to the concept of social class by means of which Marx so often determined, particularly in *The German Ideology*, the forces that are fighting for control of the hegemony. And even quite simply of the State. When, for example, in evoking the history of ideas, the *Manifesto* declares that the "ruling ideas [*die herrschenden Ideen*] of each age have ever been the ideas of its ruling class [*der herrschenden Klasse*]" (p. 26), it is not out of the question for a selective critique to filter the inheritance of this utterance so as to keep this rather than that. One may continue to speak of domination in a field of forces not only while suspending the reference to this ultimate support that would be the identity and the self-identity of a social class, but even while suspending the credit extended to what Marx calls the idea, the determination of the superstructure as idea, ideal or ideological representation, indeed even the discursive form of this representation. All the more so since the concept of idea implies this irreducible genesis of the spectral that we are planning to re-examine here.

But let us retain provisionally, for this very preliminary moment of our introduction, the schema of the dominant discourse. If such a discourse tends today to be getting the upper hand on the new stage of geopolitics (in the rhetoric of the politician, in the consensus of the media, over the most visible and resonant part of intellectual or academic space), it is the one that diagnoses, in all sorts of tones and with an unshakeable assurance, not only the end of societies constructed on the Marxist model but the end of the whole Marxist tradition, even of the reference to the works of Marx, not to say the end of history, period. All of this would have finally come to term in the euphoria of liberal democracy and of the market economy. This triumphant discourse seems relatively homogeneous, most often dogmatic, sometimes politically equivocal and, like dogmatisms, like all conjurations, secretly worried and manifestly worrisome. The protocol of our conference evokes the example of the book by Francis Fukuyama, *The End of History and the Last Man.*[3] Is not what we have here a new gospel, the noisiest, the most mediatized [*médiatique*], the most "successful" one on the subject of the death of Marxism as the end of history? This work frequently resembles, it is true, the disconcerting and tardy by-product of a "footnote": *nota bene* for a certain Kojève who deserved better. Yet the book is not as bad or as naive as one might be led to think by the frenzied exploitation that exhibits it as the finest ideological showcase of victorious capitalism in a liberal democracy which has finally arrived at the plenitude of its ideal, if not of its reality. In fact, although it remains essentially, in the tradition of Leo Strauss relayed by Allan Bloom, the grammar school exercise of a young, industrious, but come-lately reader of Kojève (and a few others), one must recognize that here or there this book goes beyond nuance and is sometimes suspensive to the point of indecision. To the questions elaborated in its own fashion, it on occasion ingenuously adds, so as to cover all the bases, what it calls "two broad responses, from the Left and the Right, respectively" (p. xxii). It would thus merit a very close analysis. This evening we will have to limit ourselves to what concerns the *general structure* of a thesis indispensable, precisely in the very structure of its logic, in the formulation of its formula, to the anti-Marxist conjuration.

It is by design, of course, that we called it a moment ago a "gospel."

Why a gospel? Why would the formula here be neo-testamentary? This book claims to bring a "positive response" to a question whose formation and formulation are never interrogated in themselves. It is the question of whether a "coherent and directional History of mankind" will eventually lead "the

(We are thus going to underscore it, as well as the figure of the Promised Land, which is at once close to it and dissociated from it for two reasons that we can only indicate here in parentheses. *On the one hand,* these biblical figures play a role that seems to exceed the simple rhetorical cliché they appear to be. *On the other hand,* they demand attention all the more so in that, in a fashion that is not fortuitous, the greatest symptomatic or metonymic concentration of what remains irreducible in the worldwide conjuncture in which the question of "whither Marxism" is inscribed today has its place, its figure, or the figure of its place in the Middle East: three other messianic eschatologies mobilize there all the forces of the world and the whole "world order" in the ruthless war they are waging against each other, directly or indirectly; they mobilize simultaneously, in order to put them to work or to the test, the old concepts of State and nation-State, of international law, of tele-techno-medio-economic and scientifico-military forces, in other words, the most archaic and the most modern spectral forces. One would have to analyze, in the limitless breadth of their worldwide historical stakes, since the end of the Second World War, in particular since the founding of the State of Israel, the violence that preceded, constituted, accompanied, and followed it on every side, *at the same time* in conformity with *and* in disregard of an international law that therefore appears today to be *at the same time* more contradictory, imperfect, and thus more perfectible and necessary than ever. Such an analysis can no longer avoid granting a determining role to this war of messianic eschatologies in what we will sum up with an ellipsis in the expression "appropriation of Jerusalem." The war for the "appropriation of Jerusalem" is today the world war. It is happening everywhere, it is the world, it is today the singular figure of its being "out of joint." Now, still in too elliptical a fashion, let us say that in order to determine in its radical premises Middle-Eastern violence as an unleashing of messianic eschatologies and as infinite combinatory possibilities of holy alliances [a word that must be put in the plural to account for what makes the triangle of the three religions said to be religions of the Book turn in these alliances], Marxism remains at once indispensable and structurally insufficient: it is still necessary *but* provided it be transformed and adapted to new conditions and to a new thinking of the ideological, provided it be made to analyze the new articulation of techno-economic causalities and of religious ghosts, the dependent condition of the juridical at the service of socio-economic powers or States that are themselves never totally independent with regard to capital [but there is no longer, there never was just capital, nor capitalism in the singular, but capitalisms plural—whether State or private, real or symbolic, always linked to spectral forces—or rather *capitalizations* whose antagonisms are irreducible].

This transformation and this opening up of Marxism are in conformity with what we were calling a moment ago the *spirit of Marxism*. If analysis of the Marxist type remains, then, indispensable, it appears to be radically insufficient there where the Marxist ontology grounding the project of Marxist science or critique *also itself carries with it and must carry with it, necessarily,* despite so many modern or post-modern denials, a messianic eschatology. On this score at least, paradoxically and despite the fact that it necessarily participates in them, it cannot be *simply* classified among the ideologems or theologems whose critique or demystification it calls for. In saying that, we will not claim that this messianic eschatology common both to the religions it criticizes and to the Marxist critique must be simply deconstructed. While it is common to both of them, with the exception of the content [but none of them can accept, of course, this *epokhē* of the content, whereas we hold it here to be essential to the messianic in general, as thinking of the other and of the event to come], it is also the case that its formal structure of promise exceeds them or precedes them. Well, what remains irreducible to any deconstruction, what remains as undeconstructible as the possibility itself of deconstruction is, perhaps, a certain experience of the emancipatory promise; it is perhaps even the formality of a structural messianism, a messianism without religion, even a messianic without messianism, an idea of justice—which we distinguish from law or right and even from human rights—and an idea of democracy—which we distinguish from its current concept and from its determined predicates today [permit me to refer here to "Force of Law" and *The Other Heading*]. But this is perhaps what must now be thought and thought otherwise in order to ask oneself where Marxism is going, which is also to say, where Marxism is leading and where is it to be led [*où conduire le Marxisme*]: where to lead it by interpreting it, which cannot happen without transformation, and not where can it lead us such as it is or such as it will have been.

We return to the *neo-evangelistic* rhetoric of Fukuyama: "we have become so accustomed by now to expect that the future will contain bad news with respect to the health and security of decent, democratic political practices that we have problems recognizing *good news* when it comes. And yet, the *good news* has come" [p. xv]. The neo-evangelistic insistence is significant for more reasons than one. A little further on, this Christian figure crosses the Jewish prefiguration of the Promised Land. But in order to take its distance from it right away. If the development of modern physics is not for nothing in the advent of the good news, notably, Fukuyama tells us, inasmuch as it is linked to a technology that permits "the limitless accumulation of wealth" and "an increasing homogenization of all human societies," it is "in the first place" because this "technology confers decisive military advantages on those countries that possess it" [p. xiv]. Now, although it is essential and indispensable to the advent or the "good news" proclaimed by Fukuyama, this physico-techno-military given only leads us as far, he says, as the gates of this "Promised Land": "But while modern natural science guides us to the gates of the Promised Land of liberal democrary, it does not deliver us to the Promised Land itself, for there is no economically necessary reason why advanced industrialization should produce political liberty" [p. xv].

We must be careful not to overinterpret, but let us take seriously the insistence of this rhetoric. What does it seem to be saying to us? That the language of the Promised Land, and thus of the land promised but refused [to Moses] is, *at least by itself,* better fitted to the materialism of physics and economism. If one takes into account the fact that Fukuyama associates a certain Jewish discourse of the Promised Land with the powerlessness of economist materialism or of the rationalism of natural science; and if one takes into account that elsewhere he treats as an almost negligible exception the fact that what he with equanimity calls "the Islamic world" does not enter into the "general consensus" that, he says, seems to be taking shape around "liberal democracy" [p. 211], one can form at least an hypothesis about which angle Fukuyama chooses to privilege in the eschatological triangle. The model of the liberal State to which he explicitly lays claim is not only that of Hegel, the Hegel of the struggle for recognition, it is that of a Hegel who privileges the "Christian vision." If "the existence of the State is the coming of God into the world," as one reads in *The Philosophy of Right* invoked by Fukuyama, this coming has the sense of a Christian event. The French Revolution would have been "the event that took the Christian vision of a free and equal society, and implanted it here on earth" [p. 199 and *passim*]. This end of History is essentially a Christian eschatology. It is consonant with the current discourse of the Pope on the European community: destined to become a Christian State or super-

State, this community would still belong therefore to some Holy Alliance. It is thus not unconnected with the alliance spoken of explicitly in the *Manifesto* which also named the Pope at that point. After having distinguished between the Anglo-Saxon model of the liberal State [Hobbes, Locke] and Hegelian "liberalism" that pursues first of all "rational recognition," Fukuyama distinguishes between two gestures by Kojève. When the latter describes the perfection of the universal and homogeneous State, he is depending too much on Locke and on an Anglo-Saxon model criticized by Hegel. On the other hand, he is right to affirm that postwar America or the European Community constitutes "the embodiment of Hegel's state of universal recognition" [p. 203].

In other words, consequently and in all good logic, a Christian State. A Holy Alliance.

We will not oppose some vulgarly "empirical" evidence to these predictive and predictable predications. We will come upon the problem of empiricity again later. If one considers, today, in Europe, the date of these declarations, those of Kojève *and* those of Fukuyama, one has difficulty pleading attenuating circumstances for a book published and widely translated in 1992. And let us specify once again that it is in the name of a Christian interpretation of the struggle for recognition [p. 199], and thus of the exemplary European Community, that the author of *The End of History and the Last Man* [Christian man] criticizes Marx and proposes to correct his materialist economism, to "complete it": the latter would be lacking that Hegeliano-Christian "pillar" of recognition or that "thymotic" element of the soul. The universal and homogeneous State, the State of the end of History, should rest on "the twin pillars of economics and recognition" [p. 204]. As at the time of the *Manifesto,* a European alliance is formed which is haunted by what it excludes, combats, or represses. End of this parenthesis. The import—past or future—of this neo-evangelism will be spelled out later.)

The economist materialism or the materialism of modern physics should then, in this logic, yield the stage to the spiritualist language of the "good news." Fukuyama thus deems it necessary to have recourse to what he calls "Hegel's non-materialist account of History, based on the 'struggle for recognition'." In truth, the whole book is inscribed in the unexamined axiomatics of this simplified—and highly Christianized—outline of the master-slave dialectic in the *Phenomenology of Spirit.* The dialectic of desire and of consciousness is nevertheless presented, with an imperturbable confidence, as the continuation of a Platonic theory of *thymos,* relayed all the way up to Hegel, and beyond him, by a tradition that would pass by way of Machiavelli, Hobbes, Locke, and so on, despite so many differences and disagreements among all these political thinkers. The Anglo-Saxon conception of modern liberalism would also be exemplary in this regard. It would in fact have sought to exclude all this *megalothymia* (characteristic of Stalin, Hitler, and Saddam Hussein [p. 190]), even if "the desire for recognition remains all around us in the form of *isothymia.*" Any contradiction would be cancelled once a State has succeeded in conjugating what Fukuyama calls the "twin pillars," that of economic rationality and that of the *thymos* or the desire for recognition. This would be the case, and *the thing would have already happened,* according to Kojève at least as he is interpreted—and seconded—by Fukuyama. The latter credits Kojève with having "identified an important truth when he asserted that postwar America or the members of the European Community constituted the embodiment of Hegel's state of universal recognition" (p. 203).

Let us underscore the words "important truth." They give a pretty good translation of the sophisticated naïveté or the crude sophism that impels the movement of such a book and sets its tone. They also deprive it of any credibility. For Fukuyama wants to find grist for the mill of his argument everywhere: in the "good news" as empirical and supposedly observable event (this is the "important truth" of the "embodiment of Hegel's state of universal recognition") *and/or* in the "good news" as simple sign of an *as yet inaccessible* regulating ideal that cannot be measured against any historical event and especially against any so-called "empirical" failure.

On the one hand, the gospel of politico-economic liberalism needs the event of the good news that consists in what has putatively *actually* happened (what has happened in this last quarter of the century, in particular, the supposed death of Marxism and the supposed realization of the State of liberal democracy). It cannot do without the recourse to the event; however since, *on the other hand,* actual history and so many other realities that have an empirical appearance contradict this advent of the perfect liberal democracy, one must at the same time pose this perfection as simply a regulating and trans-historical ideal. Depending on how it works to his advantage and serves his thesis, Fukuyama defines liberal democracy here as an actual reality and there as a

indispensable for a long time yet. For a long time and why not forever? We indeed say a problematics from the Marxian tradition, in its opening and the constant transformation that should have and will have to characterize it, and not from the Marxist dogmatics linked to the apparatuses of orthodoxy.)

Since he cannot deny, without inviting ridicule, all the violence, all the injustices, all the tyrannical and dictatorial manifestations of what he calls "megalothymia" (excess or asymmetry in the desire for recognition), since he must concede that they are raging in the capitalist world of a very imperfect liberal democracy, since these "facts" contradict the "identification" that he had nevertheless qualified as "an important truth," Fukuyama does not hesitate to slip one discourse in under the other. For the announcement of the *de facto* "good news," for its effective, phenomenal, historical, and empirically observable event, he substitutes the announcement of an *ideal* good news, the teleo-eschatological good news, which is inadequate to any empiricity. Once obliged to de-historicize it in this way, he recognizes in this good news the language of a "Nature" (this is his word and one of the major concepts of the book) and identifies it according to "criteria" which he qualifies as "trans-historical." In the face of so many disasters, in the face of all the *de facto* failures to establish liberal democracy, Fukuyama reminds us that he is speaking only on the "level of principles." He would limit himself, he says, to defining only the *ideal* of liberal democracy. Recalling his first article from 1989, "The End of History?", he writes in fact: "While some present-day countries might fail to achieve stable liberal democracy, and others might lapse back into other, more primitive forms of rule like theocracy or military dictatorship, the *ideal* of liberal democracy could not be improved on" (p. xi; the italics are Fukuyama's). It would be too easy to show that, measured by the failure to establish liberal democracy, the gap between fact and ideal essence does not show up only in these so-called primitive forms of government, theocracy, and military dictatorship (supposing even, *concesso non dato*, that all theocracy is foreign to the ideal State of liberal democracy, or heterogeneous to its very concept). But this failure and this gap also characterize, *a priori* and by definition, *all* democracies, including the oldest and most stable of so-called Western democracies. At stake here is the very concept of democracy as concept of a promise that can only arise in such a *diastema* (failure, inadequation, disjunction, disadjustment, being "out of joint"). That is why we always propose to speak of a democracy *to come*, not of a *future* democracy in the future present, not even of a regulating idea, in the Kantian sense, or of a utopia—at least to the extent that their inaccessibility would still retain the temporal form of a *future present*, of a future modality of the *living present.*

[Even beyond the regulating idea in its classic form, the idea, if that is still what it is, of democracy to come, its "idea" as event of a pledged injunction that orders one to summon the very thing that will never present itself in the form of full presence, is the opening of this gap between an infinite promise (always untenable at least for the reason that it calls for the infinite respect of the singularity *and* infinite alterity of the other as much as for the respect of the countable, calculable, subjectal equality between anonymous singularities) and the determined, necessary, but also necessarily inadequate forms of what has to be measured against this promise. To this extent, the effectivity or actuality of the democratic promise, like that of the communist promise, will always keep within it, and it must do so, this absolutely undetermined messianic hope at its heart, this eschatological relation to the to-come of an event *and* of a singularity, of an alterity that cannot be anticipated. Awaiting without horizon of the wait, awaiting what one does not expect yet or any longer, hospitality without reserve, welcoming salutation accorded in advance to the absolute surprise of the *arrivant*[4] from whom or from which one will not ask anything in return and who or which will not be asked to commit to the domestic contracts of any welcoming power (family, State, nation, territory, native soil or blood, language, culture in general, even humanity), *just* opening which renounces any right to property, any right in general, messianic opening to what is coming, that is, to the event that cannot be awaited *as such*, or recognized in advance therefore, to the event as the foreigner itself, to her or to him for whom one must leave an empty place, always, in memory of the hope—and this is the very place of spectrality. It would be easy, too easy, to show that such a hospitality without reserve, which is nevertheless the condition of the event and thus of history (nothing and no one would arrive otherwise, a hypothesis that one can never exclude, of course), is the impossible itself, and that this *condition of possibility* of the event is also its *condition of impossibility*, like this strange concept of messianism without content, of the messianic without messianism, that guides us here like the blind. But it would be just as easy to show that without this experience of the impossible, one might as well give up on both justice and the event. That would be still more just or more honest. One might as well give up also on whatever good conscience one still claims to preserve. One might as well confess the economic calculation and declare all the checkpoints that ethics, hospitality, or the various messianisms would still install at the borders of the event in order to screen the *arrivant*.]

Let us return to Fukuyama. What is more original than indisputable in his logic is the fact that this ideal is not posed as an infinite regulating ideal and the pole of an endless task or approximation, although often, and this is yet another incoherency, he declares that this "current trend toward liberalism," despite its tendency to "recede," "*promises* to be victorious in the long run" (p. 212; emphasis added). Fukuyama considers this ideal also as an event. Because it would have *already happened*, because the ideal would have presented itself in its form as ideal, this event would have already marked the end of a finite history. This ideal is at once *infinite and finite: infinite*, since it is distinguished from any determined empirical reality or remains a tendency "in the long run," it is nevertheless *finite* since it has happened, already, as ideal, and therefore history is over. That is why this book also defines itself as Hegelian *and* Marxist, like a kind of exercise in the discipline of these two masters of the end of history, Hegel and Marx. After having called to the witness stand and heard the testimony of the two masters in his own fashion (which, it must be said, is rather hurried), Fukuyama has made his choice. He writes:

> Both Hegel and Marx believed that the evolution of human societies was not open-ended, but would end when mankind had achieved a form of society that satisfied its deepest and most fundamental longings. Both thinkers thus posited an "end of history": for Hegel this was the liberal state, while for Marx it was a communist society. (P. xii)

So the disciple has chosen between the two masters and he chooses the thinker of the liberal State. In a Christian tradition, as we have already seen,[5] but also, whether or not it seems consistent with this essential Christianity, in a naturalist tradition.

Here one would have to analyze minutely this or that page, but we must be satisfied with just referring to them, not, however, without having quoted at least a few sentences. For example these:

In the end, it would appear impossible to talk about "history," much less a "Universal History," without reference to a permanent, trans-historical standard, i.e., without reference to nature. For "history" is not a given, not merely a catalogue of everything that happened in the past, but a deliberate effort of abstraction in which we separate out important from unimportant events. (P. 138)

Solid and durable tradition of a logic according to which naturalism and tele-ologism are founded one upon the other. Fukuyama rejects what he serenely considers to be "the 'empirical' evidence presented to us by the contemporary world."[6] "We must instead," he continues, "raise directly and explicitly the nature of the trans-historical standards by which we evaluate the goodness or badness of any regime or social system" (p. 139). The measure of all things has a single name: the *trans-historical and natural* criterion against which Fukuyama ultimately proposes to measure everything is called "man as *man*." It is a little as if he had never come across any worrisome question about such a Man, or read either a certain Marx or the Stirner whom the latter goes after in *The German Ideology* regarding the properly ghostly abstraction of such a concept of man, not to mention Nietzsche (constantly caricatured and reduced to a few miserable stereotypes: for example, the "relativist"! and not the thinker of a "last man" whom he so often named as such), not to mention Freud (evoked only once as having put "human dignity" in doubt by reducing man to "deeply hidden sexual urges" [p. 297]), not to mention Husserl—simply passed over in silence—or Heidegger (who would be but the "follower" of the relativist Nietzsche [p. 333]), not to mention a few thinkers who are even closer to us, and first of all, and especially, not to mention a certain Hegel, about whom the least one can say is that he is not a philosopher of natural and trans-historical man. If the reference to Hegel dominates this book, that reference is never bothered by this obvious fact. To define this supposedly natural entity, this man as Man whom he talks about so blithely, Fukuyama claims to come back to what he calls "the first man," that is, to "natural man." On the concept of nature, on the genealogy of this concept, Fukuyama moreover seems unforthcoming (almost as much as Marx, one must add, even if the critical treatment to which the latter subjects the abstract concepts of Nature and Man as man remains a rich and fertile one). And when, so as to speak of this "natural man," Fukuyama claims to have recourse to an "entirely non-materialist" dialectic issued by what he calls "a new, synthetic philosopher named Hegel-Kojève," the *artifact* he proposes to us seems so inconsistent and insubstantial that we will give up devoting too much time to it this evening. Beyond its philosophical naïveté, it must no doubt be treated precisely as an *artifact*, a symptomatic *montage* that responds to a demand, in order to reassure it; one could almost say it responds on demand. It doubtless owes its success to this soothing confusion and to this opportunist logic of the "good news" which the confusion opportunely smuggles in as contraband.

In spite of all that, it would be, it seems, neither just nor even interesting to accuse Fukuyama of the fate reserved for his book. One would do better to ask oneself why this book, with the "good news" it claims to bring, has become such a media gadget, and why it is all the rage in the ideological supermarkets of a worried West where it is bought up just as, at the first rumors of war, people buy sugar and oil, when there is any left.[7] Why this amplification by the media? And how is it that a discourse of this type is sought out by those who celebrate the triumph of liberal capitalism and its predestined alliance with liberal democracy only in order to hide, and first of all from themselves, the fact that this triumph has never been so critical, fragile, threatened, even in certain regards catastrophic, and in sum bereaved? Bereaved by what the specter of Marx represents still today and which it would be a matter of conjuring away one more time in a jubilatory and manic fashion (a necessary phase of unsuccessful mourning work, according to Freud), but also virtually bereaved for itself. By hiding from themselves all these failures and all these threats, people would like to hide from the potential—force and virtuality—of what we will call the principle and even, still in the figure of irony, the *spirit* of the Marxist critique. We would be tempted to distinguish this *spirit* of the Marxist critique, which seems to be more indispensable than ever today, at once from Marxism as ontology, philosophical or metaphysical system, as "dialectical materialism,"[8] from Marxism as historical materialism or method, and from Marxism incorporated in the apparatuses of party, State, or workers' International. But we will also distinguish it from what could be called, to go quickly, a deconstruction, there where the latter is no longer simply a *critique* and where the questions it poses to any critique and even to any question have never been in a position either to identify with or especially to oppose symmetrically something like Marxism, the Marxist ontology, or the Marxist critique.

If a discourse of the Fukuyama type plays to good effect the role of channel-jamming and doubly bereaved disavowal expected of it, it is because, cleverly for some, crudely for others, it performs a sleight-of-hand trick: *with the one hand*, it accredits a logic of the empirical event which it needs whenever it is a question of certifying the finally final defeat of the so-called Marxist States and of everything that bars access to the Promised Land of economic and political liberalisms; but *with the other hand*, in the name of the trans-historic and natural ideal, it discredits this same logic of the so-called empirical event, it has to suspend it to avoid chalking up to the account of this ideal and its concept precisely whatever contradicts them in such a cruel fashion: in a word, all the *evil*, all that is *not going well* in the capitalist States and in liberalism, in a world dominated by other forces whose hegemony is linked to this supposedly trans-historical or natural (let us say rather naturalized) ideal. We will say a few words later about the major outlines of what is going so badly in the world today. As for the sleight-of-hand trick between history and nature, between historical empiricity and teleological transcendentality, between the supposed empirical reality of the event and the absolute ideality of the liberal *telos*, it can only be undone on the basis of a new thinking or a new experience of the event, and of another logic of its relation to the phantomatic. We will approach this later. The logic of this novelty is not necessarily opposed to the most ancient ancientness.

But once again one should not be unfair to this book. Although such works remain fascinating, their very incoherence and sometimes their distressing primitivity play the role of symptomatic signal which one must account for as well as possible. Arousing our attention to a geopolitics of the ideological stakes of the moment, deploying them on the scale of the worldwide cultural market, works like these have the value of reminding us of a complication to which I alluded a moment ago. Let's be specific. If all these themes of the end (end of history, end of man, figure of the "last man," entry into a certain post-Marxism, and so forth) were, already at the beginning of the '60s, part of the elementary culture of the philosophers of my generation, we are not stuck today in their simple and static repetition. For it is also true that from this fundamental event it was not possible to deduce, and still less to date, this other event, this other series of events in progress and still unanalyzed which came about, three decades later, at a *rhythm* that no one in the world could calculate in advance, not even a few months before. (In 1981, while I was imprisoned in Prague by those then in power, I said to myself with a naive sense of near certainty: "This barbarism could last for centuries…") It is this latter event-ness that one must think, but that best resists what is called the concept, if not thinking. And it will not be thought as long as one relies on the simple (ideal, mechanical, or dialectical) opposition of the real presence of the real present or the living present to its ghostly simulacrum, the opposition of the effective or actual (*wirklich*) to the non-effective, inactual, which is also to say, as long as one relies on a general temporality or an historical temporality made up of the *successive* linking of presents identical to themselves and contemporary with themselves.

This neo-liberal rhetoric, both jubilant and worried, manic and bereaved, often obscene in its euphoria, obliges us, then, to interrogate an event-ness inscribed in the gap between the moment in which the ineluctable of a certain end was heralded and the actual collapse of those totalitarian States or societies that gave themselves the figure of Marxism. This latency period, which no one managed to represent to themselves much less to calculate in advance, is not just a temporal medium. No objective and homogeneous chronology can measure it. A set of transformations of all sorts (in particular, techno-scientifico-economico-media) exceeds both the traditional givens of the Marxist discourse and those of the liberal discourse opposed to it. Even if we have inherited some essential resources for projecting their analysis, we must first recognize that these mutations perturb the onto-theological schemas or the philosophies of technics as such. They disturb political philosophies and the common concepts of democracy, they oblige us to reconsider all relations between State and nation, man and citizen, the private and the public, and so forth.

This is where another thinking of historicity calls us beyond the metaphysical concept of history and the end of history, whether it be derived from Hegel or from Marx. This is where one could put to work in a more demanding fashion the two moments of the Kojevian postscript on post-history and post-historical animals. It would be necessary, of course, to take into account Kojève's sometimes genial, often naively joking baroquism. Fukuyama does not do so enough, even if the irony of certain provocations does not entirely escape him. But it would also have been necessary to analyze with all possible rigor the numerous chronological and logical articulations of that long and famous footnote. As he tells us in the postscript to his Note, Kojève went to Japan in 1959. (There is a French tradition, a kind of "French specialty" of peremptory diagnoses upon returning from a quick trip to a faraway land whose language one does not even speak and about which one knows next to nothing. Charles Péguy already made fun of this vice in 1913 when Gustave Lanson dared to claim expertise after a trip of a few weeks to the United States.) Upon returning from this visit which he made as an important public official of the European Community, Kojève concluded that "post-historical" Japanese civilization had set out on a path diametrically opposed to the "American path," and this because of what he then names, in that profoundly offhand, nutty, and pataphysician manner which is, to be sure, his genius but which is also his entire responsibility, "the Snobism in the pure state" of the cultural formalism of Japanese society. But he nevertheless maintains what is most important in his view, namely his previous diagnosis concerning properly American post-history. It's just that he will have had to revise something in an incredible and indecent tableau: the United States as the "final stage of Marxist 'communism'." The only thing Kojève now puts in question is the idea that this American end represents, if one may say so, the ultimate figure of the ultimate, namely of "the Hegelian-Marxist end of History" as present and not as future. Revising and contesting his first hypothesis, Kojève comes around to thinking that there is an even more final end of history, an even more eschatological end than the American (and even Californian, as he says somewhere) "happy end," and it is the more than extreme Japanese extremity (in the competition between the two capitalisms whose war will have inaugurated, let us not forget, the era of nuclear destruction!). According to Kojève, the final stage of communism in the postwar United States does indeed, as it must, reduce man to animality. But there is something even more chic, "snobbier," there is a *nec plus ultra* in the end of history and that is Japanese post-historicity. The latter succeeds, thanks to the "snobism" of its culture, in saving post-historical man from his return to animal naturality. Nevertheless, and one must emphasize this, despite the regret that caused him to think, after his 1959 trip, that Japan had *gone further*, so to speak, in its race *after* the end of history, Kojève does not put in question again his description of man's return to animality in the postwar United States. An extravagant description, not because it compares man to animals, but in the first place because it puts an imperturbable and arrogant ignorance to work in the service of doubtful effects; and it is on this point that it would be appropriate to compare Kojève's impudence to the incantation of those who, like Fukuyama, sing (as for Kojève, he is not singing) "the universalization of Western liberal democracy as end-point of human government" and the victory of capitalism that would have "successfully resolved" the "class problem," and so forth.[9] Why and how was Kojève able to think that the United States had already reached the "final stage" of "Marxist 'communism'"? What did he think he perceived there, what did he want to perceive there? Answer: the appropriation, in abundance, of everything that can respond to need or desire, the cancelation of the gap between desire and need suspends any excess, any disadjustment, in partic-ular in work. It is not at all surprising that this end of the disadjustment (of the being "out of joint") "prefigures [an] eternal present." But what about the gap between this prefiguration and what it represents before its presence itself?

> Practically [this "practically" is the grotesque signature of this senten-tious verdict], all the members of a "classless society" can appropriate there as of now [1946] whatever they like, without having for all that to work any more than they wish to.
>
> Several comparative trips (between 1948 and 1958) to the United States and the USSR have left me with the impression that if Americans appear to be Sino-Soviets who have gotten rich, it is because the Russians and the Chinese are still but impoverished Americans, moreover on a rapid road toward wealth. I was led to conclude that the *American way of life* [in English in the original] was the kind of life proper to the post-historical period and that the presence today of the United States in the World prefigures the future "eternal present" of all of humanity. Thus Man's return to animality seemed no longer a possibility still to come, but an already present certainty.
>
> It was after a recent trip to Japan (1959) that I radically changed my opinion on this point....[10]

Who could deny that the neo-Marxist and para-Heideggerian reading of the *Phenomenology of Spirit* by Kojève is interesting? It played a formative and not negligible role, from many standpoints, for a certain generation of French intellectuals, just before or just after the war. Things are not as simple in this regard as people generally maintain, but that is not our point here. On the other hand, if one wants to read with some seriousness that which is not alto-gether serious, namely Kojève's note and postscript on post-Marxism as post-history of humanity, then one must still underscore at least a few points. First of all, the last and also most enigmatic sentence of this note, which we are going to quote, remains a prescriptive utterance. Who has ever read it? It is perhaps the most irresistible opening in this "Postscript." It defines a task and a duty [*devoir*] for the *future* of post-historical man, once what Kojève calls the "Japanization" of the West (including the Russians) will have been realized. "Post-historical man *doit*...," writes Kojève. "Doit" what? Is "doit" to be translated here as "must" or "should"? *Whatever may be the case concerning the modality or the content* of this "devoir," whatever may be the necessity of this prescription, even if it calls for eternities of interpretation, there is an "it is necessary" for the future. Whatever may be its indetermination, be it that of "it is necessary [that there be] the future" ["*il faut l'avenir*"], there is some future and some history, there is perhaps even the beginning of historicity for post-historical Man, beyond man and beyond history such as they have been represented up until now. We must insist on this specific point precisely because it points to an essential lack of specificity, an indetermination that remains the ultimate mark of the future: *whatever may be the case concerning the modality or the content* of this duty, this necessity, this prescription or this injunction, this pledge, this task, also therefore this promise, this necessary promise, *this "it is necessary" is necessary, and that is the law.* This indifference to the content here is not an indifference, it is not an *attitude* of indifference, on the contrary. Marking any opening to the event and to the future as such, it therefore conditions the interest in and not the indifference to anything whatsoever, to all content in general. Without it, there would be neither intention, nor need, nor desire, and so on. The concept of this singular indifference (difference itself) is not projected by our reading onto Kojève's text. The latter speaks of it. It characterizes in his view a *future* that would carry beyond what has up until now been called history. Apparently "formalist," this indifference to the content has perhaps the value of giving one to think the necessarily pure and purely necessary form of the future as such, in its being-necessarily-promised, prescribed, assigned, enjoined, in the necessarily formal necessity of its possibility—in short, in its law. It is this law that dislodges any present out of its contemporaneity with itself. Whether the promise promises this or that, whether it be fulfilled or not, or whether it be unfilfillable, there is necessarily some promise and therefore some historicity as future-to-come. It is what we are nicknaming the messianic without messianism. For lack of time, let us do no more than read this sentence to which, in another context and at another rhythm, it would have been necessary to devote all the meditative attention it demands:

> Which means that even while he speaks from now on in an *adequate* fash-
> ion of all that he has been given, post-historical Man *must/should* [doit]
> [we underscore this *doit* that doubtless takes us back to the common con-
> dition of possibility of the two forms of the necessary, *must* and *should*]
> continue to *detach* [underscored by Kojève] "forms" from their "con-
> tents," doing this not in order to trans-form the latter actively, but in
> order to *oppose himself* [underlined by Kojève] as a pure "form" to him-
> self and to others, taken as whatever sorts of "contents." (P. 437)

   Is it possible to reread this text of Kojève's otherwise? Is it possible to rescue
it from the crude manipulation it has received in the hands not so much of
Fukuyama himself (who, moreover, is not interested in this enigmatic conclusion), but of those who exploit him? Read with some sense of the actor's
ploy, the one demanded by Kojève, and therefore with more philosophical,
political, or "ideological" vigilance, this text resists. It survives perhaps those
who waste no time translating it and putting it on display as a weapon of
philosophical propaganda or an object of prime-time media consumption.
The "logic" of the proposition just quoted might indeed correspond to a law,
the law of the law. This law would signify the following to us: in the same
place, on the same limit, where history is finished, there where a certain determined concept of history comes to an end, precisely there the historicity of
history begins, there finally it has the chance of heralding itself—of promising
itself. There where man, a certain determined concept of man, is finished,
there the pure humanity of man, of the *other man* and of man *as other* begins
or has finally the chance of heralding itself—of promising itself. In an apparently inhuman or else a-human fashion. Even if these propositions still call
for critical or deconstructive questions, they are not reducible to the vulgate of
the capitalist paradise as end of history.
   (Permit me to recall very briefly that a certain deconstructive procedure, at
least the one in which I thought I had to engage, consisted from the outset in
putting into question the onto-theo- but also archeo-teleological concept of
history—in Hegel, Marx, or even in the epochal thinking of Heidegger. Not
in order to oppose it with an end of history or an anhistoricity, but, on the
contrary, in order to show that this onto-theo-archeo-teleology locks up, neutralizes, and finally cancels historicity. It was then a matter of thinking another

historicity—not a new history or still less a "new historicism," but another opening of event-ness as historicity that permitted one not to renounce, but on the contrary to open up access to an affirmative thinking of the messianic and emancipatory promise as promise: as *promise* and not as onto-theological or teleo-eschatological program or design. Not only must one not renounce the emancipatory desire, it is necessary to insist on it more than ever, it seems, and insist on it, moreover, as the very indestructibility of the "it is necessary." This is the condition of a re-politicization, perhaps of another concept of the political.

But at a certain point promise and decision, which is to say responsibility, owe their possibility to the ordeal of undecidability which will always remain their condition. And all the grave stakes we have just named in a few words would come down to the question of what one understands, with Marx and after Marx, by effectivity, effect, operativity, work, labor [*Wirklichkeit, Wirkung,* work, operation], living work in their supposed opposition to the spectral logic that also governs the effects of virtuality, of simulacrum, of "mourning work," of ghost, *revenant,* and so forth. And of the justice that is their due. To put it in a few words, deconstructive thinking of the trace, of iterability, of prosthetic synthesis, of supplementarity, and so forth, goes beyond this opposition, beyond the ontology it presumes. Inscribing the possibility of the reference to the other, and thus of radical alterity and heterogeneity, of dif-fer*a*nce, of technicity, and of ideality in the very event of presence, in the presence of the present that it dis-joins *a priori* in order to make it possible [thus impossible in its identity or its contemporaneity with itself], it does not deprive itself of the means with which to take into account, or to render an account of, the effects of ghosts, of simulacra, of "synthetic images," or even, to put it in terms of the Marxist code, of ideologems, even if these take the novel forms to which modern technology will have given rise. That is why such a deconstruction has never been Marxist, no more than it has ever been non-Marxist, although it has remained faithful to a certain spirit of Marxism, to at least one of its spirits for, and this can never be repeated too often, there is *more than one* of them and they are heterogeneous.)

3

wears and tears

(tableau of an ageless world)

The time is out of joint. The world is going badly. It is worn but its wear no longer counts. Old age or youth—one no longer counts in that way. The world has more than one age. We lack the measure of the measure. We no longer realize the wear, we no longer take account of it as of a single age in the progress of history. Neither maturation, nor crisis, nor even agony. Something else. What is happening is happening to age itself, it strikes a blow at the teleological order of history. What is coming, in which the untimely appears, is happening to time but it does not happen in time. Contretemps. *The time is out of joint.* Theatrical speech, Hamlet's speech before the theater of the world, of history, and of politics. The age is off its hinges. Everything, beginning with time, seems out of kilter, unjust, dis-adjusted. The world is going very badly, it wears as it grows, as the Painter also says at the beginning of *Timon of Athens* (which is Marx's play, is it not). For, this time, it is a painter's speech, as if he were speaking of a spectacle or before a tableau: "How goes the world? —It wears, sir, as it grows."[1]

This wearing in expansion, in growth itself, which is to say in the becoming worldwide [*mondialisation*] of the world, is not the unfolding of a normal, normative, or normed process. It is not a phase of development, one more crisis, a growth crisis because growth is what is bad ("it wears as it grows"); it is no longer an end-of-ideologies, a last crisis-of-Marxism, or a new crisis-of-capitalism.

The world is going badly, the picture is bleak, one could say almost black. Let us form an hypothesis. Suppose that, for lack of time (the spectacle or the tableau is always "for lack of time"), we propose simply to paint, like the Painter in *Timon of Athens*. A black picture on a blackboard. Taxonomy or freeze-frame image. Title: "The time is out of joint" or "What is going so badly today in the world." We would leave this banal title in its neutral form so as to avoid speaking of crisis, a very insufficient concept, and so as to avoid deciding between the bad as suffering and the bad as wrong or as crime.

We would add to this title of a possible blackboard picture merely a few subtitles. What are they?

One might already have been shocked by the Kojevian picture of the state of the world and the state of the United States after the war. The optimism of the picture was tainted by cynicism. It was *already* insolent to say then that "all the members of a 'classless society' can appropriate there as of now whatever they like, without having for all that to work any more than they wish to." But what is one to think today of the imperturbable thoughtlessness that consists in singing the triumph of capitalism or of economic and political liberalism, "the universalization of Western liberal democracy as the endpoint of human government," the "end of the problem of social classes"? What cynicism of good conscience, what manic disavowal could cause someone to write, if not believe, that "everything that stood in the way of the reciprocal recognition of human dignity, always and everywhere, has been refuted and buried by history"?[2]

Provisionally and for the sake of convenience, let us rely on the outdated opposition between civil war and international war. Under the heading of civil war, is it still necessary to point out that liberal democracy of the parliamen-

in all Western democracies no longer to respect the professional politician or even the party member as such, it is no longer only because of some personal insufficiency, some fault, or some incompetence, or because of some scandal that can now be more widely known, amplified, and in fact often produced, if not premeditated by the power of the media. Rather, it is because politicians become more and more, or even solely characters in the media's representation at the very moment when the transformation of the public space, precisely by the media, causes them to lose the essential part of the power and even of the competence they were granted before by the structures of parliamentary representation, by the party apparatuses that were linked to it, and so forth. However competent they may personally be, professional politicians who conform to the old model tend today to become *structurally* incompetent. The same media power accuses, produces, and amplifies *at the same time* this incompetence of traditional politicians: on the one hand, it takes aways from them the legitimate power they held in the former political space (party, parliament, and so forth), but, on the other hand, it obliges them to become mere silhouettes, if not marionettes, on the stage of televisual rhetoric. They were thought to be actors of politics, they now often risk, as everyone knows, being no more than TV actors.[3] Under the heading of international or civil-international war, is it still necessary to point out the economic wars, national wars, wars among minorities, the unleashing of racisms and xenophobias, ethnic conflicts, conflicts of culture and religion that are tearing apart so-called democratic Europe and the world today? Entire regiments of ghosts have returned, armies from every age, camouflaged by the archaic symptoms of the paramilitary and of the postmodern excess of arms (information technology, panoptical surveillance via satellite, nuclear threat, and so forth). Let us accelerate things. Beyond these two types of war (civil and international) whose dividing line cannot even be distinguished any longer, let us blacken still more the picture of this wearing down beyond wear. Let us name with a single trait that which could risk making the euphoria of liberal-democrat capitalism resemble the blindest and most delirious of hallucinations, or even an increasingly glaring hypocrisy in its formal or juridicist rhetoric of human rights. It will not be a matter of merely accumulating, as Fukuyama might say, "empirical evidence," it will not suffice to point one's finger at the mass of undeniable facts that this picture could describe or denounce. The question posed too briefly would not even be that of the analysis with which one would then have to proceed in all these directions, but of the *double interpretation*, the concurrent readings that the picture seems to call for and to oblige us to associate. If one were permitted to name these plagues of the "new world order" in a ten-word telegram, one might perhaps choose the following ten words.

1. Unemployment, that more or less well-calculated deregulation of a new market, new technologies, new worldwide competitiveness, would no doubt, like labor or production, deserve another name today. All the more so in that tele-work inscribes there a new set of givens that perturbs both the methods of traditional calculation and the conceptual opposition between work and non-work, activity, employment, and their contrary. This regular deregulation is at once mastered, calculated, "socialized" (that is, most often disavowed), and irreducible to prediction—like suffering itself, a suffering that suffers still more, and more obscurely, for having lost its habitual models and language once it no longer recognizes itself in the old word unemployment and in the scene that word named for so long. The function of social inactivity, of non-work or of underemployment is entering into a new era. It calls for another politics. And another concept. The "new unemployment" no more resembles unemployment, in the very forms of its experience and its calculation, than what in France is called the "new poverty" resembles poverty.

2. The massive exclusion of homeless citizens from any participation in the democratic life of States, the expulsion or deportation of so many exiles, stateless persons, and immigrants from a so-called national territory already herald a new experience of frontiers and identity—whether national or civil.

3. The ruthless economic war among the countries of the European Community themselves, between them and the Eastern European countries, between Europe and the United States, and between Europe, the United States, and Japan. This war controls everything, beginning with the other wars, because it controls the practical interpretation and an inconsistent and unequal application of international law. There have been too many examples in the last decade or more.

4. The inability to master the contradictions in the concept, norms, and reality of the free market (the barriers of a protectionism and the interventionist bidding wars of capitalist States seeking to protect their nationals, or even Westerners or Europeans in general, from cheap labor, which often has no comparable social protection). How is one to save one's own interests in the global market while claiming to protect one's "social advantages"

and so forth?

5. The aggravation of the foreign debt and other connected mechanisms are starving or driving to despair a large portion of humanity. They tend thus to exclude it simultaneously from the very market that this logic nevertheless seeks to extend. This type of contradiction works through many geopolitical fluctuations even when they appear to be dictated by the discourse of democratization or human rights.

6. The arms industry and trade (whether it be "conventional" arms or at the cutting edge of tele-technological sophistication) are inscribed in the normal regulation of the scientific research, economy, and socialization of labor in Western democracies. Short of an unimaginable revolution, they cannot be suspended or even cut back without running major risks, beginning with the worsening of the said unemployment. As for arms trafficking, to the (limited) degree that it can still be distinguished from "normal" commerce, it remains the largest in the world, larger than the drug traffic, from which it is not always dissociated.

7. The spread ("dissemination") of nuclear weapons, maintained by the very countries that say they want to protect themselves from it, is no longer even controllable, as was the case for a long time, by statist structures. It exceeds not only statist control but every declared market.

8. Inter-ethnic wars (have there ever been another kind?) are proliferating, driven by an *archaic* phantasm and concept, by a *primitive conceptual phantasm* of community, the nation-State, sovereignty, borders, native soil and blood. Archaism is not a bad thing in itself, it doubtless keeps some irreducible resource. But how can one deny that this conceptual phantasm is, so to speak, made more outdated than ever, in the very *ontopology* it supposes, by tele-technic dis-location? (By *ontopology* we mean an axiomatics linking indissociably the ontological value of present-being [*on*] to its *situation*, to the stable and presentable determination of a locality, the *topos* of territory, native soil, city, body in general). For having spread in an unheard-of fashion, which is more and more differentiated and more and more accelerated (it is acceleration itself, beyond the norms of speed that have until now informed human culture), the process of dislocation is no less arch-originary, that is, just as "archaic" as the archaism that it has always dislodged. This process is, moreover, the positive condition of the stabilization that it constantly relaunches. All stability in a place being but a stabilization or a sedentarization, it will

have to have been necessary that the local differ*a*nce, the spacing of a displacement gives the movement its start. And gives place and gives rise [*donne
lieu*]. All national rootedness, for example, is rooted first of all in the memory
or the anxiety of a displaced—or displaceable—population. It is not only time
that is "out of joint," but space, space in time, spacing.

9. How can one ignore the growing and undelimitable, that is, worldwide
power of those super-efficient and properly capitalist phantom-States that are
the mafia and the drug cartels on every continent, including in the former so-
called socialist States of Eastern Europe? These phantom-States have infil-
trated and banalized themselves everywhere, to the point that they can no
longer be strictly identified. Nor even sometimes clearly dissociated from the
processes of democratization (think—for example—of the schema, telegraphically simplified here, that would associate them with the history-of-a-
Sicilian-mafia-harassed-by-the-fascism-of-the-Mussolinian-State-thus-intim-
ately-and-symbiotically-allied-to-the-Allies-in-the-democratic-camp-on-
both-sides-of-the-Atlantic-as-well-as-in-the-reconstruction-of-the-Italian-
Christian-democratic-State-which-has-today-entered-into-a-new-configura-
tion-of-capital, about which the least one can say is that we will understand
nothing of what is happening there if we do not take account of its genealogy). All these infiltrations are going through a "critical" phase, as one says,
which is no doubt what allows us to talk about them or to begin their analysis. These phantom-States invade not only the socioe-conomic fabric, the general circulation of capital, but also statist or inter-statist institutions.

10. For above all, above all, one would have to analyze the present state of
international law and of its institutions. Despite a fortunate perfectibility,
despite an undeniable progress, these international institutions suffer from at
least two limits. The first and most radical of the two stems from the fact that
their norms, their charter, the definition of their mission depend on a certain
historical culture. They cannot be dissociated from certain European philosophical concepts, and notably from a concept of State or national sovereignty
whose genealogical closure is more and more evident, not only in a theoreti-
co-juridical or speculative fashion, but concretely, practically, and practically
quotidian. Another limit is strictly linked to the first: This supposedly universal international law remains, in its application, largely dominated by
particular nation-States. Almost always their techno-economic and military
power prepares and applies, in other words, *carries* the decision. As one says in

English, it *makes the decision.* Countless examples, recent or not so recent, would amply demonstrate this, whether it is a question of deliberations and resolutions of the United Nations or of the putting into practice or the "enforcement" of these decisions: the incoherence, discontinuity, inequality of States before the law, the hegemony of certain States over military power in the service of international law, this is what, year after year, day after day, we are forced to acknowledge.[4]

These facts do not suffice to disqualify international institutions. Justice demands, on the contrary, that one pay tribute to certain of those who are working within them in the direction of the perfectibility and emancipation of institutions that must never be renounced. However insufficient, confused, or equivocal such signs may still be, we should salute what is heralded today in the reflection on the right of interference or intervention in the name of what is obscurely and sometimes hypocritically called the *humanitarian*, thereby limiting the sovereignty of the State in certain conditions. Let us salute such signs even as one remains vigilantly on guard against the manipulations or appropriations to which these novelties can be subjected.

Let us return now to the immediate vicinity of the subject of our conference. My subtitle, "the New International," refers to a profound transformation, projected over a long term, of international law, of its concepts, and its field of intervention. Just as the concept of human rights has slowly been determined over the course of centuries through many socio-political upheavals (whether it be a matter of the right to work or economic rights, of the rights of women and children, and so forth), likewise international law should extend and diversify its field to include, if at least it is to be consistent with the idea of democracy and of human rights it proclaims, the *worldwide* economic and social field, beyond the sovereignty of States and of the phantom-States we mentioned a moment ago. Despite appearances, what we are saying here is not simply anti-statist: in given and limited conditions, the super-State, which might be an international institution, may always be able to limit the appropriations and the violence of certain private socio-economic forces. But without necessarily subscribing to the whole Marxist discourse (which, moreover, is complex, evolving, heterogeneous) on the State and its appropriation by a dominant class, on the distinction between State power and State apparatus, on the end of the political, on "the end of politics," or on the withering away of the State,[5] and, on the other hand, without suspecting the juridical idea in itself, one may still find inspiration in the Marxist "spirit" to criticize the presumed autonomy of the juridical and to denounce endlessly the *de facto* take-over of international authorities by powerful Nation-States, by concentrations of techno-scientific capital, symbolic capital, and financial capital, of State capital and private capital. A "new international" is being sought through these crises of international law; it already denounces the limits of a discourse on human rights that will remain inadequate, sometimes hypocritical, and in any case formalistic and inconsistent with itself as long as the law of the market, the "foreign debt," the inequality of techno-scientific, military, and economic development maintain an effective inequality as monstrous as that which prevails today, to a greater extent than ever in the history of humanity. For it must be cried out, at a time when some have the audacity to neo-evangelize in the name of the ideal of a liberal democracy that has finally realized itself as the ideal of human history: never have violence, inequality, exclusion, famine, and thus economic oppression affected as many human beings in the history of the earth and of humanity. Instead of singing the advent of the ideal of liberal democracy and of the capitalist market in the euphoria of the end of history, instead of celebrating the "end of ideologies" and the end of the great emancipatory discourses, let us never neglect this obvious macroscopic fact, made up of innumerable singular sites of suffering: no degree of progress allows one to ignore that never before, in absolute figures, never have so many men, women, and children been subjugated, starved, or exterminated on the earth. (And provisionally, but with regret, we must leave aside here the nevertheless indissociable question of what is becoming of so-called "animal" life, the life and existence of "animals" in this history. This question has always been a serious one, but it will become massively unavoidable.)

The "New International" is not only that which is seeking a new international law through these crimes. It is a link of affinity, suffering, and hope, a still discreet, almost secret link, as it was around 1848, but more and more visible, we have more than one sign of it. It is an untimely link, without status, without title, and without name, barely public even if it is not clandestine, without contract, "out of joint," without coordination, without party, without country, without national community (International before, across, and beyond any national determination), without co-citizenship, without common belonging to a class. The name of new International is given here to what calls to the friendship of an alliance without institution among those who, even if they no longer believe or never believed in the socialist-Marxist International, in the dictatorship of the proletariat, in the messiano-eschato-logical role of the universal union of the proletarians of all lands, continue to be inspired by at least one of the spirits of Marx or of Marxism (they now know that there is *more than one*) and in order to ally themselves, in a new, concrete, and real way, even if this alliance no longer takes the form of a party or of a workers' international, but rather of a kind of counter-conjuration, in the (theoretical and practical) critique of the state of international law, the concepts of State and nation, and so forth: in order to renew this critique, and especially to radicalize it.

There are at least *two ways to interpret* what we have just called the "blackboard picture," the ten plagues, the mourning and promise it announces while pretending to expose or to count. Between these two interpretations, which are at once in competition and incompatible, how is one to choose? Why can we not choose? Why must we not choose? In both cases, it is a matter of fidelity to *a* certain spirit of Marxism: one, this one, and not the other.

1. The *first interpretation*, the most classical and paradoxical at the same time, would still remain within the *idealist* logic of Fukuyama. But so as to draw other consequences. Let us accept provisionally the hypothesis that all that is *going badly* in the world today is but a measure of the gap between an empirical reality and a regulating ideal, whether the latter is defined as Fukuyama does or whether one refines and transforms the concept. The value and the obviousness of the ideal would not be compromised, intrinsically, by the historical inadequation of empirical realities. Well, even within this idealist hypothesis, the recourse to a certain *spirit* of the Marxist critique remains urgent and will have to remain indefinitely necessary in order to denounce and reduce the gap *as much as possible*, in order to adjust "reality" to the "ideal" in the course of a necessarily infinite process. This Marxist critique can still be fruitful if one knows how to adapt it to new conditions, whether it is a matter of new modes of production, of the appropriation of economic and techno-scientific powers and knowledge, of juridical formality in the discourse and the practices of national or international law, of new problems of citizenship and nationality, and so forth.

2. The *second interpretation* of the blackboard picture would obey another logic. Beyond the "facts," beyond the supposed "empirical evidence," beyond all that

is inadequate to the ideal, it would be a question of putting into question again, in certain of its essential predicates, the very concept of the said ideal. This would extend, for example, to the economic analysis of the market, the laws of capital, of types of capital (financial or symbolic, therefore spectral), liberal parliamentary democracy, modes of representation and suffrage, the determining content of human rights, women's and children's rights,[6] the current concepts of equality, liberty, especially fraternity (the most problematic of all), dignity, the relations between man and citizen. It would also extend, in the quasi-totality of these concepts, to the concept of the human (therefore of the divine and the animal) and to a *determined* concept of the democratic that supposes it (let us not say of *all* democracy or, precisely [*justement*], of democracy to come). Now, even in this last hypothesis, fidelity to the inheritance of a certain Marxist *spirit* would remain a duty.

Here are two different reasons to be faithful to a spirit of Marxism. They must not be added together but intertwined. They must be implicated with each other in the course of a complex and constantly re-evaluated strategy. There will be no re-politicization, there will be no politics otherwise. Without this strategy, each of the two reasons could lead back to the worst, to worse than the bad, if one can put it that way, namely to a sort of fatalist idealism or abstract and dogmatic eschatology in the face of the world's evil.

Which Marxist spirit, then? It is easy to imagine why we will not please the Marxists, and still less all the others, by insisting in this way on the *spirit of Marxism*, especially if we let it be understood that we intend to understand *spirits* in the plural and in the sense of specters, of untimely specters that one must not chase away but sort out, critique, keep close by, and allow to come back. And of course, we must never hide from the fact that the principle of selectivity which will have to guide and hierarchize among the "spirits" will fatally exclude in its turn. It will even annihilate, by watching (over) its ancestors rather than (over) certain others.[7] At this moment rather than at some other moment. By forgetfulness (guilty or innocent, it little matters here), by foreclosure or murder, this watch itself will engender new ghosts. It will do so by choosing already among the ghosts, its own from among its own, thus by killing the dead: law of finitude, law of decision and responsibility for finite existences, the only living-mortals for whom a decision, a choice, a responsibility has meaning and a meaning that will have to pass through the ordeal of the undecidable. Which is why what we are saying here will not please any-

one. But who ever said that someone ever had to speak, think, or write in order
to please someone else? And if one interprets the gesture we are risking here
as a belated-rallying-to-Marxism, then one would have to have misunder-
stood quite badly. It is true, however, that I would be today, here, now, less
insensitive than ever to the appeal of the contretemps or of being out-of-step,
as well as to the style of an untimeliness that is more manifest and more
urgent than ever. Already I hear people saying: "You picked a good time to
salute Marx!" Or else: "It's about time!" "Why so late?" I believe in the political virtue of the contretemps. And if a contretemps does not have the good
luck, a more or less calculated luck, to come *just in time*, then the inoppor-
tuneness of a strategy (political or other) may still *bear witness*, precisely
[*justement*], to justice, bear witness, at least, to the justice which is demanded
and about which we were saying a moment ago that it must be disadjusted,
irreducible to exactness [*justesse*] and to law. But that is not the decisive moti-
vation here and we need finally to break with the simplism of these slogans.
What is certain is that I am not a Marxist, as someone said a long time ago,
let us recall, in a witticism reported by Engels. Must we still cite Marx as an
authority in order to say "I am not a Marxist"? What is the distinguishing trait
of a Marxist statement? And who can still say "I am a Marxist"?

To continue to take inspiration from a certain spirit of Marxism would be to
keep faith with what has always made of Marxism in principle and first of all a
radical critique, namely a procedure ready to undertake its self-critique. This
critique *wants itself* to be in principle and explicitly open to its own transformation, re-evaluation, self-reinterpretation. Such a critical "wanting-itself"
necessarily takes root, it is involved in a ground that it not yet critical, even if
it is not, not yet, pre-critical. This latter spirit is more than a style, even though
it is also a style. It is heir to a spirit of the Enlightenment which must not be
renounced. We would distinguish this spirit from other spirits of Marxism,
those that rivet it to the body of Marxist doctrine, to its supposed systemic,
metaphysical, or ontological totality (notably to its "dialectical method" or
to "dialectical materialism"), to its fundamental concepts of labor, mode of
production, social class, and consequently to the whole history of its apparatuses (projected or real: the Internationals of the labor movement, the
dictatorship of the proletariat, the single party, the State, and finally the totalitarian monstrosity). For, let us speak as "good Marxists," the deconstruction of

Marxist ontology does not go after only a theoretico-speculative layer of the Marxist corpus but everything that articulates this corpus with the most concrete history of the apparatuses and strategies of the worldwide labor movement. And this deconstruction is not, in the last analysis, a methodical or theoretical procedure. In its possibility as in the experience of the impossible that will always have constituted it, it is never a stranger to the event, that is, very simply, to the coming of that which happens. Certain Soviet philosophers told me in Moscow a few years ago: the best translation of *perestroika* was still "deconstruction."

For this apparently chemical analysis that will isolate in sum the spirit of Marxism to which one ought to remain faithful by dissociating it from all the other spirits—and one will observe perhaps with a smile that the latter include *almost everything*—our guiding thread this evening will be precisely the question of the ghost. How did Marx himself treat the ghost, the concept of the ghost, the specter or *revenant?* How did he determine it? How did he *bind* it, finally, after so many hesitations, through so many tensions and contradictions, to an ontology? What is this attachment of the ghost? What is the bind of this bind, of this ontology, with materialism, the party, the State, the becoming-totalitarian of the State?

To critique, to call for interminable self-critique is still to distinguish between everything and almost everything. Now, if there is a spirit of Marxism which I will never be ready to renounce, it is not only the critical idea or the questioning stance (a consistent deconstruction must insist on them even as it also learns that this is not the last or first word). It is even more a certain emancipatory and *messianic* affirmation, a certain experience of the promise that one can try to liberate from any dogmatics and even from any metaphysico-religious determination, from any *messianism.* And a promise must promise to be kept, that is, not to remain "spiritual" or "abstract," but to produce events, new effective forms of action, practice, organization, and so forth. To break with the "party form" or with some form of the State or the International does not mean to give up every form of practical or effective organization. It is exactly the contrary that matters to us here.

In saying that, one is in opposition to two dominant tendencies: *on the one hand,* the most vigilant and most modern reinterpretations of Marxism by certain Marxists (notably French Marxists and those around Althusser) who believed that they must instead try to dissociate Marxism from any teleology or from any messianic eschatology (but my concern is precisely to distinguish the latter from the former); *on the other hand*, anti-Marxist interpretations that determine their own emancipatory eschatology by giving it a metaphysical or onto-theological content that is always deconstructible. A deconstructive thinking, the one that matters to me here, has always pointed out the irreducibility of affirmation and therefore of the promise, as well as the undeconstructibility of a certain idea of justice (dissociated here from law[8]). Such a thinking cannot operate without justifying the principle of a radical and interminable, infinite (both theoretical and practical, as one used to say) critique. This critique belongs to the movement of an experience open to the absolute future of what is coming, that is to say, a necessarily indeterminate, abstract, desert-like experience that is confided, exposed, given up to its waiting for the other and for the event. In its pure formality, in the indetermination that it requires, one may find yet another essential affinity between it and a certain messianic spirit. What we have said here or elsewhere about *exappropriation* (the radical contradiction of all "capital," of all property or appropriation, as well as all the concepts that depend on it, beginning with that of free subjectivity, thus of emancipation as ordered by these concepts) does not justify any bondage. It is, if we may say so, exactly the opposite. Servitude binds (itself) to appropriation.

Now, this gesture of fidelity to a certain spirit of Marxism is a responsibility incumbent in principle, to be sure, on anyone. Barely deserving the name community, the new International belongs only to anonymity. But this responsibility appears today, at least within the limits of an intellectual and academic field, to return *more imperatively* and, let us say so as not to exclude anyone, *by priority, in urgency* to those who, during the last decades, managed to *resist* a certain hegemony of the Marxist dogma, indeed of its metaphysics, in its political or theoretical forms. And still more particularly to those who have insisted on conceiving and on practicing this resistance without showing any leniency toward reactionary, conservative or neoconservative, anti-scientific or obscurantist temptations, to those who, on the contrary, have ceaselessly proceeded in a hyper-critical fashion, I will dare to say in a deconstructive fashion, in the name of a new Enlightenment for the century to come. And without renouncing an ideal of democracy and emancipation, but rather by trying to think it and to put it to work otherwise.

The responsibility, once again, would here be that of an heir. Whether they wish it or know it or not, all men and women, all over the earth, are today to a certain extent the heirs of Marx and Marxism. That is, as we were saying a moment ago, they are heirs of the absolute singularity of a project—or of a promise—which has a philosophical and scientific form. This form is in principle non-religious, in the sense of a positive religion; it is not mythological; it is therefore not national—for beyond even the alliance with a chosen people, there is no nationality or nationalism that is not religious or mythological, let us say "mystical" in the broad sense. The form of this promise or of this project remains absolutely unique. Its event is at once singular, total, and uneffaceable—uneffaceable except by a denegation and in the course of a work of mourning that can only displace, without effacing, the effect of a trauma.

There is no precedent whatsoever for such an event. In the whole history of humanity, in the whole history of the world and of the earth, in all that to which one can give the name of history in general, such an event (let us repeat, the event of a discourse in the philosophico-scientific form claiming to break with myth, religion, and the nationalist "mystique") has been bound, for the first time and inseparably, to worldwide forms of social organization (a party with a universal vocation, a labor movement, a confederation of states, and so forth). All of this while proposing a new concept of the human, of society, economy, nation, several concepts of the State and of its disappearance. Whatever one may think of this event, of the sometimes terrifying failure of that which was thus begun, of the techno-economic or ecological disasters, and the totalitarian perversions to which it gave rise (perversions that some have been saying for a long time are precisely not perversions, that is, they are not pathological and accidental corruptions but the necessary deployment of an essential logic present at the birth, of an originary disadjustment—let us say, for our part, in a too-elliptical fashion and without contradicting this hypothesis, they are the effect of an *ontological* treatment of the spectrality of the ghost), whatever one may think also of the trauma in human memory that may follow, this unique attempt took place. A messianic promise, even if it was not fulfilled, at least in the form in which it was uttered, even if it rushed headlong toward an ontological content, will have imprinted an inaugural and unique mark in history. And whether we like it or not, whatever consciousness we have of it, we cannot not be its heirs. There is no inheritance without a call to responsibility. An inheritance is always the reaffirmation of a debt, but a critical, selective, and filtering reaffirmation, which is why we distinguished several spirits. By inscribing in our subtitle such an equivocal expression as "the State of the debt," we wanted to announce, to be sure, a certain number of ineluctable themes, but above all that of an uneffaceable and insoluble debt toward one of the spirits inscribed in historical memory under the proper names of Marx and Marxism. Even where it is not acknowledged, even where it remains unconscious or disavowed, this debt remains at work, in particular in political philosophy which structures implicitly all philosophy or all thought on the subject of philosophy.

Let us limit ourselves, for lack of time, to certain traits, for example, of what is called deconstruction, in the figure that it intially took over the course of these last decades, namely the deconstruction of the metaphysics of the "proper," of logocentrism, linguisticism, phonologism, the demystification or the de-sedimentation of the autonomic hegemony of language (a deconstruction in the course of which is elaborated another concept of the text or the trace, of their originary technization, of iterability, of the prosthetic supplement, but also of the proper and of what was given the name exappropriation). Such a deconstruction would have been impossible and unthinkable in a pre-Marxist space. Deconstruction has never had any sense or interest, in my view at least, except as a radicalization, which is to say also *in the tradition* of a certain Marxism, in a certain *spirit of Marxism*. There has been, then, this attempted radicalization of Marxism called deconstruction (and in which, as some have noted, a certain economic concept of the differantial economy and of exappropriation, or even of the gift, plays an organizing role, as does the concept of work tied to differance and to the work of mourning in general). If this attempt has been prudent and sparing but rarely negative in the strategy of its references to Marx, it is because the Marxist ontology, the appellation Marx, the legitimation by way of Marx had been in a way too solidly *taken over* [arraisonnées]. They appeared to be welded to an orthodoxy, to apparatuses and strategies, whose least fault was not only that they were, as such, deprived of a future, deprived of the future itself. By "welded" one may understand an artifactual but solid adherence whose very event constituted the whole history of the world for the last century and a half, and thus the whole history of my generation.

But a radicalization is always indebted to the very thing it radicalizes.[9] That is why I spoke of the Marxist memory and tradition of deconstruction, of its

Marxist "spirit." It is not the only one and it is not just any one of the Marxist spirits, of course. One ought to extend and refine these examples, but time is lacking.

If my subtitle specified the *State of the debt*, it was also in view of problematizing the concept of the State or the state, with or without capital initial, and in *three ways*.

First of all, we have said it often enough, one cannot *establish* the *state* of a debt, for example as regards Marx and Marxism, as one would a balance sheet or an exhaustive record, in a *static and statistical* manner. These accounts cannot be tabulated. One makes oneself accountable by an engagement that selects, interprets, and orients. In a practical and performative manner, and by a decision that begins by getting caught up, like a responsibility, in the snares of an injunction that is already multiple, heterogeneous, contradictory, divided— therefore an inheritance that will always keep its secret. And the secret of a crime. The secret *of* its very author. The secret of the one who says to Hamlet:

> *Ghost:* I am thy Fathers Spirit,
> Doom'd for a certaine terme to walke the night;
> And for the day confin'd to fast in Fires,
> Till the foule crimes done in my dayes of Nature
> Are burnt and purg'd away: But that I am forbid
> To tell the secrets of my Prison-House;
> I could a Tale unfold… (I,v).[10]

Every *revenant* seems here to come from and return to *the earth*, to come from it as from a buried clandestinity (humus and mold, tomb and subterranean prison), to return to it as to the lowest, toward the humble, humid, humilated. We must pass by here, we too, we must pass over in silence, as low as possible to the earth, the return of an animal: not the figure of the old mole ("Well said, old Mole"), nor of a certain hedgehog, but more precisely of a "fretfull Porpentine" that the spirit of the Father is then getting ready to conjure away by removing an "eternal blazon" from "ears of flesh and blood."

Secondly, another debt, all the questions concerning democracy, the universal discourse on human rights, the future of humanity, and so forth, will give rise only to formal, right-thinking, and hypocritical alibis as long as the "foreign Debt" has not been treated head-on, in as responsible, consistent, and systematic manner as possible. With this name or with this emblematic figure, we are pointing to the *interest* and first of all the interest of capital in general, an interest that, in the order of the world today, namely the world-wide market, holds a mass of humanity under its yoke and in a new form of slavery. This happens and is authorized always in the statist or inter-statist forms of an organization. Now, these problems of the foreign Debt—and everything that is metonymized by this concept—will not be treated without at least the spirit of the Marxist critique, the critique of the market, of the multiple logics of capital, and of that which links the State and international law to this market.

Thirdly, lastly, and consequently, a profound and critical re-elaboration of the concepts of the State, of the nation-State, of national sovereignty, and of citizenship must correspond to a phase of decisive mutation. The latter would be impossible without vigilant and systematic reference to a Marxist problematic, if not to the Marxist conclusions regarding the State, the power of the State, and the State apparatus, the illusions of its legal autonomy as concerns socio-economic forces, but also regarding new forms of a withering or rather a reinscription, a re-delimitation of the State in a space that it no longer dominates and that moreover it never dominated by itself.

4

in the name of the revolution, the double barricade

(impure "impure impure history of ghosts")

June, 1848, was, let us hasten to say, a thing apart, and almost
impossible to class in the philosophy of history.... But, at
bottom, what was June, 1848? A revolt of the people against
itself...; let us then be permitted for a moment to arrest the
reader's attention upon the two absolutely unique barricades of
which we have just spoken...these two frightful masterpieces of
civil war.... The barricade Saint Antoine was monstrous....
Ruin. You might say: who built that? You might also say:
who destroyed that?.... It was great and it was little. It was the
bottomless pit parodied upon the spot by chaos come again....
This barricade was furious.... It was huge and living; and, as
from the back of an electric beast, there came from it a crackling
of thunders. The spirit of revolution covered with its cloud that
summit whereon growled this voice of the people which is like
the voice of God; a strange majesty emanated from that titanic
hodful of refuse. It was a garbage heap and it was Sinaï.

As we have said before, it attacked in the name of the
Revolution, what? the Revolution....

A mile from there, at the corner of the Rue du Temple...rose
this obstruction, which made of the street a cul-de-sac; an
immovable and quiet wall; nobody could be seen, nothing could
be heard; not a cry, not a sound, not a breath. A sepulchre...the
chief of that barricade was a geometer or a spectre....

The barricade St. Antoine was the tumult of thunders; the
barricade du Temple was silence. There was between these two
redoubts the difference between the terrible and the ominous.
The one seemed a gaping mouth; the other a mask.

> Admitting that the gloomy and gigantic insurrection of June
> was composed of an anger and an enigma; you felt in the first
> barricade the dragon, and behind the second the sphinx.
>
> WHAT CAN BE DONE IN THE ABYSS BUT TO TALK
>
> Sixteen years tell in the subterranean education of the
> émeute, and June 1848 understood it far better than June
> 1832....
> There were no longer giants against colossi. It resembled
> Milton and Dante rather than Homer. Demons attacked, spec-
> tres resisted....
> A voice from the most obscure depths of the groups,
> cried..."Citizens, let us offer the protest of corpses...."
> The name of the man who thus spoke was never known...that
> great anonymous always found in human crises and in social
> births....
> After the man of the people, who decreed "the protest of
> corpses," had spoken and given the formula of the common
> soul, from all lips arose a strangely satisfied and terrible cry,
> funereal in meaning and triumphant in tone: "Long live death!
> Let us all stay!"
> "Why all?" said Enjolras.
> "All! All!"....
>
> —Victor Hugo, *Les Misérables*

Specters of Marx: The title of this lecture would commit one to speak first of all about Marx. About Marx himself. About his testament or his inheritance. And about a specter, the shadow of Marx, the *revenant* whose return so many raised voices today are attempting to conjure away. For it does resemble a conjuration or conspiracy, because of the agreement or the contract signed by so many political subjects who subscribe to the more or less clear or more or less secret clauses (the point is always to conquer or to keep the keys to a power), but first of all because such a conjuration is meant to conjure away. One must, magically, chase away a specter, exorcise the possible return of a power held to be baleful in itself and whose demonic threat continues to haunt the century.

Since such a conjuration today insists, in such a deafening consensus, that what is, it says, indeed dead, remain dead indeed, it arouses a suspicion. It awakens us where it would like to put us to sleep. Vigilance, therefore: the cadaver is perhaps not as dead, as simply dead as the conjuration tries to delude us into believing. The one who has disappeared appears still to be *there*, and his apparition is not nothing. It does not do nothing. Assuming that the remains can be identified, we know better than ever today that the dead must be able to work. And to cause to work, perhaps more than ever. There is also a mode of production of the phantom, itself a phantomatic mode of production. As in the work of mourning, after a trauma, the conjuration has to make sure that the dead will not come back: quick, do whatever is needed to keep the cadaver localized, in a safe place, decomposing right where it was inhumed, or even embalmed as they liked to do in Moscow. Quick, a vault to which one keeps the keys! These keys would be nothing other than those of the power that the conjuration would like thus to reconstitute upon the death of Marx. We were speaking earlier of an *unlocking*. The logic of the key in which I hoped to orient this keynote address was one of a politico-logic of trauma and a topology of mourning. A mourning in fact and by right interminable, without possible normality, without reliable limit, in its reality or in its concept, between introjection and incorporation. But the same logic, as we suggested, responds to the injunction of a justice which, beyond right or law, rises up in the very respect owed to whoever *is not*, no longer or not yet, living, presently living.

Mourning always follows a trauma. I have tried to show elsewhere that the work of mourning is not one kind of work among others. It is work itself, work in general, the trait by means of which one ought perhaps to reconsider the very concept of production—in what links it to trauma, to mourning, to the idealizing iterability of exappropriation, thus to the spectral spiritualization that is at work in any *tekhnē*. There is the temptation to add here an aporetic postscript to Freud's remark that linked in a same comparative history three of the traumas inflicted on human narcissism when it is thus de-centered: the *psychological* trauma (the power of the unconscious over the conscious ego, discovered by psychoanalysis), after the *biological* trauma (the animal descent of man discovered by Darwin—to whom, moreover, Engels alludes in the Preface to the 1888 *Manifesto*), after the *cosmological* trauma (the Copernican Earth is no longer the center of the universe, and this is more and more the case one could say so as to draw from it many consequences concerning the limits of geopolitics). Our aporia would here stem from the fact that there is no longer any name or teleology for determining the Marxist *coup* and its subject. Freud thought he knew, for his part, what man and his narcissism were. The Marxist blow is as much the projected unity of a thought and of a labor movement, sometimes in a messianic or eschatological form, as it is the history of the totalitarian world (including Nazism and fascism, which are the inseparable adversaries of Stalinism). This is perhaps the deepest wound for mankind, in the body of its history and in the history of its concept, still more traumatizing than the "psychological" lesion (*Kränkung*) produced by the blow of psychoanalysis, the third and most serious in Freud's view.[1] For we know that the *blow* struck enigmatically in the name of Marx also accumulates and gathers together the other three. It thus presupposes them today, even if such was not the case in the last century. It carries beyond them by carrying them out, just as it bears the name of Marx by exceeding it infinitely. The century of "Marxism" will have been that of the techno-scientific and effective decentering of the earth, of geopolitics, of the *anthropos* in its onto-theological identity or its genetic properties, of the *ego cogito*—and of the very concept of narcissism whose aporias are, let us say in order to go too quickly and save ourselves a lot of references, the explicit theme of deconstruction. This trauma is endlessly denied by the very movement through which one tries to cushion it, to assimilate it, to interiorize and incorporate it. In this mourning work in process, in this interminable task, the ghost remains that which gives one the most to think about—and to do. Let us insist and spell things out: to do and to make come about, as well as to let come (about).

But the specters *of* Marx come on stage from the other side. They are named according to the other path of the genitive—and this other grammar says more than grammar. The specters *of* Marx are also his. They are perhaps first of all the ghosts that inhabited him, the *revenants* with which Marx himself will have been occupied, and which he will have wanted in advance to make his thing; which does not mean that he knew their secrets, nor even that he thematized in his turn the obsessive recurrence of what would be a theme if one could say of the *revenant* that it lets itself be *posed there, exposed before you,* as a theme or a system, a thesis or a synthesis ought to do. All of these values are disqualified by the specter, if there is any.

The specters of Marx: with these words we will name from now on certain figures whose coming Marx will have been the first to apprehend, sometimes to describe. Those that herald the best and whose event he will have greeted, those that arise from or threaten the worst, whose testimony he will have rejected. There are several times of the specter. It is a proper characteristic of the specter, if there is any, that no one can be sure if by returning it testifies to a living past or to a living future, for the *revenant* may already mark the promised return of the specter of living being. Once again, untimeliness and disadjustment of the contemporary. In this regard, communism has always been and will remain spectral: it is always still to come and is distinguished, like democracy itself, from every living present understood as plenitude of a presence-to-itself, as totality of a presence effectively identical to itself. Capitalist societies can always heave a sigh of relief and say to themselves: communism is finished since the collapse of the totalitarianisms of the twentieth century and not only is it finished, but it did not take place, it was only a ghost. They do no more than disavow the undeniable itself: a ghost never dies, it remains always to come and to come-back.

In the *Manifesto of the Communist Party*, let us recall, a first noun returned three times on the same first page, the noun "specter" (*Gespenst*): "A specter is haunting Europe," says Marx in 1848, "the specter of communism [*Ein Gespenst geht um in Europa—das Gespenst des Kommunismus*]". Marx, unless it is the other one, Engels, then puts on stage, for the time of a few paragraphs, the terror that this specter inspires in all the powers of old Europe. No one speaks of anything anymore but this specter. All phantasms are projected onto the screen of this ghost (that is, on something absent, for the screen itself is phantomatic, as in the television of the future which will have no "screenic" support and will project its images—sometimes synthetic images—directly on the eye, like the sound of the telephone deep in the ear). One watches for the signals, the tables that turn, the dishes that move. Is it going to answer? As in the space of a salon during a spiritualist séance, but sometimes that space is what is called the street, one looks out for one's goods and furniture, attempting to adjust all of politics to the frightening hypothesis of a visitation.[2] Politicians are seers or visionaries. They desire and fear an apparition which they know will not present anyone in person but will strike a series of blows to be deciphered. All possible alliances are thus forged to conjure away this common adversary, "the specter of communism." The alliance signifies: death to the specter. It is convoked to be revoked, everyone swears [*jure*] only on the specter, but in order to conjure it away. No one talks of anything else. But what else can you do, since it is not there, this ghost, like any ghost worthy of the name? And even when it is there, that is, when it is there without being there, you feel that the specter is looking, although through a helmet; it is watching, observing, staring at the spectators and the blind seers, but you do not see it seeing, it remains invulnerable beneath its visored armor. So one speaks of nothing else but in order to chase it away, to exclude it, to exorcise it. The salon, then, is old Europe which is gathering all its forces (*alle Mächte des alten Europas*). If the conspirators attempt to exorcise or conjure away the specter, it is without knowing at bottom what or whom they are talking about. For the conspirators, communism is a name, the holy alliance is a holy hunt: "All the powers of old Europe have joined [*verbündet*] into a holy hunt [*zu einer heiligen Hetzjagd*] against this specter [*gegen dies Gespenst*]."

Who could deny it? If an alliance is in the process of being formed against communism, an alliance of the old or the new Europe, it remains a holy alliance. The paternal figure of the Holy Father the Pope, who is then cited by Marx, still figures today in a prominent place in this alliance, in the person of a Polish bishop who boasts, and in this he is confirmed by Gorbachev, that he was not for nothing in the collapse of communist totalitarianism in Europe and in the advent of a Europe that from now on will be what it should always have been according to him, a Christian Europe. As in the Holy Alliance of the nineteenth century, Russia could once again take part. That is why we insisted on the neo-evangelism—Hegelian neo-evangelism—of a rhetoric of the "Fukuyama" type. It was a Hegelian neo-evangelism that Marx denounced with great verve and vehemence in the Stirnerian theory of ghosts. We will get to this later, but already here we must point out the intersection. We believe it is significant.

The specter that Marx was talking about then, communism, was there without being there. It was not yet there. It will never be there. There is no *Dasein* of the specter, but there is no *Dasein* without the uncanniness, without the strange familiarity (*Unheimlichkeit*) of some specter. What is a specter? What is its history and what is its time?

The specter, as its name indicates, is the *frequency* of a certain visibility. But the visibility of the invisible. And visibili*ty*, by its essence, is not seen, which is why it remains *epekeina tes ousias*, beyond the phenomenon or beyond being. The specter is also, among other things, what one imagines, what one thinks one sees and which one projects—on an imaginary screen where there is nothing to see. Not even the screen sometimes, and a screen always has, at bottom, in the bottom or background that it is, a structure of disappearing apparition. But now one can no longer get any shut-eye, being so intent to watch out for the return. Whence the theatricalization of speech itself and the spectacularizing speculation on time. The perspective has to be reversed, once again: ghost or *revenant*, sensuous-non-sensuous, visible-invisible, the specter first of all sees *us*. From the other side of the eye, *visor effect*, it looks at us even before we see *it* or even before we see period. We feel ourselves observed, sometimes under surveillance by it even before any apparition. Especially— and this is the event, for the specter is *of* the event—it sees us during a *visit*. It (re)pays us a visit [*Il nous rend visite*]. Visit upon visit, since it returns to see us and since *visitare*, frequentative of *visere* (to see, examine, contemplate), translates well the recurrence or returning, the frequency of a visitation. The latter does not always mark the moment of a generous apparition or a friendly vision; it can signify strict inspection or violent search, consequent persecution, implacable *concatenation*. The social mode of haunting, its original style could also be called, taking into account this repetition, *frequentation*. Marx lived more than others, we are going to make this clear, in the frequentation of specters.

The specter *appears* to present itself during a visitation. One represents it to oneself, but it is not present, itself, in flesh and blood. This non-presence of the specter demands that one take its times and its history into consideration, the singularity of its temporality or of its historicity. When, in 1847–48, Marx names the specter of communism, he inscribes it in an historical perspective that is exactly the reverse of the one I was initially thinking of in proposing a title such as "the specters of Marx." Where I was tempted to name thereby the persistence of a present past, the return of the dead which the worldwide work of mourning cannot get rid of, whose return it runs away from, which it *chases* (excludes, banishes, and at the same time pursues), Marx, for his part, announces and calls for a presence to come. He seems to predict and pre- scribe: What for the moment figures only as a specter in the ideological representation of old Europe must become, in the future, a present reality, that is, a living reality. The *Manifesto* calls, it calls for this presentation of the living reality: we must see to it that in the future this specter—and first of all an association of workers forced to remain secret until about 1848—becomes a *reality*, and a *living* reality. This real life must show itself and manifest itself, it must *present itself* beyond Europe, old or new Europe, in the universal dimension of an International.

But it must also manifest itself in the form of a manifesto that will be the *Manifesto* of a party. For Marx already gives the party form to the properly political structure of the force that will have to be, according to the *Manifesto*, the motor of the revolution, the transformation, the appropriation then finally the destruction of the State, and the end of the political as such. (Since this singular end of the political would correspond to the presentation of an absolutely living reality, this is one more reason to think that the essence of the political will always have the inessential figure, the very anessence of a ghost.)

Here is perhaps one of the strange motifs we should talk about this evening: What tends perhaps to disappear in the political world that is shaping up, and perhaps in a new age of democracy, is the domination of this form of organization called the party, the party-State relation, which finally will have lasted, strictly speaking, only two centuries, barely longer than that, a period to which belong as well certain determined types of parliamentary and liberal democracy, constitutional monarchies, Nazi, fascist, or Soviet totalitarianisms. *Not one* of these regimes was possible without what could be called the axiomatics of the party. Now, as one can see foreshadowed, it seems, everywhere in the world today, the structure of the party is becoming not only more and more suspect (and for reasons that are no longer always, necessarily, "reactionary," those of the classical individualist reaction) but also radically unadapted to the new—tele-techno-media—conditions of public space, of political life, of democracy, and of the *new* modes of representation (both parliamentary and non-parliamentary) that they call up. A reflection on what will become of Marxism tomorrow, of its inheritance or its testament, should include, among so many other things, a reflection on the finitude of a certain concept or of a certain reality of the party. And, of course, of its State correlative. A movement is underway that we would be tempted to describe as a deconstruction of the traditional concepts of State, and thus of party and labor union. Even though they do not signify the withering away of the State, in the Marxist or Gramscian sense, one cannot analyze their historical singularity outside of the Marxist inheritance—where inheritance is more than ever a critical and transformative filter, that is, where it is out of the question to be for or against the State in general, its life or its death *in general*. There was a moment, in the history of European (and, of course, American) politics, when it was a reactionary gesture to call for the end of the party, just as it was to analyze the inadequation of existing parliamentary structures to democracy itself. Let us put forward here with many precautions, both theoretical and practical, the hypothesis that this is no longer the case, *not always* the case (for these old forms of struggle against the State may survive for a long time); one must do away with this equivocation so that it will no longer be the case. The hypothesis is that this mutation has already begun; it is irreversible.

The universal Communist Party, the Communist International will be, said the *Manifesto* in 1848, the final incarnation, the real presence of the specter, thus the end of the spectral. This future is not described, it is not foreseen in the constative mode; it is announced, promised, called for in a performative mode. From the symptom, Marx draws a diagnosis and a prognosis. The symptom that authorizes the diagnosis is that the fear of the communist ghost *exists*. One gets signs of this if one observes the Holy European Alliance. These signs must mean something, namely that the European powers recognize, through the specter, the power of communism ("Communism is already acknowledged by all European powers to be itself a power [*als eine Macht*]"). As for the prognosis, it does not consist in merely forseeing (a gesture of the constative type) but in calling for the advent, in the future, of a manifesto of the communist party which, precisely in the performative form of the call, will transform the legend of the specter not yet into the reality of communist society but into that other form of real event (between the legendary specter and its absolute incarnation) that is the Manifesto of the Communist Party. Parousia of the manifestation of the manifest. As party. Not as party that in addition would be, in this case, communist, or whose communism would be only a predicate. But as party that would accomplish the essence of the party as communist party. Here is the call, namely the Manifesto in view of the Manifesto, the self-manifestation of the manifesto, in which consists the essence of any manifesto that calls itself: by saying "it is time," time rejoins and adjoins itself here, now, a now that happens to itself in the act and the body of this manifestation: it is "high time" that I become manifest, that become manifest the manifesto that is no other than this one here, now, me, the present is coming to pass, itself conjoined witness, here precisely is the manifesto that I am or that I operate in the work, in an act, I am myself but this manifestation, at this very moment, in this book, here I am: "It is high

time [*Es ist hohe Zeit*] that communists should openly, in the face of the whole
world, publish their views, their aims, their tendencies, and meet [or oppose:
entgegenstellen] this nursery tale of the specter of communism [*den Märchen vom
Gespenst des Kommunismus*] with a Manifesto of the party itself." What does this
manifesto testify to? And who testifies to what? In which languages? The following sentence speaks of the multiplicity of languages: not of all languages
but of a few, and of communists of different nationalities gathered in London.
The Manifesto, says *The Manifesto* in German, will be published in English,
French, German, Italian, Flemish, and Danish. Ghosts also speak different
languages, national languages, like the money from which they are, as we shall
see, inseparable. As circulating currency, money bears local and political character, it "uses different national languages and wears different national
uniforms."[3] Let us repeat our question of the manifesto as speech or language
of testimony. Who testifies to what? In what way does the "what" determine
the "who," the one never preceding the other? Why does this absolute manifestation of self *attest* to itself [s'atteste-*t-elle elle-même*], while taking the side of
the party, only by contesting and detesting the ghost? What about the ghost,
therefore, in this struggle? The ghost that finds itself called upon to take sides,
as well as to testify, with the helmet and visor effect?

The structure of the event thus called for remains difficult to analyze. The
legend of the specter, the story, the fable (*Märchen*) would be abolished in the
Manifesto, as if the specter itself, after having embodied a spectrality in legend and without becoming a reality (communism itself, communist society),
came out of itself, called for an exit from the legend without entering into the
reality of which it is the specter. Since it is neither real nor legendary, some
"Thing" will have frightened and continues to frighten in the equivocation of
this event, as in the singular spectrality of this performative utterance, namely, of Marxism itself (and the question this evening could be summed up as
follows: what is a Marxist utterance? a so-called Marxist utterance? or more
precisely: what *will be from now on* such an utterance? and who could say "I am
a Marxist" or "I am not a Marxist"?).

To make fear, to make oneself fear.[4] To cause fear in the enemies of the
Manifesto, but perhaps also in Marx and the Marxists themselves. For one
could be tempted to explain the whole totalitarian inheritance of Marx's
thought, but also the other totalitarianisms that were not just by chance or
mechanical juxtaposition its contemporaries, as a reaction of panic-ridden

fear before the ghost in general. To the ghost that communism represented for the capitalist (monarchist, imperial, or republican) States of old Europe in general, came the response of a frightened and ruthless war and it was only in the course of this war that Leninism and then Stalinist totalitarianism were able to constitute themselves, harden themselves monstrously into their cadaverous rigor. But since Marxist ontology was *also* struggling against the ghost in general, in the name of living presence as material actuality, the whole "Marxist" process of the totalitarian society was also responding to the same panic. We must, it seems to me, take such an hypothesis seriously. Later, between Stirner and Marx, we will get around to this essential ineluctability of the reflexive reflex, of the "make oneself fear" in the experience of the ghost. It is as if Marx and Marxism had run away, fled from themselves, and had scared themselves. In the course of the same *chase*, the same persecution, the same infernal pursuit. Revolution against the revolution as the figure of *Les Misérables* suggests. More precisely, given the number and the *frequency*, it is as if they had been frightened by *someone* within themselves. They should not have done so, we might think a little hastily. Nazi and fascist totalitarianisms found themselves now on one side, now on the other in this war of ghosts, but in the course of a sole and same history. And there are so many ghosts in this tragedy, in the charnel houses of all the camps, that no one will ever be sure of being on a single and same side. It is better to know that. In a word, the whole history of European politics at least, and at least since Marx, would be that of a ruthless war between solidary camps that are equally terrorized by the ghost, the ghost of the other, and its own ghost as the ghost of the other. The Holy Alliance is terrorized by the ghost of communism and undertakes a war against it that is still going on, but it is a war against a camp that is itself organized by the terror of the ghost, the one in front of it and the one it carries within itself.

There is nothing "revisionist"[5] about interpreting the genesis of totalitarianisms as reciprocal reactions to the fear of the ghost that communism inspired beginning in the last century, to the terror that it inspired in its adversaries but that it turned inside out and felt sufficiently within itself to precipitate the monstrous realization, the magical effectuation, the animist incorporation of an emancipatory eschatology which ought to have respected the promise, the being-promise of a promise—and which could not have been a simple ideological phantasm since the critique of ideology itself was inspired by nothing else.

For, finally we must get around to this, the *revenant* was the persecution *of* Marx. As it was that *of* Stirner. *Both of them,* as is quite understandable, kept on persecuting their persecutor, their own persecutor, their most intimate stranger. Marx loved the figure of the ghost, he detested it, he called it to witness his contestation, he was haunted by it, harassed, besieged, obsessed by it. In him, but of course in order to repulse it, outside of him. In him outside of him: this is the place outside of place of ghosts wherever they feign to take up their abode. More than others, perhaps, Marx had ghosts in his head and knew without knowing what he was talking about ("Mensch, es spukt in Deinem Kopfe!" one might say to him in a parody of Stirner). But for this very reason he also did not love the ghosts he loved. And who loved him—and observed him from beneath the visor. He was doubtless *obsessed* by them (the word is his, as we will see) but, as he did against the adversaries of communism, he waged a merciless battle against them.

Like all obsessives, he harassed the obsession. There are countless signs of this, each one more explicit than the other. To cite only two very different examples from this rich spectrology, one could evoke in passing his 1841 Dissertation (*The Difference in the Philosophy of Nature of Democritus and Epicurus*). There the very young Marx signs a filial dedication (for it is always to the father, the secret of a father that a frightened child calls for help against the specter: "I am thy Fathers Spirit...I am forbid/ To tell the secrets of my Prison-House"). In this dedication, Marx addresses himself as son to Ludwig von Westphalen, "personal adviser to the government" in Trier, this "very dear paternal friend [*seinen theuren väterlichen Freund*]." He then speaks of a sign of filial love (*diese Zeilen als erste Zeichen kindlicher Liebe*) as regards someone before whom "all the spirits of the world are called to appear [*vor dem alle Geister der Welt erscheinen*]" and who never recoiled in fear from the shadows of retrograde ghosts (*Schlagschatten der retrograden Gespenster*) or from skies often covered with dark clouds. The last words of this dedication name the spirit (*Der Geist*) as the "great magical physician [*der grosse Zauberkundig Arzt*]" to whom this spiritual father entrusted himself (*anvertraut*) and from whom he draws all his strength to struggle against the evil of the ghost. It is the spirit against the specter. In this adoptive father, in this hero of the struggle against retrograde ghosts (which Marx seems implicitly to distinguish from the specter of progress that communism will be for example), the young Marx sees the living and visible proof (*argumentum ad oculos*) that "idealism is not a fiction but a truth."

Youthful dedication? Conventional language? Surely. But the words are not so common, they appear calculated and the statistical accounting can begin. Frequency counts. The experience, the apprehension of the ghost is tuned into *frequency*: number (more than one), insistence, rhythm (waves, cycles, and periods). The youthful dedication continues to speak and to proliferate itself, it appears more significant and less conventional when one notices, in the years that follow, the relentless determination to denounce, that is, to conjure (away), and with great verve, but also with great fascination, what *The German Ideology* will call the history of ghosts (*Gespenstergeschichte*). We will come back to this text in a moment, it is crawling with them, a crowd of *revenants* are waiting for us there: shrouds, errant souls, clanking of chains in the night, groanings, chilling bursts of laughter, and all those heads, so many invisible heads that look at us, the greatest concentration of all specters in the history of humanity. Marx (and Engels) try to straighten things out, they seek to identify, they pretend to count. They have trouble.

A little later, in fact, *The Eighteenth Brumaire of Louis Bonaparte* deploys once again, on the same frequency, something like a spectropolitics and a genealogy of ghosts, more precisely a *patrimonial* logic of the *generations of ghosts*. Marx never stops conjuring and exorcising there. He separates out the good from the bad "ghosts." Sometimes in the same sentence, he desperately tries to oppose (but how difficult it is and how risky), the "spirit of the revolution [*Geist der Revolution*]" to its specter (*Gespenst*). Yes, it is difficult and risky. Because of the lexicon, first of all: like *esprit* and like "spirit," *Geist* can also signify "specter" and Marx thinks he can exploit, even as he controls, its rhetorical effects. The semantics of *Gespenst* themselves haunt the semantics of *Geist*. If there is some ghost, it is to be found precisely where, between the two, reference hesitates, undecidably, or else no longer hesitates where it should have. But if it is so difficult and risky, beyond any possible mastery, if the two remain indiscernible and finally synonymous, it is because, in Marx's own view, the specter will first have been necessary, one might say even vital to the historical unfolding of spirit. For, first of all, Marx himself *inherits* from the Hegelian remark on the repetition of history, whether one is talking about great events, revolutions, or heroes (the remark is well known: first tragedy, then farce). Victor Hugo was also attentive, as we have seen, to the revolutionary repetition. A revolution repeats, and it even repeats the revolution against the revolution. *The Eighteenth Brumaire* concludes from this that men make their *own* history, that is the condition of *inheritance*. Appropriation in general, we would say, is *in the condition of the other* and of the *dead* other, of more than one dead, a generation of the dead. What is said about appropriation is also valid for freedom, liberation, or emancipation.

> Men make their own history [*ihre eigene Geschichte*] but they do not make it just as they please [*aus freien Stücken*]; they do not make it under circumstances chosen by themselves, but under circumstances directly encountered, given and transmitted from the past [*überlieferten Umständen*]. The tradition of all the dead generations [*aller toten Geschlechter*] weighs [*lastet*] like a nightmare on the brain of the living.

(Marx writes "lastet wie ein Alp," that is, weighs like one of those ghosts that give nightmares; the French translation reads simply "pèse d'un poids très lourd," weighs very heavily; as often happens in translations, the ghost drops off into oblivion or, in the best of cases, it is dissolved into approximate figures, for example "phantasmagoria," a word that moreover is generally relieved of its literal sense which links it to speech and to public speech.)

> And just when they seem engaged in revolutionizing themselves and things, in creating something that has never yet existed [*noch nicht Dagewesenes zu schaffen*], precisely in such periods of revolutionary crisis they anxiously conjure up [*beschwören sie ängstlich*] the spirits of the past to their service [*die Geister der Vergangenheit zu ihrem Dienste herauf*] and *borrow* [*entlehnen*] from them *names*, battle-cries [*Schlachtparole*] and costumes in order to present the new scene of world history in this time-honoured disguise and this *borrowed language* [*mit dieser erborgten Sprache*].[6]

It is indeed a matter of convoking or conjuring (*beschwören*) the spirits as specters in a gesture of positive conjuration, the one that swears in order to call up and not to drive away. But can one uphold this distinction? For if such a conjuration seems welcoming and hospitable, since it calls forth the dead, makes or lets them come, it is never free of anxiety. And thus of a movement of repulsion or restriction. Not only is the conjuration characterized by a certain anxiety, it does not let itself be determined merely *in addition* by this anxiety (as the word *ängstlich* suggests), it is destined to the anxiety *that it is*.

The conjuration is anxiety from the moment it calls upon death to invent the quick and to enliven the new, to summon the presence of what is not yet there (*noch nicht Dagewesenes*). This anxiety in the face of the ghost is properly revolutionary. If death weighs on the living brain of the living, and still more on the brains of revolutionaries, it must then have some spectral density. To weigh (*lasten*) is also to charge, tax, impose, indebt, accuse, assign, enjoin. And the more life there is, the graver the specter of the other becomes, the heavier its imposition. And the more the living have to answer for it. *To answer for the dead, to respond to the dead.* To correspond and have it out with [*s'expliquer avec*] obsessive haunting, in the absence of any certainty or symmetry. Nothing is more serious and nothing is more true, nothing is more exact [*juste*] than this phantasmagoria. The specter weighs [*pèse*], it thinks [*pense*], it intensifies and condenses itself within the very inside of life, within the most living life, the most singular (or, if one prefers, individual) life. The latter therefore no longer has and must no longer have, insofar as it is living, a pure identity to itself or any assured inside: this is what all philosophies of life, or even philosophies of the living and real individual, would have to weigh carefully.[7]

The paradox must be sharpened: the more the new erupts in the revolutionary crisis, the more the period is in crisis, the more it is "out of joint," then the more one has to convoke the old, "borrow" from it. Inheritance from the "spirits of the past" consists, as always, in borrowing. Figures of borrowing, borrowed figures, figurality as the figure of borrowing. And the borrowing *speaks*: borrowed language, borrowed names, says Marx. A question of credit, then, or of faith. But an unstable and barely visible dividing line crosses through this law of the fiduciary. It passes between a parody and a truth, but one truth as incarnation or living repetition of the other, a regenerating reviviscence of the past, of the spirit, of the spirit of the past from which one inherits. The dividing line passes between a mechanical reproduction of the specter and an appropriation that is so alive, so interiorizing, so assimilating of the inheritance and of the "spirits of the past" that it is none other than the life of forgetting, life as forgetting itself. And the forgetting of the maternal in order to make the spirit live in oneself. These are Marx's words. It is his language, and the example of the language is not just any example among others. It designates the very element of these rights of succession.

> Thus Luther donned the mask of the Apostle Paul, the revolution of

1789 to 1814 draped itself alternately as the Roman Republic and the
Roman Empire, and the revolution of 1848 knew nothing better to do
than to parody [*parodieren*], now 1789, now the revolutionary tradition of
1793 to 1795. In like manner a beginner who has learnt a new language
always translates it back into his mother tongue, but he has assimilated
[appropriated: *hat er sich nur angeeignet*] the spirit of the new language
and can freely express himself in it [produce in it: *in ihr produzieren*] only
when he finds his way in it without recalling the old and forgets his
native tongue in the use of the new. (P. 104)

From one inheritance to the other. The living appropriation of the spirit,
the assimilation of a new language is already an inheritance. And the appropriation of another language here figures the revolution. This revolutionary
inheritance supposes, to be sure, that one ends up forgetting the specter, that
of the primitive or mother tongue. In order to forget not what one inherits
but the pre-inheritance on the basis of which one inherits. This forgetting is
only a forgetting. For what one must forget will have been indispensable. One
must pass through the pre-inheritance, even if it is to parody it, in order to
appropriate the life of a new language or make the revolution. And while the
forgetting corresponds to the moment of living appropriation, Marx nevertheless does not valorize it as simply as one might think. Things are very
complicated. One must forget the specter and the parody, Marx seems to say,
so that history can continue. But if one is content to forget it, then the result is
bourgeois platitude: life, that's all. So one must not forget it, one must remember it but while forgetting it enough, in this very memory, in order to "find
again the *spirit* of the revolution without making its *specter* return [*den* Geist *der*
revolution wiederzufinden, nicht ihr Gespenst *wieder umgehen machen*; emphasis
added]."

This is the fold of "a striking difference [*ein springender Unterschied*]," says
Marx, between two modalities or two temporalities in the conjuration of the
dead (*Totenbeschwörung*), in the evocation or convocation of the specter. One
has to admit that they resemble each other. They contaminate each other
sometimes in such a troubling manner, since the simulacrum consists precisely in miming the phantom or in simulating the phantasm of the other, that
the "striking" difference strikes, precisely, at the origin, and leaps into view
only in order to jump up and down before your eyes. To disappear by appearing, in the phenomenon of its phantasm. Marx holds to this difference, all the

same, as he holds to life; he illustrates it in one of those eloquent revolutionary epics to which one can only do justice by reading it aloud, until one is out of breath. It begins thus, by the *conjuration (Beschwörung)* of the dead on the scale of worldwide history (*weltgeschichtliche Totenbeschwörung*):

> Consideration of this world-historical necromancy [*Totenbeschwörung*] reveals at once a striking difference. Camille Desmoulins, Danton, Robespierre, Saint-Just, Napoleon, the heroes as well as the parties and the masses of the old French Revolution, performed the task of their time [*die Aufgabe ihrer Zeit*] in Roman costume and with Roman phrases, the task of unchaining and setting up modern *bourgeois* society. The first ones knocked the feudal basis to pieces and mowed off the feudal heads which had grown on it. The other created inside France the conditions under which free competition could first be developed, parcelled landed property exploited...and beyond the French borders... (Ibid.)

But synchrony does not have a chance, no time is contemporary with itself, neither the time of the Revolution, which finally never takes place in the present, nor the times that follow or follow from it. What happens? Nothing, nothing other at least than forgetting. First of all this task, which was moreover the task of their time (*die Aufgabe ihrer Zeit*), appears in a time that is already dislocated, disjointed, off its hinges ("out of joint" or "aus den Fugen"): it can *present itself only* through the Roman haunting, in the anachrony of antique costume and phrases. Then, once the revolutionary task is accomplished, amnesia necessarily sets in. It was already on the program of the anachrony, in the "task of their time." Anachrony practices and promises forgetting. Bourgeois society forgets, in its sober platitude, "that ghosts from the days of Rome had watched over its cradle [*dass die Gespenster der Römerzeit ihre Wiege gehütet hatten*]. A question of the head, as always according to Marx, a question of the head or the cap- and the spirit: in the amnesiac order of capitalist bourgeoisie (the one that lives, like an animal, on the forgetting of ghosts), the muzzle [*gueule*] replaces the head at the summit, the lard-head of a fattened, sedentary, bourgeois king, replaces the political and vigorous head of revolutionaries on the march.[8]

> [I]ts real commanders [*ihre wirklichen Heerführer*] sat behind the counter, and the hogheaded [*Speckkopf*] Louis XVIII was its political chief [*ihr politisches Haupt*]. Wholly absorbed in the production of wealth and in peaceful competitive struggle, it no longer comprehended that ghosts

from the days of Rome had watched over its cradle. But unheroic as bourgeois society is, it nevertheless took heroism, sacrifice, terror, civil war and battles of peoples to bring it into being. (Ibid.).

Marx then accumulates the examples of this rhythmic *anachrony*. He analyzes its pulses and impulsions. He takes pleasure in it, the pleasure of repetition; on seeing him so sensitive to these compulsive waves, one gets the impression that he is not just pointing his finger: he is taking the pulse of history. And he is listening to a revolutionary *frequency*. In regular bursts, the latter alternates conjuration and abjuration of the specters. The great specter of the classical tradition (Rome) is convoked (this is the positive conjuration) so as to allow one to rise to the height of the historic tragedy, but already also so as to hide, in the illusion, the mediocre content of bourgeois ambition. Then, this done, the phantasm is revoked, which is the abjuration; one forgets the ghost as if one were waking up from an hallucination. Cromwell had already spoken the language of the Hebrew prophets. The bourgeois revolution accomplished, the English people prefer Locke to Habakkuk. Then comes the Eighteenth Brumaire and the repetition repeats itself. It is at this point that Marx intends to distinguish between the spirit (*Geist*) of the revolution and its specter (*Gespenst*), as if the former did not already call up the latter, as if everything, and Marx all the same recognizes this himself, did not pass by way of differences *within a fantastics as general as it is irreducible*. Far from organizing the good schematics of a constitution of time, this other transcendental imagination is the law of an invincible *anachrony*. Untimely, "out of joint," even and especially if it appears to come in due time, the spirit of the revolution is *fantastic and anachronistic through and through*. It has to be so— and among all the questions that this discourse assigns to us, one of the most necessary would no doubt concern the articulation among these indissociable concepts which must, if not identify with each other, at least pass one into the other without crossing any rigorous conceptual border: spirit of revolution, actual reality, (productive or reproductive) imagination, specter (*Geist der Revolution, Wirklichkeit, Phantasie, Gespenst*):

> Thus the resurrection of the dead [*Die Totenerweckung*] in those revolutions served the purpose of glorifying [*verherrlichen*] the new struggles, not of parodying [*parodieren*] the old; of magnifying the given task in imagination [*in der Phantasie*], not of fleeing from its solution in reality; of

finding once more the spirit of revolution, not of making its ghost walk
about again.
    From 1848 to 1851 only the ghost [*Gespenst*] of the old revolution
walked about, from Marrast, the *républicain en gants jaunes*, who disguised
himself as the old Bailly, down to the adventurer who hides his com-
monplace repulsive features under the iron death mask of Napoleon.
(P. 105)

Marx often aims at the head—and the chief. The figures of the ghost are
first of all faces. It is a matter then of masks, if not, this time, of a helmet and a
visor. But between the spirit and the specter, between tragedy and comedy,
between the revolution on the march and what installs it in parody, there is
only the difference of a time between two masks. It is a matter of spirit when
Luther takes the mask (*maskierte sich*) of the Apostle Paul, it is a matter of
specter, "parody," and "caricature" with the lard-head Louis XVIII or the
death mask of Napoleon the Great on the face of Napoleon "le Petit."

One must take another step. One must think the future, that is, life. That
is, death. Marx recognizes, of course, the law of this fatal anachrony and, finally, he is perhaps as aware as we are of the essential contamination of spirit
(*Geist*) by specter (*Gespenst*). But he wants to be done with it, he deems that
one can, he declares that one should be done with it. He detests all ghosts,
the good and the bad, he thinks one can break with this frequentation. It is as
if he were saying to us, we who do not believe a word of it: What you think
you are calling so subtly the law of anachrony is precisely anachronistic. That
fate weighed on revolutions of the past. Those that are coming, *at present and in
the future* (namely, what Marx always prefers, like everyone, like life itself, and
this is the tautology of preference), those that are heralded already in the
nineteenth century must turn away from the past, from its *Geist* as well as its
Gespenst. In sum, they must cease to inherit. They must no longer even do that
mourning work in the course of which the living maintain the dead, play dead,
busy themselves with the dead, let themselves be entertained and occupied
and *played or tricked* [jouer] by the dead, speak *them* and speak *to them*, bear their
name and hold forth in their language. No, no more revolutionary memory,
down with the monument, bring down the curtain on the shadow theater and
funerary eloquence, destroy the mausoleum for popular crowds, shatter the
death masks beneath the glass caskets. All of that is the revolution of the past.
Already, still in the nineteenth century. Already in the nineteenth century,

one must stop inheriting in this way, one must forget this form of forgetting on
the frequency of what is called mourning work, the haunting of the spirit as
much as the haunting of the specter:

> The *social* revolution of the nineteenth century cannot draw its poetry
> [*ihre Poesie*] from the past, but only from the future. It cannot begin with
> itself before it has stripped off all superstition about the past. Earlier rev-
> olutions required recollections of past world history in order to dull
> themselves to their own content [*um sich über ihren eigenen Inhalt zu
> betäuben*]. In order to arrive at its own content [*um bei ihrem eignen Inhalt
> anzukommen*], the revolution of the nineteenth century must let the dead
> bury their dead. There the words went beyond the content; here the con-
> tent goes beyond the words [*Dort ging die Phrase über den Inhalt, hier geht der
> Inhalt über die Phrase hinaus*]. (P. 106; my emphasis)

Things are not simple by a long shot. One must lend an ear and read closely, reckon with every word of the language; we are still in the cemetery, the
gravediggers are working hard, digging up skulls, trying to identify them, one
by one, and Hamlet recalls that this one "had a tongue" and it used to sing.
What does Marx mean? He too has died, let us not forget, and more than
once, precisely [*justement*], we ought to know it, it is not so easy given that this
happens too often; we inherit from him in our fashion, at least from each one
of his surviving words, which he could never have wanted us to forget without having at least some respectful attention for them, without having, for
example, heard the revolutionary injunction to let the dead bury their dead,
the imperative of an "active forgetting," as a certain Nietzsche will soon put
it. What does Marx mean, the dead Marx? He knew very well that the dead
have never buried anyone. Nor have the living who were not also *mortals*, that
is, who properly bear within themselves, that is, outside themselves, and
before themselves, the impossible possibility of their death. It will always be
necessary that still living mortals bury the already dead living. The dead have
never buried anyone, but neither have the living, the living who would be
only living, the immortal living. The gods never bury anyone. Neither the
dead as such, nor the living as such have ever put anyone in the ground. If
Marx cannot not know this, what then does he mean? What does he want
exactly [*au juste*]? What did he want *then*, he who is dead and buried? He
wanted first of all, it seems, to recall us to the *make-oneself-fear* of that fear of
oneself. During past revolutions, the dead ones, the conjuration convoked the

great spirits (Jewish prophets, Rome, and so forth), but only in order to forget, to repress, out of fear, to anesthesize itself (*sich betäuben*) in the face of the
violence of the blow it was striking. The spirit of the past protected the conjuration against its "own content," the spirit was there to protect it against
itself. Everything is concentrated therefore in the question of this "content"
and of this "own content" to which Marx refers so often, three times in these
few famous lines. The whole anachronistic dislocation plays in the inadequation between the phrase and the content—the *proper* content, the appropriate content. Marx believes in it.

This disadjustment will no doubt never end. Doubtless it will reverse itself,
and we'll have the revolution within the revolution, the future revolution that,
without mourning, wins out over the past revolution: it will finally be the
event, the advent of the event, the coming of the future-to-come, the victory
of an "own content" that ends up winning out over the "phrase." All the same,
in the past revolution, when the gravediggers were alive, in sum, the phrase
exceeded the content. Whence the anachrony of a revolutionary present
haunted by its antique models. But in the future, and already in the *social* revolution of the nineteenth century still to come in Marx's view (the whole
novelty of the new would inhabit this *social* dimension, beyond the political
or economic revolution), the anachrony or untimeliness will not be erased in
some plenitude of the parousia and the presence to itself of the present. Time
will still be "out of joint." But this time the inadequation will stem from the
excess of its "own content" with regard to the "phrase." The "own content" will
no longer frighten, it will not hide itself, driven back behind the bereaved
rhetoric of antique models and the grimace of death masks. It will exceed the
form, it will break out of the clothes, it will overtake signs, models, eloquence,
mourning. Nothing there will be any longer an affected mannerism, giving
itself airs [*affecté, apprêté*]: no more credit and no more borrowed figure. But as
paradoxical as it seems, it is in this unleashed overflowing, at the moment
when all the joints give way between form and content, that the latter will be
properly its "own" and properly revolutionary. By all logic, one ought to recognize it by nothing other than the excess of this untimely dis-identification,
therefore by nothing that is. By nothing that is presently identifiable. As soon
as one identifies a revolution, it begins to imitate, it enters into a death agony.
That is the poetic difference, for we recall that Marx tells us where the *social*
revolution will have to draw forth its "poetry." That is the difference of poet-

ry itself between the *over there* of the political revolution of yesterday and the *here* of the social revolution of today, more precisely of this imminent today about which, alas, we know, now, today, that in its tomorrow, for the last century and a half, it will have to have exposed itself indefinitely, imperturbably, sometimes for the best, more often for the worst, here rather than over there, to one of the most inexhaustible phraseologies of modern history: "Dort ging die Phrase über den Inhalt, hier geht der Inhalt über die Phrase hinaus." Yes and no, alas.

It would, of course, have been necessary to cite more examples of this implacable anachrony in the *Eighteenth Brumaire of Louis Bonaparte* (and this title, with the date, already furnishes the first example of bereaved parody: in what is both a family, the Bonapartes, and France, at the genealogical juncture of public and private). We will retain only one example, closest to the letter, that is, to the spectral body that takes its place. This time it is a matter in effect of a parody of the specter itself. A revolution begins itself to caricature the "red specter" that the counter-revolutionaries did everything to conjure (away). The "red specter" was also the name of a revolutionary group.[9] The supplementary fold that matters to us here is the one that regularly assures the reflexive return of a conjuration: those who inspire fear frighten themselves, they conjure the very specter they represent. The conjuration is in mourning for *itself* and turns its own force against itself.

Here is our hypothesis: well beyond an "eighteenth Brumaire" this has never stopped happening to what is called Marxism. Far from protecting it from the worst, this return conjuration, this counter-conjuration will have precipitated it more surely in that direction. In chapter 3 of the *Eighteenth Brumaire*, Marx opposes once again the Revolution of 1848 to the first French Revolution. A sure and effective rhetoric accumulates the traits of an opposition dominated by a major figure: 1789 is the ascending curve, audacity mounts, one goes ever farther (constitutionals, Girondins, Jacobins), while in 1848 things follow a descending curve, the constitutionals conspire against the constitution, the revolutionaries seek to be constitutionals, and the omnipotence of the National Assembly gets bogged down in parliamentarism. The phrase decidedly wins out over content:

> wild, inane agitation [without content: *inhaltslose Agitation*] in the name of tranquillity; most solemn preaching of tranquillity in the name of revo-

lution; passions without truth, truths without passion; heroes without
heroic deeds, history without events [*Geschichte ohne Ereignisse*]. (P. 125)

Now, in what does this absence of events, and finally this ahistoricity, consist? What does it look like? Answer: an absence of body, of course. But who or
what has lost its body? Well, not a living individual, not, as one says, a real
subject, but a specter, the red specter that was conjured (away) by the counter-
revolutionaries (in fact, by all of Europe: the *Manifesto* was yesterday). That
is why one must "reverse" things, invert the tale by Chamisso, "The Wonderful
Story of Peter Schlemihl," the man who lost his shadow. Here, Marx tells us,
"Men and events appear as inverted Schlemihls [*als umgekehrte Schlemihle*],"
the shadow has lost its body at the moment the revolution appeared in the
uniform of order. The specter itself, the red specter, has been in effect disin-
carnated. As if that were possible. But is that not also possibility, precisely
[*justement*], virtuality itself? And to understand history, that is, the event-ness
of the event, must one not reckon with this virtualization? Must one not think
that the loss of the body can affect the specter itself? To the point that it is
then impossible to discern between the specter and the specter of the specter,
the specter searching for proper content and living effectivity? Not the night
in which all cows are black, but grey on grey because red on red. For let us
never forget that in describing these overturnings, inversions, conversions
without border, Marx means to denounce appearances. His *critique* also consists in saying: these men and these events who lose flesh like an inverted
Schlemihl whose body has disappeared (*abhanden gekommen ist*), that's how they
appear (*erscheinen*), to be sure, but this is but an apparition, therefore also an
appearance and *finally an image*, in the sense of *phenomenon* and in the sense of
rhetorical *figure*. It remains the case that what seems to be finally an image is
also, provisionally, the final image, what "appears in the end" (*endlich erscheint*),
grey on grey like red on red, in the parousia of this aborted revolution:

> If any section of history has been painted grey on grey [*grau in grau*], it
> is this. Men and events appear as inverted Schlemihls [*erscheinen als
> umgekehrte Schlemihle*], as shadows that have lost their bodies. The revo-
> lution itself paralyses its own bearers and endows only its adversaries
> with passionate forcefulness. When the "red specter" [*das "rote Gespenst"*]
> continually conjured up and exorcised [*heraufbeschworen und gebannt*] by
> the counter-revolutionaries, finally appears [*endlich erscheint*], it appears

not with the Phrygian cap of anarchy on its head, but in the uniform of order, in red breeches [*in roten Plumphosen*]. (Ibid.)

On both sides, between revolution and counter-revolution, between the democrats and Bonaparte, the war does not oppose only specters and conjurations, animist spells and magic incantations, but simulacra of simulacra. On both sides, a specular reflection endlessly sends the simulacrum away, that is, defers up to the abyss the encounter with a living body, with the real, living, actual event, with the revolution itself, the revolution properly speaking, in person. This does not prevent Marx from giving a date. It is true that he points out, each time within brackets, that it is a Sunday. Now, in its very singularity, a date always repeats, resuscitates the ghost of another date for which it mourns. What is more, a Sunday is not just any day for a revolution. Hegel had already named a certain speculative Good Friday, Marx gives one to see what is seen on the Lord's day, the awaited apparition, the return of the dead, resurrection as reapparition:

> beneficial consequences of the second [Sunday of the month: *Sonntag des Monats*] May 1852. In their minds [Messieurs the Democrats] the second [Sunday of] May 1852 had become a fixed idea, a dogma, like the day on which Christ should reappear [*wiedererscheiner sollte*] and the millenium begin, in the minds of the Chiliasts. As ever, weakness had taken refuge in a belief in miracles, fancied the enemy overcome when it had only conjured him away in imagination [*in der Phantasie weghexte*]... (P. 107; the first three bracketed insertions are Marx's)

And a little later—it is still Sunday, the same day, another Sunday, the floor is turned over to phantoms, to the phantasmagoria, to anathema as formula of exorcism (*Bannformel*), to sorcery, the survival will have lasted but the blink of an eye—here is the will and testament of a people. With its own voice, with its own hand, an immediately blinded people signs its own death warrant in a Mephistophelean decree:

> the sheet lightning of the daily press, the entire literature, the political names and the intellectual reputations [*die geistigen Renommeen*], the civil law and the penal code, the *liberté, égalité, fraternité* and the second [Sunday of] May 1852—all has vanished like a phantasmagoria [*Phantasmagorie*] before the spell [*Bannformel*] of a man whom even his

enemies do not make out to be a magician [*Hexenmeister*]. Universal suffrage seems to have survived [*überlebt*] only for a moment, in order that with its own hand it may make its last will and testament before the eyes of all the world and declare in the name of the people itself: "All that comes to birth is fit for overthrow, as nothing worth." (Ibid.)

What happened in this blink of an eye? How to describe this sleight of hand? A fake magician, as insubstantial as a sort of *back-up ghost*, auxiliary specter, or *revenant* on call (Louis Bonaparte), himself haunted by the quasi-paternal figure of a great specter (Napoleon Bonaparte and the Revolution of 1789), taking advantage of a day on duty, makes the revolution disappear, like a phantasmagoria, by means of a perverse, diabolical, and non-apparent exorcism. For if his conjuration makes the people disappear, it signs in fact by the same token his own disappearance, it signs it with his own hand: absolute alienation and now without body, alienation of self that appropriates in this way only its own death and bequeaths only the patrimony of its expropriation.

Do these paradoxes correspond to a consistent and irreducible logic? Or must one make certain allowances? Must one allow for rhetoric? Is it just a matter here of seeking certain effects in what some (for example, Michel Henry[10]) have occasionally wanted to qualify among the "political" or "historical" texts of Marx, in opposition to his "philosophical" texts? Our hypothesis is different. No doubt one must take the measure of the polemic, the oratorical talent, an uncommon linguistic arsenal: a panoply of arguments but also of images, a *fantastic panoply* at a time when people had a taste for ghosts (for a *certain* theater of ghosts, according to a historically determined scenography—every age has its scenography, we have our ghosts). One must also consider, to be sure, the singular involvement in the mobility of a highly differentiated historical, tactical, and strategic context. But this should not prevent one from recognizing certain invariables beyond these limits. There is constancy, consistency, and coherence here. There are discursive layers whose stratification allows long sequences to remain subjacent to ephemeral formations. Even if a certain structural heterogeneity remains, as we are constantly suggesting here, it does not divide different types of discourse, but rather is at work within each one of them. In its philosophical form, the paradoxy of the specter was already part of the program of *The German Ideology* and will remain on the program of *Capital*. And the fantastic panoply, while it furnishes the rhetoric or the polemic with images or phantasms, perhaps gives one to think that the figure of the ghost is not just one figure among others. It is perhaps the hidden figure of all figures. For this reason, it would perhaps no longer figure as one tropological weapon among others. There would be no meta-rhetoric of the ghost.

In the face of these paradoxes, what would be the task here? One of the tasks, at least, would be for example to reconstitute a battle plan, the spectro-logical map of what was, in *The German Ideology*, the most gigantic phan-tomachia in the whole history of philosophy. One would have to follow it in detail, through the extraordinary play and the reciprocal excesses of what Marx called, in the passages we have just quoted, an "own content" and a "phrase." Pleasure ought not to lose a single spark of the wit, the spirit of Marx (and Engels) through and beyond the witticism [*mot d'esprit*], not only in the economy of the *Witz*, its features and its barbs, but through and beyond the trans-substantiation between *Gaz* and *Geist*.[11]

We will be able to isolate only a few traits in a long and witty [*spirituelle*] diatribe. Once again it is a question of a *hunt*. Anything close at hand is made to serve as arrow for the bow. There is harassment always without mercy, sometimes without respect for the rules of conduct (which is to say, without too much good faith), of someone who is accused of belonging to that lineage of neo-evangelists we were talking about above. Saint Max (Stirner), if one can believe Marx (and Engels), would have caused the Apocalypse of Saint John to lie. Where the latter heralded the whore of Babylon (that other center of our Middle-Eastern ellipsis, still today), the neo-evangelist Stirner pro-claims man, the secret (*das Geheimnis*), the unique (*den Einzigen*). And then follows, in the desert of the spirit (*die Wüste des Geistes*), the whole history of spirits, ghosts, or *revenants*: first the pure history of spirits (*reine Geistergeschichte*), then the history of the possessed (*die Besessenen*) as impure history of phantoms (*unreine Geistergeschichte*), then the impure impure history of spirits (*unreine unreine Geistergeschichte*). Stirner proclaims it himself: "ever since the word was made flesh, since the world *was* spiritualized [*vergeistigt*], bewitched [*verzaubert*], it is a ghost [*ein Spuk*]."[12] Marx ironizes on the "Stirner" case (the proper name in quotation marks because, as everyone knows, it is a pseudonym): "'Stirner' sees spirits [*sieht Geister*]." For, like a tourist guide or a professor, Stirner would claim to teach us the rules of method for a good introduction to ghosts. After having determined the spirit to be something other than (the) self ("*Der Geist ist* etwas Andres als Ich"), a definition, we dare say, not lacking in insight, Stirner poses yet another excellent question ("But this other, what is it? [*Dieses Andre aber, was ist's?*]"), a big question which Marx, it seems, is too quick to scoff at and too eager to do whatever necessary to exorcise in his turn. All the more so in that, as Marx himself remarks in order to mock it easily, this question does no more than modify, with a supplementary "metamorphosis" (*Wandlung*), the originary question (*die urpsprüngliche Frage*), the abyssal question that bore in effect on the non-identity to self, on the inadequation and thus the non-presence to self, the dis-adjusted untimeliness of this thing that is called *spirit*. Marx should not have made fun of it, but he does, and maliciously, with an ingenuousness that would like to appear feigned. Perhaps it is less so than it appears. (So let us not try to hide the fact here, although this is not exactly the right moment, that we take seriously the originality, audacity, and, precisely, the philosophico-political seriousness of Stirner who also should be read without Marx or against him; but this is not our topic here). Marx:

> Now, therefore, the question arises: What is the spirit other than the ego? whereas the original question was: What is the spirit, owing to its creation out of nothing, other than itself [*Was ist der Geist durch seine Schöpfung aus Nichts anderes als er selbst*]? With this Saint Max jumps to the next "transformation." (P. 152; another equivalent reading: spirit is created from nothing other than itself)

In its first and simple "impurity," the history of ghosts unfolds in several moments. Even before one watches from the comfort of one's chair[13] what is called the theory of specters, the procession of the ghosts of concepts that would be these concepts of ghosts (their mere names, Marx thinks), it is important to underscore that this theory *betrays* its origin, namely, father Hegel. It betrays and it betrays: It allows one to see its ancestral line and it is unworthy of that ancestor. It denounces that ancestor. Stirner's Hegelian genealogy would also be a decline of the son. Stirner descends from Hegel, he is haunted by the author of *The Phenomenology of Spirit* and he cannot stand it. He spits out living ghosts like a whale suffering from indigestion. In other words, he does not comprehend Hegel as well as another one of the descendants, guess who. The latter, just as persecuted by the shadow of this great father who comes back every night, ready also to betray him or to avenge him (it is sometimes the same thing), is busy giving a lesson here in Hegelianism to brother Stirner. Stirner always slips into Hegelian language, he slides his words into "the long-familiar orthodox-Hegelian phrases" (p. 149). But this unworthy heir has not understood the essentials of the will and testament, he has not read very well *The Phenomenology of Spirit* which is his inspiration and which he wants to give to us in a Christian version ("Saint Max intends to give us a phenomenology of the Christian spirit" [p. 153]). What has he not understood? What is the essential? On the subject of the becoming-specter of the spirit, he has not seen that, for Hegel, the world was not only spiritualized (ver*geistigt*) but de-spiritualized (ent*geistigt*), a thesis that the author of *The German Ideology* seems to approve: this de-spiritualization is quite correctly (*ganz richtig*) recognized by Hegel, we read. Hegel managed to relate the two movements, but our "saintly dialectician," who is ignorant of the "historical method," has not learned how to do so. What is more, if he had been a better historian, he would have ended up breaking with Hegel. For the reproach against Stirner is both that he does not understand Hegel and—this is not necessarily a contradiction—that he is too Hegelian in his genealogy of the ghost. This bad brother sees himself accused at once of being the too filial son and a bad son of Hegel.[14] A docile son listens to his father, he mimes him but does not understand him at all, implies Marx—who would have liked to do not the opposite, that is, become another bad son, but something else by interrupting filiation. Easier said than done. In any case, the work of Stirner remains null and void. "But even if he had given us this phenomenology (which after Hegel is moreover superfluous), he would all the same have given us nothing" (pp. 153–54).

A bad son and a bad historian, Stirner would be unable to break with the ancestor and the precedent of the *Phenomenology* (and what is a *phenomenology* if not a logic of the *phainesthai* and of the *phantasma*, therefore of the phantom? Unless one goes to desperate lengths, as Marx finally does himself, to try to distinguish between spirit and specter). The author of *The Ego and His Own* does not see that concepts as abstract as Self-Consciousness or Man are religious in nature. He makes of religion a *causa sui*, as if specters could move about on their own. He does not see that "'Christianity' has no history whatsoever," no history of its own. It does not manage to explain, as it should have done, the "self-determinations" and the "developments" of "the religious spirit" based on "empirical conditions" and "empirical causes," on "a determined form of society," "determined relations of exchange and industry." He missed both the being-determined, therefore "necessary," he missed the *determina-tion* (the master-word of the accusation) and more precisely the empiricity of this determination. He thus misapprehended what determines this determination of spirit as hetero-determination. The apparently declared empiricism that inspires this critique always leads it back, in fact, to a law of alterity. As always, empiricism has a vocation for heterology. One recognizes actual experience by its encounter with some other. Now, for having overlooked this hetero-determination of the Christian spirit, Stirner is under a spell, he hallucinates, he phantomalizes, one might say he fantasizes the spirit. In truth, he is haunted by the Hegelian frequency. He is inhabited only by that. The only "alterity" of which he is capable is the "being-other" of the professorial chair, "a 'being-other' of the thoughts of the Berlin professor." The "metamorphoses" of Stirnerian man and world are universal history incarnated in the shadow of Hegel, incorporated into "the body of Hegelian philosophy [*in den Leib der Hegelschen Philosophie*]," metamorphosed and incorporated "into ghosts, which only apparently are a 'being-other' of the thoughts of the Berlin professor." They are only that, and they are apparently that. In *The Phenomenology of Spirit*, in this Bible or this Book, Hegel transfigures the individual into "consciousness" and the world into "object." Life and history are thus transfigured, in their very diversity, into *relations of consciousness to the object*. It is still a matter of truth and it is a phenomenologization of the truth as truth of *consciousness* that is here put in question. The history of the ghost remains a history of phantomalization and the latter will indeed be a history of truth, a history of the becoming-true of a fable, unless it is the reverse, a fabulation of truth, in any case a history of ghosts. The phenomenology (of spirit) describes (1) the relation of consciousness to the object *as truth* or as relation *to the truth* as mere object; (2) the relation of consciousness, insofar as it is *the true*, to the object; (3) the *true relation* of consciousness with truth (*wahres Verhalten des Bewusstseins zur Wahrheit*).

This tripleness reflects the Trinity: God the Father, Christ, and the Holy Spirit. The spirit provides mediation, thus passage and unity. It gives rise, by the same token, to the metamorphosis of the spiritual into the spectral: this is the very error of Saint Max. One therefore has the feeling that, in the critique of Stirner in any case, Marx is out to get the specter above all and not the spirit, as if he still believed in some de-contaminating purification in this regard, as if the ghost were not watching the spirit, as if it were not haunting

spirit, it participates in the latter and stems from it even as it follows it as its ghostly double. The difference between the two is precisely what tends to disappear in the ghost effect, just as the concept of such a difference or the argumentative movement that puts it to work in the rhetoric tends to vanish. All the more so in that this rhetoric is in advance devoted to the polemic, in any case to the strategy of a hunt or chase [*une chasse*]. And even to a counter-sophistics that at every moment runs the risk of replicating the *reply*: reproducing in a mirror the logic of the adversary at the moment of the retort, piling it on there where one accuses the other of abusing language. This counter-sophistics (Marx as paradoxical heir of Plato, as we shall see) has to manipulate simulacra, mimemes, phantasms. It has to watch out for, so as to denounce, the maneuvers of an illusionist, the "conjuring tricks" of a pres-tidigitator of the concept, or the sleights of hand of a nominalist rhetor.

We can try to grasp this strategy as close as possible to its literality, and first of all its Stirnerian literality, in what Marx calls the series of "conjuring tricks" (French: *escamotage*; German, *Eskamotage*), which he intends to take apart at the beginning of "Saint Max" ("The Leipzig Council III").[1] The production of the ghost, the constitution of the *ghost* effect is not simply a spiritualization or even an autonomization of spirit, idea, or thought, as happens *par excellence* in Hegelian idealism. No, once this autonomization is effected, with the cor-responding expropriation or alienation, and only then, the ghostly moment *comes upon* it, adds to it a supplementary dimension, one more simulacrum, alienation, or expropriation. Namely, a body! In the flesh (*Leib*)! For there is no ghost, there is never any becoming-specter of the spirit without at least an appearance of flesh, in a space of invisible visibility, like the dis-appearing of an apparition. For there to be ghost, there must be a return to the body, but to a body that is more abstract than ever. The spectrogenic process corresponds therefore to a paradoxical *incorporation*. Once ideas or thoughts (*Gedanke*) are detached from their substratum, one engenders some ghost by *giving them a body*. Not by returning to the living body from which ideas and thoughts have been torn loose, but by incarnating the latter in *another artifactual body, a pros-thetic body*, a ghost of spirit, one might say a ghost of the ghost if, as Marx sometimes leads one to think, the first spiritualization also, and already, pro-duces some specter. But a more acute specificity belongs to what could be called the "second" ghost, as incorporation of autonomized spirit, as objec-tivizing expulsion of interior idea or thought. (In this sense, there is always some mourning work in this incorporation of interiority, and death is on the program. The theory of ideology depends in many of its features, as we will emphasize, on this theory of the ghost. As Stirnerian theorem critiqued, corrected, or reversed by Marx, it formalizes less a process of spiritualization, the autonomization of spiritual ideality, than a paradoxical law of *incorporation*: the ideological as well as, *mutatis mutandis*, the fetish would be the given, or rather lent, borrowed body, the second incarnation conferred on an initial idealization, the incorporation in a body that is, to be sure, neither perceptible nor invisible, but remains flesh, in a body without nature, in an *a-physical* body that could be called, if one could rely on these oppositions, a technical body or an institutional body. Like the one who says, from the safety of his visor, "I am thy Fathers Spirit," it is even a visible-invisible body, sensuous-non-sensuous, and always under the tough institutional or cultural protection of some artifact: the helmet of the ideologem or the fetish under armor.)

But that is not all. The specificity of the process can still capitalize the spectralization. Once the ghost is produced by the incarnation of spirit (the autonomized idea or thought), when this *first* ghost effect has been operated, it is in turn negated, integrated, and incorporated by the very subject of the operation who, claiming the uniqueness of its *own* human body, then becomes, according to Marx as critic of Stirner, the absolute ghost, in fact the ghost of the ghost of the specter-spirit, simulacrum of simulacra without end. This would be, if one believes Marx, the delirious and hallucinogenic moment of the properly Stirnerian *hubris*: in the name of critique, and sometimes political critique (for Stirner also maintains a political discourse; one must recall the infinite entanglement of the debate that formed the context of this "Leipzig Council III: Saint Max"), this would be but a raising of the ante of negativity, a rage for reappropriation, an accumulation of ghostly layers. Marx denounces the sophistics of this "conjuring trick" in one of the clearest moments of this verbose and sometimes vertiginous argumentation—which itself seems to give into the vertigo to which such tropics necessarily lead, for a specter does not only cause séance tables to turn, but sets heads spinning. In truth it is a matter of another "Eskamotage." Marx loves this word. Why does this proliferation of ghosts proceed by so many *conjuring tricks*? A conjuring trick in fact multiplies itself, it gets carried away with itself, and is unleashed in a series. Marx begins to count them and then gives up. The word "Eskamotage" speaks of subterfuge or theft in the exchange of merchandise, but first of all the sleight of hand by means of which an illusionist makes the most perceptible body disappear. It is an art or a technique of *making disappear*. The *escamoteur* knows how to *make inapparent*. He is expert in a hyper-phenomenlogy. Now, the height of the conjuring trick here consists in causing to disappear while producing "apparitions," which is only contradictory in appearance, precisely, since one causes to disappear by provoking hallucinations or by inducing visions. Stirner has just been quoted at length and there then follows a nearly literal commentary, a paraphrase:

> Thus, the man, identified here with the "unique," having first given thoughts [*den Gedanken*] corporeality [*Leibhaftigkeit*], i.e., having transformed them into specters [*d.h. sie zu Gespenstern gemacht hat*] now destroys this corporeality again [*zerstört er nun wieder diese Leibhaftigkeit*], by taking them back into his own body, which he thus makes into a body of specters [*indem er sie in seinen eignen Leib zurücknimmt und diesen somit als den Leib der Gespenster setzt*]. The fact that he arrives at his own corporeality only through the negation of the specters, shows the nature of this constructed corporeality of the man [*Leibhaftigkeit des Mannes*], which he has first to "announce" to "himself," in order to believe in it. But what he "announces to himself" he does not even "announce" correctly. The fact that apart from his "unique" body there are not also to be found in his head all kinds of independent bodies, spermatozoa, he transforms into the *"fable"*: I *alone* am corporeal [*Ich* allein *bin leibhaftig*]. Another conjuring trick. (Pp. 125–26)

The spectral effect corresponds then, according to Marx, to a position (*Setzung*) of the ghost, a *dialectical* position of the ghostly body as body proper. All of this would take place *among ghosts*, between *two ghosts*. Two according to Marx, while for Stirner only the first moment would be spectral, and the ego or I would sublate it in the reappropriation of a living and unique body. The living body, the "mine," "my property" returns by annulling or taking back into it the phantomatic projections, the ideal prostheses. This second moment marks the "destruction" or "negation" of a ghost previously posed, exposed on the outside, objectified, namely, the idea or the thought that has been incorporated *a first time*. This *first* spectral incorporation is then negated and interiorized. The self is what takes it back within (*zurücknimmt*): "I" incorporates the initial incorporation by negating or destroying, by deposing the previous position from its objective exteriority, by de-objectifying the ghost. Obviously, Marx is here paraphrasing Stirner in his description of the discovery of self by the adolescent becoming an adult. But only up to the point where Marx, and not Stirner, determines the ultimate moment to be a ghost, the body proper of the I, the mine, my property (*als die Meinige, als Mein Eigentum*). There where Stirner sees a carnal and living reappropriation, *more life* (there where there would be *no more death*), Marx denounces a hyperbolic surplus of spectrality, *more death* (there where there would be *no more life*): since the living body, mine, the unique, is but the common place, the space in which thoughts or ideal, autonomized entities are gathered, is it not itself the "body of ghosts [*Leib der Gespenster*]"?

In this whirling dance of ghosts, let us try to hold on to the at least apparent firmness of a few obvious facts. What Stirner and Marx seem to have in common is the critique of the ghostly. Both of them want to have done with the *revenant*, both of them hope to get there. Both of them aim at some reappropriation of life in a body proper. This hope at least is what impels the prescriptive injunction or the promise of their discourses. It is perhaps even what gives its first determining content to the messianic formality of their call. But whereas Stirner seems to entrust this reappropriation to a simple conversion of the self that *takes back into itself* (a self that in truth *is* nothing but this movement of interiorizing gathering) and authentically reanimates, in some fashion, the objectified ghosts, the ghost at large, Marx, for his part, denounces this egological body: there, he cries, is the ghost of all ghosts! There is the gathering place toward which all the repatriated specters run: the forum or agora for all those who come back, for there is a lot of talking going on. Marx then prescribes that one proceed with the reappropriation while taking into account all the practical and social structures, all the empirico-technical detours that had produced the initial ghosts. It is not enough to destroy as if with a spell, in an instant, the "corporeality" (*Leibhaftigkeit*) of the ghosts in order to reincorporate them alive. This magic of immediacy, which would give life back to the specters by simple transition from exterior to interior body, from the objective to the subjective, in the simple auto-affection of the "I-Me," "creator and owner" of these thoughts, that is what Stirner seems to recommend. In the absolute certitude of the pure contact with itself, the immediacy of an "I-Me" would have exorcised the ghost by depriving it from then on of any interstice, lodging, or spacing favorable to haunting. This resembles an *epokhē*, a phenomenological reduction *of the* ghost, but Marx criticizes it as a phenomenological reduction *to the* ghost (to the phenomenality or phantasm of a phantom). The reduction as subjectivization of the corporeal form of the external phantom is but a super-idealization and a supplementary spectralization. Marx quotes and comments on Stirner:

> "How I find myself" (it should read: "how the youth finds himself") "behind the *things* [Dinge], and indeed as *spirit* [Geist], so subsequently, too, I must find myself" (it should read "the man must find himself") "behind the *thoughts* [Gedanken], i.e., as their creator and owner [*als ihr Schöpfer une Eigner*]. In the period of spirits [*In der Geisterzeit*], thoughts outgrew me" (the youth), "although they were the offspring of my brain; like delirious fantasies [*wie Fieberphantasien*], they floated around me and agitated me greatly, a dreadful power. The thoughts became themselves *corporeal* [leibhaftig], they were specters [*Gespenster*], like God, the Emperor, the Pope, the Fatherland, etc.; by destroying their corporeality [*Leibhaftigkeit*], I take them back into my own corporeality and *announce*: I alone am corporeal [*zerstöre Ich irhe Leibhaftigkeit, so nehme Ich sie in die Meinige zurück und sage: Ich* allein *bin leibhaftig*]. And now I take the world as it is for me, as *my* world, as my property: I relate everything to myself [*Und nun nehme Ich die Welt als das, was sie Mir ist, als die* Meinige *als Mein Eigentum: Ich beziehe Alles auf Mich*]." (P. 125)

In the story of what is *being said* here, in this fabulous reconstruction that often proceeds by simple *nomination* and is content to substitute a "pompous series of resounding names" for proper names (p. 131), Marx denounces a surplus of hallucination and a capitalization of the ghost: what is really (*wirklich*) destroyed are merely the representations in their form as representation (*Vorstellung*). The youth may indeed destroy his hallucinations or the phantomatic appearance of the bodies—of the Emperor, the State, the Fatherland. He does not actually (*wirklich*) destroy them. And if he stops relating to these realities through the prostheses of his representation and the "spectacles of his fantasy [*durch die Brille seiner Phantasie*]," if he stops transforming these realities into objects, objects of theoretical intuition, that is, into a spectacle, then he will have to take into account the "practical structure" of the world: Work, production, actualization, techniques. Only this practicality, only this actuality (work, the *Wirken* or the *Wirkung* of this *Wirklichkeit*) can get to the bottom of a purely imaginary or spectral flesh (*phantastische…gespenstige Leibhaftigkeit*).

Marx seems to be warning Stirner: If you want to conjure away these ghosts, then believe me, I beg you [*je vous en conjure*], the egological conversion is not

enough, nor is the change in the direction of a gaze, nor a putting into parentheses, nor the phenomenological reduction; one must work—practically,
actually. One must think work and work at it. Work is necessary, as is an
account of reality as practical actuality. One does not chase away the *real*
emperor or pope in a single blow by exorcising or by conjuring away
[*escamotant*] the mere *ghostly* form of their bodies. Marx is very firm: when one
has destroyed a phantomatic body, the real body remains. When the *ghostly*
body (*die gespenstige Leibhaftigkeit*) of the emperor disappears, it is not the
body that disappears, merely its phenomenality, its phantomality
(*Gespensterhaftigkeit*). The emperor is then more real than ever and one can
measure better than ever his actual power (*wirkliche Macht*). When one has
negated or destroyed the fantastic or phantomatic form (*die phantastische und
gespenstige Gestalt*) of the fatherland, one has not yet touched upon the "actual
relations [*wirkliche Verhältnisse*]" that constitute it. In his abstract reconstruction
of the various stages of life, Stirner gives us but a "spectral shade" that we
ought to "confront" with its disappeared body, for what he has lost in this supposed destruction of specters is quite simply his body, "life" and "actual reality
[*Wirlichkeit*]." He lost his body out of love of his body. For this whole history
remains under the control of the paradoxes of narcissism and the work of
mourning. Everything begins, everything ought to begin and begin again,
according to the Stirnerian axiomatics, with the love of one's own body ("*wenn
man sich* leibhaftig *liebgewonnen*"; "only when *one* has grown fond of oneself
corporeally"). One then mourns for the ghosts in which one had already expro-
priated oneself (ideas, objectified thoughts, and so forth), in which one had
already lost one's body and one's life. To this *immediate* work of mourning, to
this mourning for work, to this work of mourning without work, to this immediately narcissistic conversion, Marx opposes a work on this work of mourning
that liberates us from this hyper-phantomality: the *ego* of the Stirnerian body.
This critique does not eliminate the death and expropriation at the heart of
the living; it calls one back to what always defers the work of mourning,
mourning itself and narcissism. Marx merely determines the differ*a*nce or
deferral as practical and as a delay of reappropriation.

Has this backward glance allowed us to distinguish between the voices
which are sometimes so close? In the political dispute that Marx wants to
provoke with Stirner, these voices seem to echo each other. If there were a
confabulation for the initiated, it would turn around the question of who is

better able to have the ghost's hide: at what rhythm, according to which detours and strategies. In real time, immediately, or in deferred time. Why call this a confabulation [*conciliabule*]?[2] Beneath the absolute, infinite, apparently definitive discord, the one that Marx insists on above all and that he constantly recalls as if no one wanted to believe him, a proximity is hidden, indeed a fearsome analogy. Let us be clear: fearsome for Marx. And if there is a confabulation, it is because a common stake incites the polemic. It is called the specter. And Marx and Stirner want to be done with it. That is the common axiom, which is not open to discussion. One must have the ghost's hide and to do that, one must have it. To have it, one must see it, situate it, identify it. One must possess it without letting oneself be possessed by it, without being possessed of it (*besessen*—that is the title of one of Marx's accusations: "The Possessed," *Die Besessenen [Unreine Geistergeschichte]*). But does not a specter consist, to the extent that it consists, in forbidding or blurring this distinction? in consisting in this very undiscernability? Is not to possess a specter to be possessed by it, possessed period? To capture it, is that not to be captivated by it? And yet Marx seems to agree essentially with Stirner: one must win out over the specter, put an end to it. The disagreement is over the means to this end, and over the best solution. This disagreement [*différend*] over how to put the ghosts to death seems methodological, but by definition it knows no limit: without fail, it becomes ontological, ethical, political. The fact remains that a *conciliabule* is a schismatic or heretical council, a secret council, a lively discussion. The sworn members [*conjurés*], who are sometimes plotters, contradict each other, erect plans, ready their arms, or exchange secrets. There, whether or not they agree on strategy, all these opponents of darkness realize in vain that Europe is trembling in the face of a certain ghost, the one named by the *Manifesto* with its first noun; they too plot against an army of specters, against spectrality itself, and no doubt they all think it is a good war. We realize it better now: it will have taken more than a century before *The German Ideology* began to be exhumed, brought from beneath the earth, before one began to untangle the crossed threads of its roots and the knot of its complicities and antagonisms among Marx, Engels, Feuerbach, Stirner, Hess, Bauer, and so forth. This has begun but it is not over. And the paternal shade of Hegel continues to come back, the plot thickens with its first reapparition. To accuse the other, in this poisoned conspiracy, is always to announce or denounce the imminence of its return ("if again this apparition come…").

For if this backward glance had made us more attuned to the cunning of such a "logic," to all its disguises, to the impregnable arms or armors that it provides to the phantom body, to the endless strategy to which it gives rise, we better understand Stirner. We better understand how and why he would have given himself up to this general and precipitous spectralization. According to Marx in any case, Stirner accepted a series of disguises (*Verkleidungen*) of the Hegelian idea. Trusting them, accrediting them dogmatically (*auf Treu und Glauben*), he would have taken them for the world itself, a world before which he then had to affirm himself, assert his self-worth, and to that end oppose himself to a non-self in the face of which he would reappropriate himself as *living* and incarnate *individual* (*als leibhaftiges Individuum*).

Stirner has often been read, in fact, as a Fichtean thinker. But this Ego, this *living individual* would itself be inhabited and invaded by *its own specter*. It would be constituted by specters of which it becomes the host and which it assembles in the haunted community of a single body. Ego = ghost. Therefore "I am" would mean "I am haunted": I am haunted by myself who am (haunted by myself who am haunted by myself who am…and so forth). Wherever there is Ego, *es spukt*, "it spooks." (The idiom of this "es spukt" plays a singular role in all these texts, as it does in Freud's "Das Unheimliche." Its translation always fails, unfortunately, to render the link between the impersonality or the quasi-anonymity of an operation [*spuken*] without act, without real subject or object, and the production of a figure, that of the *revenant* [*der Spuk*]: not simply "it spooks," as we just ventured to translate, but "it returns," "it ghosts," "it specters.") The essential mode of self-presence of the *cogito* would be the haunting obsession of this "es spukt." It would be a matter there of the Stirnerian *cogito* in the logic of an accusation, to be sure, but is this limit impassable? Can one not extend this hypothesis to any cogito? The Cartesian *cogito*, the Kantian "I think," the phenomenological *ego cogito*?[3] A real presence is promised here to a eucharistic Narcissus. The Stirnerian living being, its unique Ego, would be in effect visited by its own apparition. The individual himself gives to himself his "this is my body." Sancho-Stirner and Christ resemble each other moreover as two "beings of flesh [*beleibte Wesen*]," notes Marx who is not content just to underscore incessantly the Christian-Hegelian dimension of the enterprise and thus to recall that all phenomenology is a phenomenology of spirit (let us translate here: phenomenology of the specter) and that, as such, it cannot hide its Christian vocation. He also claims

Allem Dich ein Geist anschaut!]" (p. 152).

Follow my gaze, the specter seems to say with the imperturbable authority and the rock hardness of a Commandatore. Let us follow this gaze. Right away we lose sight of it: disappeared, the departed, in the hall of mirrors where it multiplies. There is not only one spirit watching You. Since this spirit "is" everywhere, since it comes from everywhere (*aus Allem*), it proliferates *a priori*, it puts in place, while depriving them of any place, a mob of specters to which one can no longer even assign a *point of view*: they invade all of space. Number is the specter. But in order to inhabit even there where one is not, to haunt all places at the same time, to be *atopic* (mad and non-localizable), not only is it necessary to see from behind the visor, to see without being seen by whoever makes himself or herself seen (me, us), it is also necessary to speak. And to hear voices. The spectral rumor now resonates, it invades everything: the spirit of the "sublime" and the spirit of "nostalgia" cross all borders. "One hears," Marx quotes, "'millions of spirits speak through the mouths of people' [*und man hört 'aus den Menschen Millionen Geister reden'*]" (ibid.). A merciless spiraling movement then draws in a series of quotations that lead to *two conclusions*. Marx wants at the same time to extract them from Stirner's witness-text and to use them against him. As always, he grabs the weapons and turns them back against the one who thought he was their sole owner. We underscore here the objections that one might be tempted to address to the phenomenological principle in general. Two conclusions, then: (1) the phenomenal form of the world itself is spectral; (2) the phenomenological *ego* (Me, You, and so forth) is a specter. The *phainesthai* itself (before its determination as phenomenon or phantasm, thus as phantom) is the very possibility of the specter, it brings death, it gives death, it works at mourning.[6]

Consequence, concatenation, rattle of chains, endless procession of phenomenal forms that file by, all white and diaphanous, in the middle of the night. The apparition form, the phenomenal body of the spirit, that is the definition of the specter. The ghost is the phenomenon of the spirit. Let us cite Marx who, citing Stirner, wants to force him to admit that he identifies irresistibly with the witness-adversary whom he calls to appear, the poor Szeliga. The latter will have survived oblivion only in this insubstantial guise, he speaks only through this indirect voice. Everything is concentrated then in the German expression *es spukt*, which translations are obliged to circumvent. One would have to say: it haunts, it ghosts, it specters, there is some phantom there, it has the feel of the living-dead—manor house, spiritualism, occult science, gothic novel, obscurantism, atmosphere of anonymous threat or imminence. The subject that haunts is not identifiable, one cannot see, localize, fix any form, one cannot decide between hallucination and perception, there are only displacements; one feels oneself looked at by what one cannot see:

> If one has achieved this level [where talk passes through millions of spirits, *aus den Menschen Millionen Geister reden*], if one can exclaim with Stirner: "*Yes*, ghosts are teeming in the whole world [*Ja, es spukt in der Ganzen Welt*], then "it is not difficult to advance to the point" (p. 93) where one makes the further exclamation: "Only *in* it? *No*, the world itself is an apparition [*Nur* in *ihr? Nein, sie selber spukt*]" (let your communication be, Yea, yea; Nay, nay: for whatsoever is more than these cometh of evil, i.e., a logical transition), "it is the wandering pseudo-body of a spirit, it is an apparition [*sie ist der wandelnde Scheinleib eines Geistes, sie ist ein Spuk*]." Then cheerfully "look near at hand or into the distance, you are surrounded by a ghostly world.... You see spirits [*in die Nähe oder in die Ferne, Dich umgibt eine gespenstige Welt—Du siehst Geister*]".... [A]nd then "you should not be surprised" if, in these circumstances and from the heights of Szeligality, you discover also that "your spirit is a ghost haunting your body [*Deine Geist in Deinem Leibe spukt*]," that you yourself are a ghost [*Du selbst ein Gespenst bist*] which "awaits salvation, that is, a spirit." Thereby you will have arrived at the point where you are capable of seeing "spirits" and "ghosts" in "all" people, and therewith spirit-seeing "reaches its final goal" (Pp. 46–47).
>
> The basis of this instruction, only much more correctly expressed, is to be found in Hegel, *inter alia*, in the *Geschichte der Philosophie*, III, pp. 124, 125. (P. 153)

This passage will have clarified, among other things, the difference between specter and spirit. It is a differ*a*nce. The specter is not only the carnal apparition of the spirit, its phenomenal body, its fallen and guilty body, it is also the impatient and nostalgic waiting for a redemption, namely, once again, for a spirit (*auf Erlösung harrt, nämlich ein Geist*). The ghost would be the deferred spirit, the promise or calculation of an expiation. What is this differance? All or nothing. One must reckon with it but it upsets all calculations, interests, and capital. A transition between the two moments of spirit, the ghost is just passing through. Stirner, notes Marx while citing him, takes "seriously" this passage of the "spirits" (in the plural) that are the "offspring of spirit" in the singular (*Sankt Max macht jetzt Ernst mit den "Geistern," welche die*

"Kinder des Geistes sind"). He at least imagines this spectrality of everything (*Gespensterhaftigkeit Aller*). To this whole progeniture, to all these children whose sex is never determined, neither by Max nor Marx (but everything suggests that they are brothers of the same Son, thus sons of the same Father, through the mediation of the same Holy Spirit), he is content just to give names. Incantatory magic of onomastics and *appellations contrôlées*. The names are new, the concepts have aged, they drag along behind them a single idea: the idea that men *represent*, precisely by means of new appellations, general concepts. The whole debate here concerns, of course, the status of conceptual generality and the rough treatment it receives from Stirner, who according to Marx, phantomalizes it. These "representatives" (*Repräsentanten*) that are men present or represent the generality of concepts in "the Negroid form" (*im negerhaften Zustande*). Perfidious, bifid, the word "Negroid" does double duty. On the one hand, it denounces the confusion within which Stirner maintains the concept, more precisely the *presentation* of the concept, the manner in which concepts "come onstage" in the intuition: the indetermination of the homogeneous, in the dark element of a nocturnal obscurity. The "Negroid state" is thus also, as some august ancestor had said just a little while earlier, the night in which all cows are black. Marx's insinuation utilizes a classic stratagem: when you accuse someone of being too generous with generality and, moreover, too preoccupied, in the penumbra, with ghosts, you try to conclude that the crime is one of obscurantism, or even occultism. Here is someone, you then exclaim, who continues to believe in ghosts: he must believe in them to expend so much energy trying to get rid of them! In the name of Enlightenment and Reason, you then rise up to condemn any *obscurity* in the presentation of the general concept: "Negroid form" equals obscurantism plus occultism, mystery plus mysticism and mystification. Blackness is never far from the obscure and the occult. Spiritualism is but a spiritism. But, on the other hand, "Negroid form" might signal the enslavement of these pseudo-concepts that have no autonomy. They are not acknowledged as having any internal necessity. For they are working merely as *objects* in the service of men, *for* men. "These general concepts appear here first of all in the Negroid form as objective spirits having for people the character of objects [*als objektive, den Menschen gegenständliche Geister*], and at this level are called specters or—*apparitions*! [*und heissen auf dieser Stufe Gespenster oder*—Spuk!]" (p. 157).[7]

If the ghost is disseminated everywhere, the question becomes a distressing one: where does one *begin* to count the progeniture? It is again a question
of the head. Who is to be put at the head of all those whom one gets in one's
head? (*Mensch, es spukt in deinem Kopfe!*) At the head of the procession comes
capital, the capital representation, the oldest Son: Man. The arch-specter, the
one who is at the beginning and at the controls, the capital ghost (*das
Hauptgespenst*) is man himself with a capital M (*das Hauptgespenst ist natürlich
"der Mensch" selbst*). But if men exist, in this logic, only as representatives
(*Repräsentanten*) of an abstract generality, an essence, a concept, or a spirit, of a
foreign (*Fremden*) sacrality or alterity, then they are present for each other
only in a ghostly fashion, as specters (*nur als gespenstige, Gespenster für einander
vorhanden sind*) (ibid.). Humanity is but a collection or series of ghosts. Docile
application of the Hegelian logic? Careful recitation of *The Phenomenology of
Spirit*? So Marx suggests and he amuses himself by having the procession,
precisely, in theory, the parade of these specters march across the page. With
the irony of a happy pamphleteer and a somewhat nervous self-satisfaction,
one whose body no doubt is worked over by some compulsive disavowal, he
pretends to count off the specters on his fingers. For there would be ten of
them, as if by chance. Marx only feigns to count them, he pretends to enu-
merate for he knows that one cannot count here. He intends precisely to give
a demonstration of the innumerable. These simulacra of identity are classed
according to a logic that uses every means to confound the adversary. *Both* the
grouping of sets *and* the discrete and ordered (in a row: *der Reihe nach*) serial-
ization of spectral singularities. There is in sum, no doubt, but a single ghost,
a ghost of ghosts, and it is but a concept, not even a concept, the obscure
"Negroid" presentation of a larger concept, more englobing than all the others, indeed it is but a name, a metonymy that lends itself to any and all sub-
stitutions (the part for the whole that it then exceeds, the effect for the cause
of which it is in turn the cause, and so forth). Nominalism, conceptualism,
realism: all of that is routed by the Thing or the Athing called ghost. The tax-
onomic order becomes too easy, at once arbitrary and impossible: one can
neither classify nor count the ghost, it is number itself, it is numerous, innumerable as number, one can neither count on it nor with it. There is but one
of them and already there are too many. It proliferates, one can no longer
count its offspring or interests, its supplements or surplus values (the same
figure in Greek—Plato knew something of this-associated the offspring of

the father and the interest of capital or the Good).[8] For the singular ghost, the ghost that generated this incalculable multiplicity, the arch-specter, is a father or else it is capital. These two abstract bodies are both visible-invisible. Apparitions without anybody [*sans personne*]. That does not prevent speculation, on the contrary. Nor the desire to count what can no longer be counted. Arithmetical desire finds there on the contrary its spur, indeed its very origin. And the desire to classify. And the hierachizing compulsion that, on the other hand, does not prevent lining the ghosts up in a row, horizontally, like so many concepts equal before the law and ready to move over a level field. They are labelled, a number is sewn on their backs as if they were playing on a soccer team the night of the big final beneath the lights, from Ghost No. 1 to Ghost No. 10. Only one of them would be missing, one may well wonder which one it is.

We are going to count the ghosts. On Marx's fingers. But we cannot help asking ourselves, once again, at the opening of this fabulous scene: Why such relentless pursuit [*acharnement*]? Why this hunt for ghosts? What is the reason for Marx's rage? Why does he harass Stirner with such irresistible irony? One has the impression, since the critique appears so insistent and redundant, both brilliant and ponderous, that Marx could go on forever launching his barbs and wounding to death. He could never leave his victim. He is bound to it in a troubling fashion. His prey captivates him. The *acharnement* of a hunter consists in setting out an animal lure, here the living lifeless body of a ghost, in order to trick the prey.[9] I have my own feeling on this subject (I insist that it is a *feeling*, *my* feeling and I have no reason to deny that it projects itself necessarily into the scene I am interpreting: my "thesis," my hypothesis, or my hypostasis, precisely, is that it is never possible to avoid this precipitation, since everyone reads, acts, writes with *his or her* ghosts, even when one goes after the ghosts of the other). My feeling, then, is that Marx scares himself [*se fait peur*], he *himself* pursues [*il s'acharne* lui-même] relentlessly someone who almost resembles him to the point that we could mistake one for the other: a brother, a double, thus a diabolical image. A kind of ghost of himself. Whom he would like to distance, distinguish: to *oppose*. He has recognized someone who, like him, appears obsessed by ghosts and by the figure of the ghost and by its names with their troubling consonance and reference (*Geist, Gespenst*). Someone who is besieged, like him, by the same and by another, by the same that is each time another, because the identity of the ghost is precisely the

"problem" (*problema*: at once question, task, program, and shield, the apotro
paic armor, armor against armor, one helmet fascinated by the other, a duel
under visors). I am describing then this feeling: that of a Marx obsessed,
haunted, possessed *like/as* Stirner, and perhaps more than him, which is even
harder to take. Now, Stirner talked about all this *before he did*, and at such great
length, which is even more intolerable. In the sense given to this word in hunting, he *poached* the specters of Marx.[10] Marx tried all the exorcisms, and with
what eloquence, what jubilation, what bliss! He so loved the words of the exorcism! For these words always cause to come back, they convoke the *revenant*
that they conjure away. Come so that I may chase you! You hear! I chase you. I
pursue you. I run after you to chase you away from here. I will not leave you
alone. And the ghost does not leave its prey, namely, its hunter. It has understood instantly that one is hunting it just to hunt it, chasing it away only so as
to chase after it. Specular circle: one chases after in order to chase away, one
pursues, sets off in pursuit of someone to make him flee, but one makes him
flee, distances him, expulses him so as to go after him again and remain in
pursuit. One chases someone away, kicks him out the door, excludes him, or
drives him away. But it is in order to chase after him, seduce him, reach him,
and thus keep him close at hand. One sends him far away, puts distance
between them, so as to spend one's life, and for as *long a time* as possible, coming close to him again. The *long time* is here the time of *this distance hunt* (a
hunt *for* distance, the prey, but also a hunt *with* distance, the lure).[11] The distance hunt can only hallucinate, or desire if you prefer, or defer proximity:
lure and prey.

This logic and this topology of the *paradoxical hunt* (whose figure, beginning before Plato, will have traversed the whole history of philosophy, more
precisely of the ontological inquest or inquisition) should not be treated as a
rhetorical ornament when one reads *The Manifesto of the Communist Party*: its
first sentences, as we saw, immediately associate the figure of haunting with
that of hunting. This is the very experience of conjuration. The conjuration is
on all sides, in the camp of the powers of old Europe (who are leading a "holy
hunt" against the communist specter), but also in the opposite camp where
they are also on a hunt. There, two great hunters, Marx and Stirner, are in
principle sworn to the same conjuration. But the first accuses the other of
betraying and serving the adversary, Christian Europe in sum. The first
begrudges the second his having been the first to place the specter at the

center of his system, his logic, and his rhetoric, even if it was only to expulse it.
Isn't that inadmissible? He begrudges him [*Il lui en veut*], he wants not to want
the same thing as him and it is not a thing: the ghost. Like him, and like all
those who are occupied by specters, he welcomes them only in order to chase
them. As soon as there is some specter, hospitality and exclusion go together.
One is only occupied with ghosts by being occupied with exorcising them,
kicking them out the door. That is what Marx and Stirner have in common:
nothing other than this ghost hunt, but nothing but this singular nothing that
a ghost remains. All the same, let us not forget that, unlike the spirit, for example, or the idea or simply thought, this nothing is a nothing that *takes on a body*.
And since the two adversaries want to conjure away this body, nothing can
efface in this regard a resemblance between them that is by definition troubling. The deconstructive critiques that Marx will address to the Stirnerian
"historical constructions" or "montages" risk coming back at him like a
boomerang. Whence the endless, relentless pursuit. Endless because it maintains itself by *itself*, it is talking with itself [*il s'entretient* de lui-même]. He wants
to classify [*classer*], he can only chase [*chasser*]. The pursuit pursues relentlessly, as we were suggesting, a kind of double or brother. Both of them love
life, which is always the case but never goes without saying for finite beings:
they know that life does not go without death, and that death is not beyond,
outside of life, unless one inscribes the beyond in the inside, in the essence of
the living. They both share, apparently like you and me, an unconditional
preference for the living body. But precisely because of that, they wage an
endless war against whatever represents it, whatever is not the body but
belongs to it, comes back to it: prosthesis and delegation, repetition, differ-
*a*nce. The living ego is auto-immune, which is what they do not want to know.
To protect its life, to constitute itself as unique living ego, to relate, as the
same, to itself, it is necessarily led to welcome the other within (so many
figures of death: differ*a*nce of the technical apparatus, iterability, non-unique-
ness, prosthesis, synthetic image, simulacrum, all of which begins with
language, before language), it must therefore take the immune defenses apparently meant for the non-ego, the enemy, the opposite, the adversary and direct
them at once *for itself and against itself*. Marx thinks he is a better expert (a better "scholar" of ghosts), let us recall that he says in effect to Saint Max: I know
my way around specters better than you; the ghost is my affair [is looking at
me: *ça me regarde*], if you want to save life and conjure away the living-dead,

you must not go at it immediately, abstractly, egologically, fantasmatically, with the word, with the language act of a *phantasmagoreuein*; you must pass through the laborious ordeal of the detour, you must traverse and *work on* the *practical* structures, the solid mediations of real, "empirical" actuality, and so forth. Otherwise, you will have conjured away only the phantomality of the body, not the body itself of the ghost, namely, the reality of the State, Emperor, Nation, Fatherland, and so on. But obviously, for the time of this detour, you must accept to take into account the autonomous, relatively autonomous body of ghostly reality.

By himself pursuing this double who is in a rush to get things over with, and who is therefore all the more insubstantial, Marx always runs the risk of going after in this way his own ghost: a specter at once speculative and spec-ular. This risk irritates him, so he has to keep endlessly piling on the traits, the distinctive traits and the polemical traits. He will never be done with it, but it is in order to be done with it, to close out his account that he counts things up.

He counts off the other's ghosts. There are ten of them. Well, anyway, he stops at ten. Is it simply so he can count on his fingers? A manual operation in view of a manual? But what is Marx's hand doing here, underhandedly so to speak, as Patrice Loraux might say?[12] Why ten?

One might read the whole *German Ideology*, we will not do it here, as the inexhaustible gloss on this table of ghosts. For one can take it in this way, as a table, a Table of the law in ten parts, the specter of a Decalogue and a deca-logue of specters. The new table is presented also as a tableau, the ironic tabularization, the fictive taxonomy, or the statistic of ghosts. A table of the categories of the object or of being as specter in general. And yet, despite the stasis that is appropriate for the exhibition of a tableau or picture, this one knows no rest in any stability. This tableau of spirits moves on the model of a séance table [*table tournante*]. It begins to dance before our eyes, like a certain "table" in *Capital* which we will later see move, when its becoming-commod-ity opens up the dimension of secrecy, mysticism, and fetishism. For in this list of ghosts, in this new table whose capital categories stand like the counts of an indictment, the concepts cannot be distinguished. They are not added one to the other, they supplement each other and thereby pass in turn one into the other, each figuring a turn of the other. We cannot read here *The German Ideology*, which at bottom is but the developed exposition of this table. Without

even quoting the mocking remarks in the exclamatory style (the curious reader is referred to them) with which Marx accompanies each one of the ten
apparitions, we will limit ourselves to a few observations about this or that
distinctive trait. Whereas in the "pure history of spirits [*reine Geistergeschichte*],"
Marx had counted "ten theses," here, a few pages later, in the "impure history
of spirits," he banks on [*table sur*] ten ghosts:

Gespenst No. 1 (ghost No. 1): the supreme being (*das höchste Wesen*), God. Not
a minute is wasted speaking of this "incredible belief," Marx notes. Neither
Stirner nor Marx, moreover, stops to consider the essence of believing, here
the essence of faith *par excellence*, which can only ever believe in the unbelievable, and would not be what it is without that, beyond any "proof of the
existence of God."

Gespenst No. 2: Being or essence (*Das Wesen*). [Apparently, we are going down:
from the highest, *das höchste Wesen*, to the less high, *das Wesen* period. An old
problem, at least since Aristotle. Descending hierarchy, from theology to
ontology. Will it be so simple? *Wesen* remains the common concept, as we shall
see, and the guiding thread of this classificaiton that therefore remains essentially ontological, in truth onto-theological.[13]]

Gespenst No. 3: the vanity of the world. Nothing to say about that, notes
Marx, except that it serves to introduce what follows, to link "easily," "lightly,"
leicht with what follows. And what is lighter, in fact, more vain, precisely, more
non-existent (here, no more *Wesen*) than the shadow and the vanity of a ghost?
The vanity of the world, then, just to make a link with what follows, namely

Gespenst No. 4: good and evil beings (*die guten und bösen Wesen*). *Das Wesen* has
come back but, notes Marx, Max has nothing to say on this score, even if there
is so much to be said. It is just to make a link with what follows, namely:

Gespenst No. 5: Being and its realm (*das Wesen und sein Reich*). This is the first
determination of Being. It possesses an empire, whence its metamorphosis
(*Verwandlung*) into a plurality of beings. This is the first birth of the plural,
birth itself, the origin of number and progeniture. Of course, the word "realm"
already transfers the table of the commandments or the table of categories
from Being to an evangelical ground.

Gespenst No. 6: beings, therefore (*die Wesen*). We have passed over into the
plural, into the proliferation of the progeniture, from 5 to 6, through metamorphosis and spontaneous generation (*dass es* "das Wesen" *ist, worauf es sich
flugs in Gespenst Nr 6:* "die Wesen" *verwandelt*).

Gespenst No. 7: the Man-God (*der Gottmensch*). In this descending hierarchy, this is, in sum, the moment of conversion or reversibility (descent *and* ascension). It is also the category of the third, the middle or the mediation, for the synthesis of speculative idealism, the *hinge* [charnière] of this onto-theology as anthropo-theology of the ghost. Does not the Man-God play the same role in *The Phenomenology of Spirit?* This articulating joint also situates the place of the becoming-flesh, the privileged moment of the spectral incarnation or incorporation. It is not at all surprising that Marx, following Max, devotes his longest commentary to it, which is also, precisely, the most relentless [*acharné*], the most captivated. Is not the Christic moment, and within it the eucharistic instant, the hyperbole of *acharnement* itself? If every specter, as we have amply seen, is distinguished from spirit by an incorporation, by the phenomenal form of a quasi-incarnation, then Christ is the most spectral of specters. He tells us something about absolute spectrality. Stirner himself would be ready to grant him the singularity of this transcendental privilege. Without this incarnation, would the concept of incarnation have any sense at all, any historical chance? Jesus is at once the greatest and the most "incomprehensible of ghosts" (*unbegreiflichste Gespenst*). Marx insists on this:

> Of him Stirner is able to say that he was "corpulent" [*dass er* "beleibt" *gewesen ist*]. If Saint Max does not believe in Christ, he at least believes in his "actual corpus" [*an seiner "wirklichen Leib"*]. According to Stirner, Christ introduced great distress into history, and our sentimental saint relates with tears in his eyes, "how the strongest Christians have racked their brains in order to comprehend him"—Yes—"there has never been a specter that caused such mental anguish…" (P. 158).[14]

It is thus easy to go from him to the "horrible being" (*zum grauenhaften Wesen*):

Gespenst No. 8: man. Here we come closest to ourselves but also to the most terrifying thing. It is of the essence of the ghost in general to be frightening. This is especially true of man, of the most "unheimlich" of all ghosts, a word Stirner uses that the French translations overlook most often and that interests us to the highest degree. It is the word of irreducible haunting or obsession. The most familiar becomes the most disquieting. The economic or egological home of the *oikos*, the nearby, the familiar, the domestic, or even the national (*heimlich*) frightens itself. It feels itself occupied, in the proper secret (*Geheimnis*) of its inside, by what is most strange, distant, threatening. We will come back to this in conclusion. If Christ, that absolute specter, causes fear and pain, the man that this *Gottmensch* becomes (and man only arrives at himself, here, in this becoming) causes even more fear as he comes closer to us. He is even more spectral than the spectral. Man *makes himself fear*. He makes himself into the fear that he inspires.[15] Hence the contradictions that render humanism untenable. We see rise up here the logic of this *fear of oneself* that is guiding our remarks. The ipseity of the self is constituted there. No one will have escaped it, neither Marx, nor the Marxists, nor of course their mortal enemies, all those who want to defend the property and integrity of their home [*chez soi*]: the body proper, the proper name, nation, blood, territory, and the "rights" that are founded thereon. Marx exposes the fatefulness of this, but he does so in the other, precisely, exposed in the opposite, on the side facing, in Saint Max.[16] It has to do with the phenomenological fold, Marx seems to suggest, with that difference, both decisive and insubstantial at the same time, that separates being from appearing. The appearing of being, as such, as phenomenality of its phenomenon, is and is not the being that appears; that is the fold of the "unheimlich":

> Specter No. 8, *man*. Here our bold writer is seized with immediate "horror"—"he is terrified of himself" [*"er erschrickt vor sich selbst"*], he sees in every man a "frightful specter" [*einen "grausigen Spuk"*], a "sinister specter" [*einen "unheimlichen Spuk"*], in which something "stalks" [*in dem es "umgeht"*; the same word as in the *Manifesto*]. He feels highly uncomfortable. The split [*Zwiespalt*] between phenomenon [*Erscheinung*] and essence [*Wesen*] gives him no peace. He is like Nabal, Abigail's husband, of whom it is written that his essence too was separated from his phenomenal appearance... (Ibid.)

Everything always happens closest to the head and to the chief. This fear of oneself could have led the writer to suicide. The writer, the man-writer could have *chased* after himself, hunted himself down, Saint Max is ready to blow his brains out (once again the sign of the hunt: *eine Kugel durch den Kopf jagt*) from the moment the persecution is internal and the other makes him suffer in the head. What saves this man from man is still another ghost. He remembers that the ancients "took no notice of anything of the kind in their slaves." He then thinks of the "spirit of the people" wherever it is incarnated. This leads him to deduce (*Dies bringt ihn auf*) the next ghost.

Gespenst No. 9: the spirit of the people (*Volksgeist*). There would be too much to say *today* about this deduction—not only about the return of national-populisms, but about what has always linked them, in the founding story they tell themselves, to apparitions of *revenants.* The founder of the spirit of a people, one could show, always has the figure of a *revenant-survivant,* a ghost-survivor. It always obeys the temporality of its return. Its reapparition is awaited but obscurely feared. Marx speaks with so much lucidity elsewhere about nationalism, but here he remains very laconic. He merely remarks the necessary transition toward the final metamorphosis:

Gespenst No. 10: Everything. Max will have succeeded in transmuting everything, the All itself, into a ghost (*"Alles" in ein Spuk zu verwandeln*). So we have to stop the counting. And the recounting. And the story, and the fable, and the gothic novel. And the numerological occultism that puts on airs of *Aufklärung.* One has to admit that, forthwith [*séance tenante*], "all enumeration ends" (*alles Zählen aufhört*) once everything comes back to haunt everything, everything is in everything, that is, "in the class of specters" (*in der Klasse Gespenster*). One could throw it all together in any order, and Stirner does not fail to do so: the Holy Spirit, truth, law, and especially, especially the "good cause" in all its forms (*die gute Sache,* which Marx, who is as always a lucid analyst of modern times, accuses Stirner of never being able to forget, as if he too had made of good conscience, already, a vocation and of rightful law a technique of personal promotion).

Stirner's exemplary fault, for which he must be judged, judged for the example, would be the vice of modern speculation. Speculation always speculates on some specter, it speculates in the mirror of what it produces, on the spectacle that it gives itself and that it gives itself to see. It believes in what it believes it sees: in representations. "All the 'specters' that have filed before us (*die wir Revue passieren liessen*) were representations (*Vorstellungen*)" (p. 160). In this sense, speculation is always theoretical and theological. To explain the origin of this "history of ghosts," Marx refers to Feuerbach and to his distinction between *ordinary theology,* which believes in the ghosts of sensuous imagination, and *speculative theology,* which believes in the ghosts of non-sensuous abstraction. But theology *in general* is "belief in ghosts" (*Gespensterglaube*). One might say belief *in general,* the belief in this alliance of the sensuous and the non-sensuous where the two theologies intersect, the ordinary and the speculative. We will talk again later about the sensuous non-sensuous, with the apparition of another table: neither the Table of the ten commandments, nor the table of the ten categories, but a wooden table this time, a table with four legs, a table with a wooden head. It is the birth, quite simply, of exchange-value. And we will have spoken of nothing other than heads, tableaux, and tables, and tables armed from head to toe. And the origin of exchange-value is the birth of capital. Of mysticism and the secret.

In their common denunciation, in what is at once most critical and onto-logical about it, Marx and Saint Max are also heirs to the Platonic tradition, more precisely to the one that associates in a strict fashion image with specter, and idol with phantasm, with the *phantasma* in its phantomatic or errant dimension as living-dead. The "phantasma," which the *Phaedo* (81d) or the *Timaeus* (71a) do not separate from the *eidola*, are figures of dead souls, they are the souls of the dead: when they are not hanging around funeral monu-ments and sepulchers (*Phaedo*), they are haunting the souls of certain living persons, day and night (*Timaeus*). Strict and recurrent, this coupling does not let itself be undone. It leads one to think that the survival and the return of the living dead belong to the essence of the idol. To its inessential essence, of course. To what gives body to the idea, but a body with a lower ontological content, a body that is less real than the idea itself. The idol appears or lets itself be determined only against the background of death. It is doubtless a hypothesis without originality, but one whose consequence can be measured by the constancy of an immense tradition, or rather one must say of the philo-sophical *patrimony* such as it is handed down, through the most parricidal mutations, from Plato to Saint Max, to Marx and beyond. The lineage of this patrimony is wrought, but never interrupted, by the question of the idea, the question of the concept and of the concept of the concept, the very one that harbors the whole problematic of *The German Ideology* (nominalism, concep-tualism, realism, but also rhetoric and logic, literal meaning, proper meaning, figural meaning, and so forth). And this question would be a question of life or death, the question of life-death, before being a question of Being, of essence, or of existence. It would open onto a dimension of irreducible *sur-vival* or *sur-viving* [survivance] and onto Being and onto some opposition between living and dying.

What is ideology? Can one translate with regard to it the logic of *surviving* that we have just glimpsed with regard to the *patrimony of the idol*, and what would be the interest of such an operation?

The treatment of the phantomatic in *The German Ideology* announces or confirms the absolute privilege that Marx always grants to religion, to ideology as religion, mysticism, or theology, in his analysis of ideology in general. If the ghost gives its form, that is to say, its body, to the ideologem, then it is the essential feature [*le propre*], so to speak, of the religious, according to Marx, that is missed when one effaces the semantics or the lexicon of the specter, as translations often do, with values deemed to be more or less equivalent (fantasmagorical, hallucinatory, fantastic, imaginary, and so on). The mystical character of the fetish, in the mark it leaves on the experience of the religious, is first of all a ghostly character. Well beyond a convenient mode of presentation in Marx's rhetoric or pedagogy, what seems to be at stake is, *on the one hand*, the irreducibly specific character of the specter. The latter cannot be derived from a psychology of the imagination or from a psychoanalysis of the imaginary, no more than from an onto- or me-ontology, even though Marx seems to inscribe it within a socio-economic genealogy or a philosophy of labor and production: all these deductions suppose the possibility of spectral survival. *On the other hand* and by the same token, at stake is the irreducibility of the religious model in the construction of the concept of ideology. When Marx evokes specters at the moment he analyzes, for example, the mystical character or the becoming-fetish of the commodity, we should therefore not see in that only effects of rhetoric, turns of phrase that are contingent or merely apt to convince by striking the imagination. If that were the case, moreover, one would still have to explain their effectiveness in this respect. One would still have to reckon with the invincible force and the original power of the "ghost" effect. One would have to say why it frightens or strikes the imagination, and what fear, imagination, their subject, the life of their subject, and so forth, are.

Let us situate ourselves for a moment in that place where the values of *value* (between use-value and exchange-value), *secret, mystique, enigma, fetish*, and the *ideological* form a chain in Marx's text, singularly in *Capital*, and let us try at least to indicate (it will be only an indicator) the *spectral* movement of this chain. The movement is staged there where it is a question, precisely, of forming the concept of what the stage, any stage, withdraws from our blind eyes at the moment we open them. Now, this concept is indeed constructed with reference to a certain haunting.

It is a great moment at the beginning of *Capital* as everyone recalls: Marx is wondering in effect how to describe the sudden looming up of the mystical character of the commodity, the mystification of the thing itself—and of the money-form of which the commodity's simple form is the "germ." He wants to analyze the equivalent whose *enigma* and mystical character only strike the bourgeois economist in the finished form of money, gold or silver. It is the moment in which Marx means to demonstrate that the mystical character owes nothing to a use-value.

Is it just chance that he illustrates the principle of his explanation by causing a table to turn? Or rather by recalling the apparition of a turning table?[17]

This table is familiar, too familiar; it is found at the opening of the chapter on the fetishism of the commodity and its secret (*Geheimnis*).[18] This table has been worn down, exploited, overexploited, or else set aside, no longer in use, in antique shops or auction rooms. The thing is at once set aside and beside itself. Beside itself because, as we will soon be surprised to see, the said table is a little mad, weird, unsettled, "out of joint." One no longer knows, beneath the hermeneutic patina, what this piece of wood, whose example suddenly looms up, is good for and what it is worth.

Will that which is going to loom up be a mere example? Yes, but the example of a thing, the table, that seems to loom up of *itself* and to stand all at once on its paws. It is the example of an apparition.

Let us take the chance, then, after so many glosses, of an ingenuous reading. Let us try to see what happens. But is this not right away impossible? Marx warns us with the first words. The point is right away to go beyond, in one fell swoop, the first glance and thus to see there where this glance is blind, to open one's eyes wide there where one does not see what one sees. One must see, at first sight, what does not let itself be seen. And this is invisibility itself. For what first sight misses is the invisible. The flaw, the error of first sight is to see, and not to notice the invisible. If one does not give oneself up to this invisibility, then the table-commodity, immediately perceived, remains what it is not, a simple thing deemed to be trivial and too obvious. This trivial thing seems to comprehend itself (*ein selbstverständliches, triviales Ding*): the thing itself in the phenomenality of its phenomenon, a quite simple wooden table. So as to prepare us to see this invisibility, to see without seeing, thus to think the body without body of this invisible visibility—the ghost is already taking shape—Marx declares that the thing in question, namely, the commodity, *is not so simple* (a warning that will elicit snickers from all the imbeciles, until the end of time, who never believe anything, of course, because they are so sure that they see what is seen, everything that is seen, only what is seen). The commodity is even very complicated; it is blurred, tangled, paralyzing, aporetic, perhaps undecidable (*ein sehr vertracktes Ding*). It is so disconcerting, this commodity-thing, that one has to approach it with "metaphysical" subtlety and "theological" niceties. Precisely in order to analyze the metaphysical and the theological that constructed the phenomenological good sense of the thing itself, of the immediately visible commodity, in flesh and blood: as what it is "at first sight" (*auf den ersten Blick*). This phenomenological good sense may perhaps be valid for use-value. It is perhaps even meant to be valid only for use-value, as if the correlation of these concepts answered to this function: phenomenology as the discourse of use-value *so as not* to think the market or in view of making oneself blind to exchange-value. Perhaps. And it is for this reason that phenomenological good sense or phenomenology of perception (also at work in Marx when he believes he can speak of a *pure and simple* use-value) can claim to foster Enlightenment since use-value has nothing at all "mysterious" about it (*nicht Mysteriöses an ihr*). If one keeps to use-value, the properties (*Eigenschaften*) of the thing (and it is going to be a question of property) are always very human, at bottom, reassuring for this very reason. They always relate to what is proper to man, to the properties of man: either they respond to men's needs, and that is precisely their use-value, or else they are the product of a human activity that seems to intend them for those needs.

For example—and here is where the table comes on stage—the wood remains wooden when it is made into a table: it is then "an ordinary, sensuous thing [*ein ordinäres, sinnliches Ding*]." It is quite different when it becomes a commodity, when the curtain goes up on the market and the table plays actor and character at the same time, when the commodity-table, says Marx, comes on stage (*auftritt*), begins to walk around and to put itself forward as a market value. *Coup de théâtre*: the ordinary, sensuous thing is transfigured (*verwandelt sich*), it becomes someone, it assumes a figure. This woody and headstrong denseness is metamorphosed into a supernatural thing, a *sensuous non-sensuous* thing, sensuous but non-sensuous, sensuously supersensible (*verwandelt er sich in ein sinnlich übersinnliches Ding*). The ghostly schema now appears indispensable. The commodity is a "thing" without phenomenon, a thing in flight that surpasses the senses (it is invisible, intangible, inaudible, and odorless); but this transcendence is not altogether spiritual, it retains that bodiless body which we have recognized as making the difference between specter and spirit. What surpasses the senses still passes before us in the silhouette of the sensuous body that it nevertheless lacks or that remains inaccessible to us. Marx does not say sensuous *and* non-sensuous, or sensuous *but* non-sensuous; he says: sensuous non-sensuous, sensuously supersensible.[19] Transcendence, the movement of *super-*, the step beyond (*über, epekeina*), is made sensuous in that very excess. It renders the non-sensuous sensuous. One touches there on what one does not touch, one feels there where one does not feel, one even suffers there where suffering does not take place, when at least it does not take place where one suffers (which is also, let us not forget, what is said about phantom limbs, that phenomenon marked with an X for any phenomenology of perception). The commodity thus haunts the thing, its specter is at work in use-value. This haunting displaces itself like an anonymous silhouette or the figure of an extra [*figurante*] who might be the principal or capital character. It changes places, one no longer knows exactly where it is, it turns, it invades the stage with its *moves*: there is a step there [*il y a là un pas*] and its allure belongs only to this mutant. Marx must have recourse to theatrical language and must describe the apparition of the commodity as a stage entrance (*auftritt*). And he must describe the table become commodity as a table that turns, to be sure, during a spiritualist séance, but also as a ghostly silhouette, the figuration of an actor or a dancer. Theo-anthropological figure of indeterminate sex (*Tisch*, table, is a masculine noun), the table has feet, the table has a head, its body comes alive, it erects its whole self like an institution, it stands up and addresses itself to others, first of all to other commodities, its fellow beings in phantomality, it faces them or opposes them. For the specter is social, it is even engaged in competition or in a war as soon as it makes its first apparition. Otherwise neither *socius*, nor conflict, nor desire, nor love, nor peace would be tenable.

One would have to put this table on the auction block, subject it to co-occurrence or concurrency, make it speak with so many other tables in our patrimony, so many that we have lost count of them, in philosophy, rhetoric, poetics, from Plato to Heidegger, from Kant to Ponge, and so many others. With all of them, the same ceremony: a séance of the table.

Marx, then, has just announced its entrance on stage and its transmutation into a sensuously supersensible thing, and now here it is standing up, not only

holding itself up but rising, getting up and lifting itself, lifting its head, re-
dressing itself and addressing itself. Facing the others, and first of all other
commodities, yes, it lifts its head. Let us paraphrase a few lines as literally as
possible before citing the translation. It is not enough for this wooden table
to stand up (*Er steht nich nur*), its feet on the ground, it also stands (*sondern er
stellt sich*—and Marx does not add "so to speak" as certain French translators
had made him concede, frightened as they were by the literal audacity of the
description)—it also stands on its head, a wooden head, for it has become a
kind of headstrong, pigheaded, obstinate animal that, standing, faces other
commodities (*er stellt sich allen andren Waren gegenüber auf den Kopf*). Facing up
to the others, before the others, its fellows, here then is the apparition of a
strange creature: at the same time Life, Thing, Beast, Object, Commodity,
Automaton—in a word, specter. This Thing, which is no longer altogether a
thing, here it goes and unfolds (*entwickelt*), it unfolds *itself*, it develops what it
engenders through a quasi-spontaneous generation (parthenogenesis and
indeterminate sexuality: the animal Thing, the animated-inanimated Thing,
the dead-living Thing is a Father-Mother), it gives birth through its head, it
extracts *from* its wooden head a whole lineage of fantastic or prodigious crea-
tures, whims, chimera (*Grille*), non-ligneous character parts, that is, the lineage
of a progeniture that no longer resembles it, inventions far more bizarre or
marvelous (*viel wunderlicher*) than if this mad, capricious, and untenable table,
its head beginning to spin, started to dance on its own initiative [*de son propre
chef, aus freien Stücken*].[20] Whoever understands Greek and philosophy could
say of this genealogy, which transfigures the ligneous into the non-ligneous,
that it also gives a tableau of the becoming-immaterial of matter. As one
knows, *hulē*, matter, is first of all wood. And since this becoming-immaterial of
matter seems to take no time and to operate its transmutation in the magic of
an instant, in a single glance, through the omnipotence of a thought, we might
also be tempted to describe it as the projection of an animism or a spiritism.
The wood comes alive and is peopled with spirits: credulity, occultism, obscurantism, lack of maturity before Englightenment, childish or primitive
humanity. But what would Enlightenment be without the market? And who
will ever make progress without exchange-value?

Capital contradiction. At the very origin of capital. Immediately or in the
end, through so many differantial relays, it will not fail to induce the "prag-
matic" double constraint of all injunctions. Moving about freely (*aus freien*

Stücken), *on its own head* [de son propre chef], with a movement of its head but that controls its whole body, from head to toe, ligneous and dematerialized, the Table-Thing appears to be at the principle, at the beginning, and at the controls of itself. It emancipates itself on its own initiative: all alone, autonomous and automaton, its fantastic silhouette moves on its own, free and without attachment. It goes into trances, it levitates, it appears relieved of its body, like all ghosts, a little mad and unsettled as well, upset, "out of joint," delirious, capricious, and unpredictable. It appears to put itself spontaneously into motion, but it also puts others into motion, yes, it puts everything around it into motion, as though "pour encourager les autres" (to encourage the others), Marx specifies in French in a note about this ghost dance: "One may recall that China and the tables began to dance when the rest of the world appeared to be standing still—*pour encourager les autres*."[21]

The capital contradiction does not have to do simply with the incredible conjunction of the sensuous and the supersensible in the same Thing; it is the contradiction of *automatic autonomy*, mechanical freedom, technical life. Like every thing, from the moment it comes onto the stage of a market, the table resembles a prosthesis of itself. Autonomy *and* automatism, *but* automatism of this wooden table that spontaneously puts itself into motion, to be sure, and seems thus to animate, animalize, spiritualize, *spiritize* itself, but while remaining an artifactual body, a sort of automaton, a puppet, a stiff and mechanical doll whose dance obeys the technical rigidity of a program. Two genres, two generations of movement intersect with each other in it, and that is why it figures the apparition of a specter. It accumulates undecidably, in its uncanniness, their contradictory predicates: the inert thing appears suddenly *inspired*, it is all at once transfixed by a *pneuma* or a *psychē*. Become like a living being, the table resembles a prophetic dog that gets up on its four paws, ready to face up to its fellow dogs: an idol would like to make the law. But, inversely, the spirit, soul, or life that animates it remains caught in the opaque and heavy thingness of the *hulē*, in the inert thickness of its ligneous body, and autonomy is no more than the mask of automatism. A mask, indeed a visor that may always be hiding no living gaze beneath the helmet. The automaton mimes the living. The Thing is neither dead nor alive, it is dead and alive at the same time. It survives. At once cunning, inventive, and machine-like, ingenious and unpredictable, this war machine is a theatrical machine, a *mekhanē*. What one has just seen cross the stage is an apparition, a quasi-divinity—fallen from the sky or come out of the earth. But the vision also *survives*. Its hyperlucidity insists.

Challenge or invitation, "encouragement," seduction countering seduction, desire or war, love or hate, provocation of other ghosts: Marx insists on this a lot for there is a *multiple* of this sociality (there is always more than one commodity, more than one spirit, and even more specters) and *number* belongs to the movement itself, to the non-finite process of spectralization (Baudelaire invoked number very well in the anthill-city of modern capitalism—ghost, crowd, money, prostitution—and Benjamin likewise in his wake). For if no use-value can *in itself* produce this mysticality or this spectral effect of the commodity, and if the secret is at the same time profound and superficial, opaque and transparent, a secret that is all the more secret in that no substantial essence hides behind it, it is because the effect is born of a *relation* (ferance, difference, reference, and differ*a*nce), as double relation, one should say as double social bond.

This double *socius* binds *on the one hand* men to each other. It associates them insofar as they have been for all times interested in time, Marx notes right away, the time or the duration of labor, and this in all cultures and at all stages of techno-economic development. This *socius*, then, binds "men" who are first of all experiences of time, existences determined by this relation to time which itself would not be possible without surviving and returning, without that being "out of joint" that dislocates the self-presence of the living present and installs thereby the relation to the other. The same socius, the same "social form" of the relation binds, on the other hand, commodity-things to each other. *On the other hand*, but how? And how is what takes place *on the one hand* among men, in their apprehension of time, explained by what takes place *on the other hand* among those specters that are commodities? How do those whom one calls "men," living men, temporal and finite existences, become subjected, in their social relations, to these specters that are relations, *equally social* relations among commodities?

[Since temporality appears to be essential here to the process of capitalization and to the *socius* in which an exchange-value is merchandized while spectralizing itself, since the existence of the men and women inscribed in this process is determined first of all, in *Capital*, as *temporal*, let us indicate quickly, in passing, the possibility of an inheritance or a filiation that would

deserve a more sustained analysis. In question is the *formula* that, at the opening of *Capital*, defines exchange-value and determines the table as
"non-sensuous sensuous" thing," sensuously supersensible. This formula literally recalls (and this literality cannot be taken as fortuitous or external) the
definition of time—of time as well as of space—in Hegel's *Encyclopedia*
(*Philosophy of Nature, Mechanics*). Hegel subjects the Kantian definition to a
dialectical interpretation, that is, to the *Aufhebung*. He analyzes time as that
which is first of all abstract or ideal (*ein Ideelles*) since it is the negative unity of
being-outside-self (like space of which it is the truth). (This ideality of time is
obviously the condition of any idealization and consequently of any ideolo-
gization and any fetishization, whatever difference one must respect between
these two processes.) Now, it is in order to make explicit the movement of
Aufhebung as temporalization of abstract and ideal time that Hegel adds this
remark: "As space, time is a pure form of sensibility or of the act of intuition,
the non-sensuous sensous [*das unsinnliche Sinnliche*]…" (¶258; I proposed a
reading of this passage in *Margins—of Philosophy*).[22]]

The commodity table, the headstrong dog, the wooden head faces up, we
recall, *to all other commodities*. The market is a front, a front among fronts, a
confrontation. Commodities have business with other commodities, these
hardheaded specters have commerce among themselves. And not only in *tête-
à-tête*. That is what makes them dance. So it appears. But if the "mystical
character" of the commodity, if the "enigmatic character" of the product of
labor *as commodity* is born of "the social form" of labor, one must still analyze
what is mysterious or secret about this process, and what the secret of the
commodity form is (*das Geheimnisvolle der Warenform*). This secret has to do
with a "quid pro quo." The term is Marx's.[23] It takes us back once again to
some theatrical intrigue: mechanical ruse (*mekhanē*) or mistaking a person,
repetition upon the perverse intervention of a prompter [*souffleur*], *parole soufflée*,[24] substitution of actors or characters. Here the theatrical *quid pro quo* stems
from an abnormal play of mirrors. There is a mirror, and the commodity form
is also this mirror, but since all of a sudden it no longer plays its role, since it
does not reflect back the expected image, those who are looking for themselves can no longer find themselves in it. Men no longer recognize in it the
social character of their *own* labor. It is as if they were becoming ghosts in their
turn. The "proper" feature of specters, like vampires, is that they are deprived

of a specular image, of the true, right specular image (but who is not so deprived?).[25] How do you recognize a ghost? By the fact that it does not recognize itself in a mirror. Now that is what happens with the *commerce* of the commodities *among themselves*. These ghosts that are commodities transform human producers into ghosts. And this whole theatrical process (visual, theoretical, but also optical, *optician*) sets off the effect of a mysterious mirror: if the latter does not return the right reflection, if, then, it phantomalizes, this is first of all because it naturalizes. The "mysteriousness" of the commodity-form as presumed reflection of the social form is the incredible manner in which this mirror sends back the image (*zurückspiegelt*) when one thinks it is reflecting for men the image of the "social characteristics of men's own labor": such an "image" objectivizes by naturalizing. Thereby, this is its truth, it shows by hiding, it reflects these "objective" (*gegenständliche*) characteristics as inscribed right on the product of labor, as the "socio-natural properties of these things" (*als gesellschaftliche Natureigenschaften dieser Dinge*). Therefore, and here the commerce among commodities does not wait, the returned (deformed, objectified, naturalized) image becomes that of a social relation among commodities, among these inspired, autonomous, and automatic "objects" that are séance tables. The specular becomes the spectral at the threshold of this objectifying naturalization: "it also reflects the social relation of the producers to the sum total of labour as a social relation between objects, a relation which exists apart from and outside the producers. Through this substitution [*quid pro quo*], the products of labour become commodities, sensuous things which are at the same time supersensible or social" (pp. 164–65).

For the thing as well as for the worker in his relation to time, socialization or the becoming-social passes by way of this spectralization. The "phantasmagoria" that Marx is working here to describe, the one that is going to open up the question of fetishism and the religious, is the very element of this social *and* spectral becoming: at the same time, by the same token. While pursuing his optical analogy, Marx concedes that, in the same way, of course, the luminous impression left by a thing on the optic nerve also presents itself as objective form before the eye and outside of it, not as an excitation of the optic nerve itself. But there, in visual perception, there is really (*wirklich*), he says, a light that goes from one thing, the external object, to another, the eye: "physical relation between physical things." But the commodity-form and the

157

relation of value between products of labor in which it presents itself have nothing to do either with its "physical nature" or with the "thingly (material) relations" (*dingliche Beziehungen*) that arise from it. "It is nothing but the definite social relation between men themselves which assumes here, for them, the fantastic form [*dies phantasmagorische Form*] of a relation between things" (p. 165). As we have just observed, this phantasmagoria of a *commerce* between market things, on the *mercatus* or the *agora*, when a piece of merchandise (*merx*) seems to enter into a relation, to converse, speak (*agoreuein*), and negotiate with another, corresponds *at the same time* to a naturalization of the human *socius*, of labor objectified in things, and to a denaturing, a denaturalization, and a dematerialization of the thing become commodity, of the wooden table when it comes on stage as exchange-value and no longer as use-value. For commodities, as Marx is going to point out, do not walk by themselves, they do not go to market on their own in order to meet other commodities. This commerce among things stems from the phantasmagoria. The autonomy lent to commodities corresponds to an anthropomorphic projection. The latter *inspires* the commodities, it breathes the spirit into them, a human spirit, the spirit of a *speech* and the spirit of a *will*.

A. Of a *speech* first of all, but what would this speech say? What would this *persona*, actor, or character say? "If commodities could speak, they would say this: our use-value may interest men, but it does not belong to us as objects. What does belong to us as objects, however, is our value. Our own intercourse [*Unser eigner Verkehr*] as commodities proves it. We relate to each other [*Wir beziehn uns*] merely as exchange-values" (pp. 176–77). This rhetorical artifice is abyssal. Marx is going to claim right away that the economist naively reflects or reproduces this fictive or spectral speech of the commodity and lets himself be in some way ventriloquized by it: he "speaks" from the depths of the soul of commodities (*aus den Warenseele heraus*). But in saying "if commodities could speak" (*Könnten die Waren sprechen*), Marx implies that they cannot speak. He makes them speak (like the economist he is accusing) but in order to make them say, paradoxically, that inasmuch as they are exchange-values, they speak, and that they speak or maintain a commerce among themselves only insofar as they speak. That to them, in any case, one can at least lend speech. To speak, to adopt or borrow speech, and to be exchange-value is here the same thing. It is use-values that do no speak and that, for this reason, are not concerned with and do not interest commodities—judging by what they seem to say. With this movement of a fiction of speech, but of speech that sells itself by saying, "Me, the commodity, I am speaking," Marx wants to give a lesson to economists who believe (but is he not doing the same thing?) that it suffices for a commodity to say "Me, I am speaking" for it to be true and for it to have a soul, a profound soul, and one which is proper to it. We are touching here on that place where, between speaking and saying "I am speaking," the differ- ence of the simulacrum is no longer operative. Much ado about nothing? Marx cites right after this the Shakespeare play while making a rather tortuous use of the opposition between fortune (chance or destiny) and nature (law, neces- sity, history, culture): "To be a well-favoured man is the gift of fortune, but to write and read comes by nature" (ibid.).

B. Of the *will* next. Since commodities do not walk in order to take themselves willingly, spontaneously, to market, their "guardians" and "possessors" pre- tend to inhabit these things. Their "will" begins to "inhabit" (*hausen*) commodities. The difference between *inhabit* and *haunt* becomes here more ungraspable than ever. Persons are personified by letting themselves be haunt- ed by the very effect of objective haunting, so to speak, that they produce by inhabiting the thing. Persons (guardians or possessors of the thing) are haunt- ed in return, and constitutively, by the haunting they produce in the thing by lodging there their speech and their will like inhabitants. The discourse of *Capital* on the "exchange process" opens like a discourse on haunting—and on the laws of its reflection:

> Commodities cannot themselves go to market and perform exchanges
> in their own right.... [T]heir guardians must place themselves in rela-
> tion to one another as persons whose will [*Willen*] resides [*haust*] in those
> objects, and must behave in such a way that each does not appropriate
> the commodity of the other, and alienate his own, except through an act
> to which both parties consent. (P. 178)[26]

From this Marx deduces a whole theory of the juridical form of the pact, the pledge, the contract, and the "economic masks" with which persons cover themselves—and which figure but "the personifications of economic rela- tions."

This description of the phantasmopoetic or phantasmagoric process is going to constitute the premise of the discourse on fetishism, in the analogy with the "religious world."[27]

But before we get to that, let us take a few steps backward and formulate a few questions. At least two.

First of all: If what *Capital* is analyzing here is not only the phantomalization of the commodity-form but the phantomalization of the social bond, its spectralization in return, by means of a perturbed reflection, then what is one to think (still retrospectively) of the stinging irony with which Marx treated Stirner when the latter dared to speak of a becoming-ghost *of* man himself, and *for himself*? Of a man who became frightened of his own ghost, a constitutive fear of the concept that he formed of himself, and thus of his whole history as a man? Of a *make-oneself-fear* by which he made himself, frightening himself with the very fear that he inspires in himself? His history as the history and work of his mourning, of the mourning for himself, of the mourning he wears right on the surface of what is proper to man? And when he describes the phantomalization of the wooden table, the ghost that engenders ghosts and gives birth to them *from its head in its head*, outside of it inside of it, beginning with itself, *departing from itself* [à partir d'elle-même], what kind of reflection causes Marx to reproduce the literal language of Stirner, which he himself cited in *The German Ideology* and turned back, in some way, against its author, that is to say, against an accuser who is then charged with the indictment count he had himself elaborated ("After the world has confronted the fantasy-making [*phantasierenden*] youth (of page 20) as a world of his 'feverish fantasies' [*Fieberphantasien*], as a world of ghosts [*als Gespensterwelt*], 'the offsprings of his own head' [*eignen Geburten seines Kopfs*] inside his head begin to dominate him")?[28]

This question could be developed endlessly. We will interrupt its course and follow one of its other relays.

Secondly: To say that the same thing, the wooden table for example, *comes on stage* as commodity *after* having been but an ordinary thing in its use-value is to grant an origin to the ghostly moment. Its use-value, Marx seems to imply, was intact. It was what it was, use-value, identical to itself. The phantasmagoria, like capital, would begin with exchange-value and the commodity-form. It is only then that the ghost "comes on stage." Before this, according to Marx, it was not there. Not even in order to haunt use-value. But whence comes the certainty concerning the previous phase, that of this supposed use-value, precisely, a use-value purified of everything that makes for exchange-value and the commodity-form? What secures this distinction for us? It is not a matter here of negating a use-value or the necessity of referring to it. But of doubting its strict purity. If this purity is not guaranteed, then one would have to say that the phantasmagoria began before the said exchange-value, at the threshold of the value of value in general, or that the commodity-form began before the commodity-form, itself before itself. The said use-value of the said ordinary sensuous thing, simple *hulē*, the wood of the wooden table concerning which Marx supposes that it has not yet begun to "dance," its very form, the form that informs its *hulē*, must indeed have at least promised it to iterability, to substitution, to exchange, to value; it must have made a start, however minimal it may have been, on an idealization that permits one to identify it as the same throughout possible repetitions, and so forth. Just as there is no pure use, there is no *use-value* which the possibility of exchange and commerce (by whatever name one calls it, meaning itself, value, culture, spirit [!], signification, the world, the relation to the other, and first of all the simple form and trace of the other) has not in advance inscribed in an *out-of-use*—an excessive signification that cannot be reduced to the useless. A culture began before culture—and humanity. Capitalization also. Which is as much as to say that, for this very reason, it is destined to survive them. (One could say as much, moreover, if we were venturing into another context, for exchange-value: it is likewise inscribed and exceeded by a promise of gift beyond exchange. In a certain way, market equivalence arrests or mechanizes the dance that it seemed to initiate. Only beyond value itself, use-value and exchange-value, the value of technics and of the market, is grace promised, if not given, but never *rendered* or given back to the dance.)

Without disappearing, use-value becomes, then, a sort of limit, the correlative of a limit-concept, of a pure beginning to which no object can or *should* correspond, and which therefore must be complicated in a general (in any case more general) theory of capital. We will draw from this only one consequence here, among all the many other possible ones: if it itself retains some use-value (namely, of permitting one to *orient* an analysis of the "phantasmagoric" process beginning at an origin that is itself fictive or ideal, thus already purified by a certain fantastics), this limit-concept of use-value is in advance contaminated, that is, pre-occupied, inhabited, haunted by its other, namely, what will be born from the wooden head of the table, the commodity-form, and its ghost dance. The commodity-form, to be sure, *is not* use-value, we must grant this to Marx and take account of the analytic power this distinction gives us. But if the commodity-form is *not, presently,* use-value, and even if it is not *actually present,* it affects *in advance* the use-value of the wooden table. It affects and bereaves it in advance, like the ghost it will become, but this is precisely where haunting begins. And its time, and the untimeliness of its present, of its being "out of joint." To haunt does not mean to be present, and it is necessary to introduce haunting into the very construction of a concept. Of every concept, beginning with the concepts of being and time. That is what we would be calling here a hauntology. Ontology opposes it only in a movement of exorcism. Ontology is a conjuration.

The "mystical character" of the commodity is inscribed before being inscribed, traced before being written out letter for letter on the forehead or the screen of the commodity. Everything begins before it begins. Marx wants to know and make known *where, at what precise moment,* at what *instant* the ghost comes on stage, and this is a manner of exorcism, a way of keeping it at bay: before this limit, it was not there, it was powerless. We are suggesting on the contrary that, before the *coup de théâtre* of this instant, before the "as soon as it comes on stage as commodity, it changes into a sensuous supersensible thing," the ghost had made its apparition, without appearing in person, of course and by definition, but having already hollowed out in use-value, in the hardheaded wood of the headstrong table, the repetition (therefore substitution, exchangeability, iterability, the loss of singularity as the experience of singularity itself, the possibility of capital) without which a use could never even be determined. This haunting is not an empirical hypothesis. Without it, one could not even form the concept either of use-value, or of value in general, or inform any matter whatsoever, or determine any table, whether a wooden table—useful or saleable—or a table of categories. Or any Tablet of commandments. One could not even complicate, divide, or fracture sufficiently the concept of use-value by pointing out, as Marx does for example, this obvious fact: for its first presumed owner, the man who takes it to market as use-value meant *for others,* the first use-value is an exchange-value. "Hence commodities must be realized as values before they can be realized as use-values" (p. 179). And vice versa, which makes the diachrony *circular* and transforms the distinction into a co-implication. "On the other hand, [commodities] must stand the test as use-values before they can be realized as values." Even if the transformation of one commodity into use-value and some other into money marks an independent stopping point, a stasis in circulation, the latter remains an infinite process. If the total circulation C-M-C is a "series without beginning or end," as the *Critique of Political Economy* constantly insists,[29] it is because the metamorphosis is possible in all directions between the use-value, the commodity, and money. Not to mention that the use-value *of* the money-commodity (*Geldware*) is also itself "dual": natural teeth can be replaced by gold prostheses, but this use-value is different from the one Marx calls "formal use-value" which arises out of the specific social function of money.[30]

Since any use-value is marked by this possibility of being used *by the other* or being used *another time*, this alterity or iterability projects it *a priori* onto the market of equivalences (which are always equivalences between non-equivalents, of course, and which suppose the double *socius* we were talking about above). In its originary iterability, a use-value is in advance promised, promised to exchange and beyond exchange. It is in advance thrown onto the market of equivalences. This is not simply a bad thing, even if the use-value is always *at risk* of losing its soul in the commodity. The commodity is a *born* "cynic" because it effaces differences, but although it is congenitally levelling, although it is "a born leveller and cynic" (*Geborner Leveller und Zyniker*) (p. 179), this original cynicism *was already being prepared* in use-value, in the wooden head of that dog standing, like a table, on its four paws. One can say of the table what Marx says of the commodity. Like the commodity that it will become, that it is in advance, the cynic already prostitutes itself, "it is always ready to exchange not only soul, but body, with each and every other commodity, be it more repulsive than Maritornes herself" (ibid.). It is in thinking of this original prostitution that, as we recall, Marx liked to cite Timon of Athens and his prophetic imprecation. But one must say that if the commodity corrupts (art, philosophy, religion, morality, law, when their works become market values), it is because the becoming-commodity already attested to the value it puts in danger. For example: if a work of art can become a commodity, and if this process seems fated to occur, it is also because the commodity began by putting to work, in one way or another, the principle of an art.

This was not a critical question, but rather a deconstruction of the critical limits, the reassuring limits that guarantee the necessary and legitimate exercise of critical questioning. Such a deconstruction is not a critique of critique, according to the typical duplication of post-Kantian German ideology. And most of all it does not necessarily entail a general phantasmagorization in which everything would indifferently become commodity, in an equivalence of prices. All the more so in that, as we have suggested here and there, the concept of commodity-form or of exchange-value sees itself affected by the same overflowing contamination. If capitalization has no rigorous limit, it is also because it comes itself to be exceeded. But once the limits of phantasmagorization can no longer be controlled or fixed by the simple opposition of presence and absence, actuality and inactuality, sensuous and supersensible, *another* approach to differences must structure ("conceptually" and "really") the field that has thus been re-opened. Far from effacing differences and analytic determinations, this other logic calls for other concepts. One may hope it will allow for a more refined and more rigorous restructuration. It alone in any case can call for this constant restructuration, as elsewhere for the very progress of the critique. And this de-limitation will also affect discourse on religion, ideology, and fetishism. But one has to realize that the ghost is there, be it in the opening of the promise or the expectation, *before its first apparition*: the latter had announced itself, from the first it will have come second. *Two times at the same time*, originary iterability, irreducible virtuality of this space and this time. That is why one must think otherwise the "time" or the date of an event. Again: "ha's this thing appear'd againe tonight?"

Would there be then some exorcism at the opening of *Capital*? When the curtain rises on the raising of a curtain? From the first chapter of its first book? However potential it may appear, and however preparatory, however virtual, would this premise of exorcism have developed enough power to sign and seal the whole logic of this great work? Would a conjuration ceremony have scanned the unfolding of an immense critical discourse? Would it have accompanied that discourse, followed or preceded it like its shadow, in secret, like an indispensable and—if one can still put it this way—vital surviving, required in advance? A surviving inherited at the origin, but at every instant afterwards? And is not this surviving conjuration a part, ineffaceably, of the revolutionary promise? Of the injunction or oath that puts *Capital* in motion?

Let us not forget that everything we have just read there was Marx's point of view on a *finite delirium*. It was his discourse on a madness destined, according to him, to come to an end, on a general incorporation of abstract human labor that is still translated, but for a finite time, into the language of madness, into a delirium (*Verrücktheit*) of expression (p. 169). We *will have to*, Marx declares, and *we will be able to, we will have to be able to* put an end to what appears in "this absurd form" (*in dieser verrückten Form*). We *will see* (translate: *we will see come*) the end of this delirium and of these ghosts, Marx obviously thinks. It is necessary, because these ghosts are bound to the categories of bourgeois economy.

This madness here? Those ghosts there? Or spectrality in general? This is more or less our whole question—and our circumspection. We do not know if Marx thought to be done with the ghost in general, or even if he really wanted that, when he declares unequivocally that this ghost here, this *Spuk* which *Capital* takes as its object, is only the effect of the market economy. And that, as such, it ought to, it will have to disappear with other forms of production.

> The categories of bourgeois economics consist precisely of forms of this kind [i.e., delirious, Marx has just said]. They are forms of thought which are socially valid, and therefore objective, for the relations of production belonging to this historically determined mode of social production, i.e. commodity production. The whole mystery of commodities, all the magic and necromancy that surrounds the products of labour on the basis of commodity production, vanishes therefore as soon as we come to [escape to: *flüchten*] other forms of production [*Aller Mystizismus der Warenwelt, all der Zauber und Spuk, welcher Arbeitsprodukte auf Grundlage der Warenproduktion umnebelt, verschwindet daher sofort, sobald wir zu andren Produktionsformen flüchten*] (Ibid.)

This translation, like so many others, manages to efface the literal reference to the ghost (*Spuk*).[31] One must also underscore the instant immediacy with which, as Marx would like at least to believe or make us believe, mysticism, magic, and the ghost would disappear: they *will vanish* (indicative), they will dissipate in truth, according to him, as if by magic, as they had come, at the very second in which one will (would) see the end of market production. Assuming even, along with Marx, that the latter will ever have a possible end. Marx does indeed say: "as soon as," *sobald*, and as always he is speaking of a disappearance to come of the ghost, the fetish, and religion as cloudy apparitions. Everything is veiled in mist, everything is enveloped in clouds (*umnebelt*), beginning with truth. Clouds on a cold night, landscape or setting of *Hamlet* upon the apparition of the ghost ("It is past midnight, bitterly cold, and dark except for the faint light of the stars").

Even if *Capital* had thus opened with a great scene of exorcism, with a bid to raise the stakes of conjuration, this critical phase would not be at all destroyed, it would not be discredited. At least it would not annul everything about its event and its inaugurality. For we are wagering here that thinking never has done with the conjuring impulse. It would instead be born of that impulse. To swear or to conjure, is that not the chance of thinking and its destiny, no less than its limit? The gift of its finitude? Does it ever have any other choice except among several conjurations? We know that the question itself—and it is the most ontological and the most critical and the most risky of all questions—still protects itself. Its very *formulation* throws up barricades or digs trenches, surrounds itself with barriers, increases the fortifications. It rarely advances headlong, at total risk to life and limb [*à corps perdu*]. In a magical, ritual, obsessional fashion, its *formalization* uses *formulas* which are sometimes incantatory procedures. It marks off its territory by setting out there strategies and sentinels under the protection of apotropaic shields. Problematization itself is careful to disavow and thus to conjure away (we repeat, *problema* is a shield, an armor, a rampart as much as it is a task for the inquiry to come). Critical problematization continues to do battle against ghosts. It fears them as it does itself.

These questions posed, or rather suspended, we can perhaps return to what *Capital* seems to want to say about the fetish, in the same passage and following the same logic. The point is also, let us not forget, to show that the enigma of the "money" fetish is reducible to that of the "commodity" fetish once the latter has become visible (*sichtbar*)—but, adds Marx just as enigmatically, *visible or evident* to the point of blinding dazzlement: the French translation to which I am referring here says the enigma of the commodity fetish "crève les yeux," literally, puts out one's eyes (*die Augenblendende Rätsel des Warenfetischs*).[32]

Now, as we know, only the reference to the religious world allows one to explain the autonomy of the ideological, and thus its proper efficacy, its incorporation in apparatuses that are endowed not only with an apparent autonomy but a sort of automaticity that not fortuitously recalls the headstrongness of the wooden table. By rendering an account of the "mystical" character and the secret (*das Geheimnisvolle*) of the commodity-form, we have been introduced into fetishism and the ideological. Without being reducible one to the other, they share a common condition. Now, says *Capital*, only the religous analogy, only the "misty realm of religion" (*die Nebelregion der religiösen Welt*) can allow one to understand the production and fetishizing autonomization of this form. The necessity of turning toward this analogy is presented by Marx as a consequence of the "phantasmagoric form" whose genesis he has just analyzed. If the objective relation between things (which we have called *commerce between commodities*) is indeed a phantasmagoric form of the social relation between men, *then* we must have recourse to the *only analogy possible*, that of religion: "It is nothing but the definite social relation between men themselves which assumes here, for them, the fantastic form of a relation between things." Consequence: "*In order, therefore, to find an analogy* [my emphasis: *Um daher eine Analogie zu finden*], we must take flight [*flüchten* again or already] into the misty realm of religion" (p. 165).

Needless to say, the stakes are enormous in the relation of fetishism to the ideological and the religious. In the statements that immediately follow, the deduction of fetishism is also applied to the ideological, to its autonomization as well as to its automatization:

> There [in the religious world] the products of the human brain [of the head, once again, of men: *des menschlichen Kopfes*, analogous to the wooden head of the table capable of engendering chimera—in its head, outside of its head—once, that is, *as soon as*, its form can become commodity-form] appear as autonomous figures endowed with a life of their own, which enter into relations both with each other and with the human race.... I call this the fetishism which attaches itself [*anklebt*] to the products of labour as soon as they are produced as commodities, and is therefore inseparable from the production of commodities.
>
> As the foregoing analysis has already demonstrated, this fetishism of the world of commodities arises from the peculiar social character of the labour which produces them. (Ibid.)

In other words, as soon as there is production, there is fetishism: idealization, autonomization and automatization, dematerialization and spectral incorporation, mourning work coextensive with all work, and so forth. Marx believes he must limit this co-extensivity to commodity production. In our view, this is a gesture of exorcism, which we spoke of earlier and regarding which we leave here once again our question suspended.

The religious is thus not just one ideological phenomenon or phantomatic production among others. On the one hand, it gives to the production of the ghost or of the ideological phantasm its originary form or its paradigm of reference, its first "analogy." On the other hand (and first of all, and no doubt for the same reason), the religious also informs, along with the messianic and the eschatological, be it in the necessarily undetermined, empty, abstract, and

to designate a structure of experience rather than a religion), there where no figure of the *arrivant*, even as he or she is heralded, should be pre-determined, prefigured, or even pre-named? Of these two deserts, which one, first of all, will have signalled toward the other? Can one conceive an atheological heritage of the messianic? Is there one, on the contrary, that is more consistent? A heritage is never natural, one may inherit more than once, in different places and at different times, one may choose to wait for the most appropriate time, which may be the most untimely—write about it according to different *lineages*, and sign thus more than one *import*. These questions and these hypotheses do not exclude each other. At least for us and for the moment. Ascesis strips the messianic hope of all biblical forms, and even all determinable figures of the wait or expectation; it thus denudes itself in view of responding to that which must be absolute hospitality, the "yes" to the *arrivant(e)*, the "come" to the future that cannot be anticipated—which must not be the "anything whatsoever" that harbors behind it those too familiar ghosts, the very ones we must practice recognizing. Open, waiting for the event *as* justice, this hospitality is absolute only if its keeps watch over its own universality. The messianic, including its revolutionary forms (and the messianic is always revolutionary, it has to be), would be urgency, imminence but, irreducible paradox, a waiting without horizon of expectation. One may always take the quasi-atheistic dryness of the messianic to be the condition of the religions of the Book, a desert that was not even theirs (but the earth is always borrowed, on loan from God, it is never possessed by the occupier, says precisely [*justement*] the Old Testament whose injunction one would also have to hear); one may always recognize there the arid soil in which grew, and passed away, the living figures of all the messiahs, whether they were announced, recognized, or still awaited. One may also consider this compulsive growth, and the furtiveness of this passage, to be the only events on the basis of which we approach and first of all name the messianic in general, that other ghost which we cannot and ought not do without. One may deem strange, strangely familiar and inhospitable at the same time (*unheimlich*, uncanny), this figure of absolute hospitality whose promise one would choose to entrust to an experience that is so impossible, so unsure in its indigence, to a quasi-"messianism" so anxious, fragile, and impoverished, to an always presupposed "messianism," to a quasi-transcendental "messianism" that also has such an obstinate interest in a materialism without substance: a materi-

alism of the *khôra* for a despairing "messianism." But without this latter despair
and if one could *count* on what is coming, hope would be but the calculation of
a program. One would have the prospect but one would not longer wait for
anything or anyone. Law without justice. One would no longer invite, either
body or soul, no longer receive any visits, no longer even think to see. To see
coming. Some, and I do not exclude myself, will find this despairing "messianism" has a curious taste, a taste of death. It is true that this taste is above all
a taste, a foretaste, and in essence it is curious. Curious of the very thing that it
conjures—and that leaves something to be desired.

B. But also at stake, indissociably, is the differantial deployment of *tekhnē*, of
techno-science or tele-technology.[36] It obliges us more than ever to think the
virtualization of space and time, the possibility of virtual events whose movement and speed prohibit us more than ever (more and otherwise than ever,
for this is not absolutely and thoroughly new) from opposing presence to its
representation, "real time" to "deferred time," effectivity to its simulacrum,
the living to the non-living, in short, the living to the living-dead of its ghosts.
It obliges us to think, from there, another space for democracy. For democ-
racy-to-come and thus for justice. We have suggested that the event we are
prowling around here hesitates between the singular "who" of the ghost and
the general "what" of the simulacrum. In the virtual space of all the tele-
technosciences, in the general dis-location to which our time is destined—as
are from now on the places of lovers, families, nations—the messianic trembles on the edge of this event itself. It is this hesitation, it has no other
vibration, it does not "live" otherwise, but it would no longer be messianic if it
stopped hesitating: how to give rise and to give place [*donner lieu*], still, to render it, this place, to render it habitable, but without killing the future in the
name of old frontiers? Like those of the blood, nationalisms of native soil not
only sow hatred, not only commit crimes, they have no future, they promise
nothing even if, like stupidity or the unconscious, they hold fast to life. This
messianic hesitation does not paralyze any decision, any affirmation, any
responsibility. On the contrary, it grants them their elementary condition. It is
their very experience.

As we must hasten the conclusion, let us schematize things. If something
seems not to have shifted between *The German Ideology* and *Capital*, it is two
axioms whose inheritance is equally important for us. But it is the inheritance
of a double bind which, moreover, signals toward the double bind of any inher-

itance and thus of any responsible decision. Contradiction and secret inhabit
the injunction (the spirit of the father, if one prefers). On the one hand, Marx
insists on respecting the originality and the proper efficacity, the autonomization and automatization of ideality as finite-infinite processes of
differance (phantomatic, fantastic, fetishistic, or ideological)—and of the
simulacrum which is not simply imaginary in it. It is an artifactual body, a
technical body, and it takes labor to constitute or deconstitute it. This movement will remain valuable, no doubt irreplaceable, provided that it is adjusted,
as it will be by any "good Marxism," to novel structures and situations. But, on
the other hand, even as he remains one of the first thinkers of technics, or
even, by far and from afar, of the tele-technology that it will always have been,
from near or from far, Marx continues to want to ground his critique or his
exorcism of the spectral simulacrum in an ontology. It is a—critical but pre-
deconstructive—ontology of presence as actual reality and as objectivity. This
critical ontology means to deploy the possibility of dissipating the phantom,
let us venture to say again of conjuring it away as representative consciousness of a subject, and of bringing this representation back to the world of labor,
production, and exchange, so as to reduce it to its conditions. Pre-deconstructive here does not mean false, unnecessary, or illusory. Rather it
characterizes a relatively stabilized knowledge that calls for questions more
radical than the critique itself and than the ontology that grounds the critique.
These questions are not destabilizing as the effect of some theoretico-speculative subversion. They are not even, in the final analysis, questions but seismic
events. *Practical* events, where thought *becomes act* [se fait agir], and body and
manual experience (thought as *Handeln*, says Heidegger somewhere), labor
but always divisible labor—and shareable, beyond the old schemas of the division of labor (even beyond the one on whose basis Marx constructed so many
things, in particular his discourse on ideological hegemony: the division
between intellectual labor and manual labor whose pertinence has certainly
not disappeared, but appears more limited than ever). These seismic events
come from the future, they are given from out of the unstable, chaotic, and
dis-located ground of the times. A disjointed or dis-adjusted time without
which there would be neither history, nor event, nor promise of justice.

The fact that the ontological and the critical are here pre-deconstructive
has political consequences which are perhaps not negligible. And they are
doubtless not negligible, to go too quickly here, with regards to the concept of

the political, as concerns the political itself.

To indicate just one example among so many others, let us evoke once again in conclusion a passage from *The German Ideology*. It puts to work a schema that *Capital* seems to have constantly confirmed. In it, Marx advances that belief in the religious specter, thus in the ghost in general, consists in autonomizing a representation (*Vorstellung*) and in forgetting its genesis as well as its real grounding (*reale Grundlage*). To dissipate the factitious autonomy thus engendered in history, one must again take into account the modes of production and techno-economic exchange:

> In religion people make their empirical world into an entity that is only
> conceived, imagined [*zu einem nur gedachten, vorgestellten Wesen*], that con
> fronts them as something foreign [*das ihnen fremd gegenübertritt*]. This
> again is by no means to be explained from other concepts, from "self-
> consciousness" and similar nonsense, but from the entire hitherto
> existing mode of production and intercourse, which is just as indepen
> dent [*unabhängig*] of the pure concept as the invention of the self-acting
> mule [in English in the text] and the use of railways are independent of
> Hegelian philosophy. If he wants to speak of an "essence" of religion, i.e.,
> of a material basis of this inessentiality, [*d.h. von einer materiellen Grundlage
> dieses Unwesen*], then he should look for it neither in the "essence of man"
> [*im "Wesen des Menschen"*], nor in the predicates of God, but in the mate
> rial world which each stage of religious development finds in existence
> (cf. above *Feuerbach*). All the "specters" which have filed before us [*die
> wir Revue passieren liessen*] were representations [*Vorstellungen*]. These rep
> resentations—leaving aside their real basis [*abgesehen von ihrer realen
> Grundlage*] (which Stirner in any case leaves aside)—understood as rep
> resentations internal to consciousness, as thoughts in people's heads,
> transferred from their objectality [*Gegenständlichkeit*] back into the subject
> [*in das Subjekt zurückgenommen*], elevated from substance into self-con
> sciousness, are obsessions [*der Sparren*] or *fixed ideas*. (P. 160–61)

If one follows the letter of the text, the critique of the ghost or of spirits would thus be the critique of a subjective representation and an abstraction, of what happens *in the head*, of what comes only out of the head, that is, of what stays there, in the head, even as it has come out of there, out of the head, and survives *outside the head*. But nothing would be possible, beginning with the critique, without the surviving, without the possible survival of this autonomy and this automatism outside the head. One may say that this is where the spirit of the Marxist critique situates itself, not the spirit that one would oppose to its letter, but the one which supposes the very movement of its letter. Like the ghost, it is neither in the head nor outside the head. Marx knows this, but he proceeds as if he did not want to know it. In *The German Ideology*, the following chapter will be devoted to this obsession that made Stirner say: "Mensch, es spukt in deinem Kopfe!" commonly translated as "Man, there are specters in your head!" Marx thinks it is enough to turn the apostrophe back against Saint Max (p. 160).

Es spukt: difficult to translate, as we have been saying. It is a question of ghost and haunting, to be sure, but what else? The German idiom seems to name the ghostly return but it names it in a verbal form. The latter does not say that there is some *revenant*, specter, or ghost; it does not say that there is some apparition, *der Spuk*, nor even that it appears, but that "it ghosts," "it apparitions." *It is a matter* [Il s'agit], in the neutrality of this altogether impersonal verbal form, of something or someone, neither someone nor something, of a "one" that does not act. *It is a matter* rather of the passive movement of an apprehension, of an apprehensive movement ready to welcome, but where? In the head? What is the head before this apprehension that it cannot even contain? And what if the head, which is neither the subject, nor consciousness, nor the ego, nor the brain, were defined first of all by the possibility of such an experience, and by the very thing that it can neither contain, nor delimit, by the indefiniteness of the "es spukt"? To welcome, we were saying then, but even while apprehending, with anxiety and the desire to exclude the stranger, to invite the stranger without accepting him or her, domestic hospitality that welcomes without welcoming the stranger, but a stranger who is already found within (*das Heimliche-Unheimliche*), more intimate with one than one is oneself, the absolute proximity of a stranger whose power is singular *and* anonymous (*es spukt*), an unnameable and neutral power, that is, undecidable, neither active nor passive, an an-identity that, *without doing anything*, invisibly occupies places belonging finally neither to us nor to it. Now, all *this*, *this* about which we have failed to say anything whatsoever that is logically determinable, *this* that comes with so much difficulty to language, *this* that seems not to mean anything, *this* that puts to rout our meaning-to-say, making us speak regularly from the place where we want to say nothing, where we know clearly what we do not want to say but do not know what we would like to say, as if *this* were no longer either of the order of knowledge or will or will-to-say, well, *this* comes back, *this* returns, *this* insists in urgency, and *this* gives one to think, but *this*, which is each time irresistible enough, singular enough to engender as much anguish as do the future and death, *this* stems less from a "repetition automatism" (of the automatons that have been turning before us for such a long time) than it gives us to think all *this, altogether other, every other,* from which the repetition compulsion arises: that every other is altogether other.[37] The impersonal ghostly returning of the "es spukt" produces an automatism of repetition, no less than it finds its principle of reason there. In an incredible paragraph of "Das Unheimliche," Freud moreover recognizes that he should have begun his research (on the *Unheimliche*, the death drive, the repetition compulsion, the beyond of the plesure principle, and so forth) with what says the "es spukt."[38] He sees there an *example* with which it would have been necessary to begin the search. He goes so far as to consider it the *strongest example* of *Unheimlichkeit* ("Wir hätten eigentlich unsere Untersuchung mit diesem, vielleicht stärksten Beispeil von Unheimlichkeit beginnen können," "We could, properly speaking, have begun our inquiry with this example of uncanniness, which is perhaps the strongest"). But one may wonder whether what he calls the strongest example lets itself be reduced to an example—merely to the strongest example, in a series of examples. And what if it were the Thing itself, the cause of the very thing one is seeking and that makes one seek? The cause of the knowledge and the search, the motive of history or of the *epistemē*? If it is from there that it drew its exemplary force? On the other hand, one must pay attention to the conjuring mechanism that Freud then puts forward to justify himself for not having thought that he ought to begin from where he *could* have begun, from where he *ought* to have begun, nevertheless, *him* for example (you understand well what I mean: Marx, *him* too).

Freud explains this to us in the serene tone of epistemological, methodological, rhetorical, in truth psychagogical caution: if he had to begin not where he could have or should have begun, it is because with the thing in question (the strongest example of *Unheimlichkeit*, the "es spukt," ghosts, and apparitions), one scares oneself too much [one makes oneself fear too much: *on se fait trop peur*]. One confuses what is *heimliche-unheimliche*, in a contradictory, undecidable fashion, with the terrible or the frightful (*mit dem Grauenhaften*). Now, fear is not good for the serenity of research and the analytic distinction of concepts. One should read also for itself and from this point of view all the rest of the text (we will try to do so elsewhere), while crossing this reading with that of numerous other texts of Heidegger.[39] We think that the frequent, decisive, and organizing recourse that the latter has to the value of *Unheimlichkeit*, in *Being and Time* and elsewhere, remains generally unnoticed or neglected. In both discourses, that of Freud and that of Heidegger, this recourse makes possible fundamental projects or trajectories. But it does so while destabilizing permanently, and in a more or less subterranean fashion, the order of conceptual distinctions that are put to work. It should disturb both the ethics and the politics that follow implicitly or explicitly from that order.

Our hypothesis is that the same is true for Marx's spectrology. Is this not our own great problematic constellation of haunting? It has no certain border, but it blinks and sparkles behind the proper names of Marx, Freud, and Heidegger: Heidegger who misjudged Freud who misjudged Marx. This is no doubt not aleatory. Marx has not yet been received. The subtitle of this address could thus have been: "Marx—*das Unheimliche*." Marx remains an immigrant *chez nous*, a glorious, sacred, accursed but still a clandestine immigrant as he was all his life. He belongs to a time of disjunction, to that "time out of joint" in which is inaugurated, laboriously, painfully, tragically, a new thinking of borders, a new experience of the house, the home, and the economy. Between earth and sky. One should not rush to make of the clandestine immigrant an illegal alien or, what always risks coming down to the same thing, to domesticate him. To neutralize him through naturalization. To assimilate him so as to stop frightening oneself (making oneself fear) with him. He is not part of the family, but one should not send him back, once again, him too, to the border.

However alive, healthy, critical, and still necessary his burst of laughter may remain, and first of all in the face of the capital or paternal ghost, the *Hauptgespenst* that is the general essence of Man, Marx, *das Unheimliche*, perhaps should not have chased away so many ghosts too quickly. Not all of them at once or not so simply on the pretext that they did not exist (of course they do not exist, so what?)—or that all this was or ought to remain past ("Let the dead bury their dead," and so forth). All the more so in that he also knew how to let them go free, emancipate them even, in the movement in which he analyzes the (relative) autonomy of exchange-value, the ideologem, or the fetish. Even if one wanted to, one could not let the dead bury the dead: that has no sense, that is *impossible*. Only mortals, only the living who are not living gods can bury the dead. Only mortals can watch over them, and can watch, period. Ghosts can do so as well, they are everywhere where there is watching; the dead *cannot do so*—it is impossible and they must not do so.

That the without-ground of this impossible can nevertheless *take place* is on the contrary the ruin or the absolute ashes, the threat that must be *thought*, and, why not, exorcised yet again. To exorcise not in order to chase away the ghosts, but this time to grant them the right, if it means making them come back alive, as *revenants* who would no longer be *revenants*, but as other *arrivants* to whom a hospitable memory or promise must offer welcome— without certainty, ever, that they present themselves as such. Not in order to grant them the right in this sense but out of a concern for *justice*. Present existence or essence has never been the condition, object, or the *thing* [chose] of justice. One must constantly remember that the impossible ("to let the dead bury their dead") is, alas, always possible. One must constantly remember that this absolute evil (which is, is it not, absolute life, fully present life, the one that does not know death and does not want to hear about it) can take place. One must constantly remember that it is even on the basis of the terrible possibility of this impossible that justice is desirable: *through* but also *beyond* right and law.

If Marx, like Freud, like Heidegger, like everybody, did not begin where he ought to have "been able to begin" (*beginnen können*), namely with haunting, before life *as such*, before death *as such*, it is doubtless not his fault. The fault, in any case, by definition, is repeated, we inherit it, we must watch over it. It always comes at a great price—and for humanity precisely. What costs humanity very dearly is doubtless to believe that one can have done in history with a general essence of Man, on the pretext that it represents only a *Hauptgespenst*, arch-ghost, but also, what comes down to the same thing—*at bottom*—to still believe, no doubt, in this capital ghost. To believe in it as do the credulous or the dogmatic. Between the two beliefs, as always, the way remains narrow.

In order for there to be any sense in asking oneself about the terrible price to pay, in order to watch over the future, everything would have to be begun again. But in memory, this time, of that impure "impure impure history of ghosts."

Can one, in order to question it, address oneself to a ghost? To whom? To him? To *it*, as Marcellus says once again and so prudently? "Thou art a Scholler; speake to *it* Horatio.... Question *it*."

The question deserves perhaps to be put the other way: Could one *address oneself in general* if already some ghost did not come back? If he loves justice at least, the "scholar" of the future, the "intellectual" of tomorrow should learn it and from the ghost. He should learn to live by learning not how to make conversation with the ghost but how to talk with him, with her, how to let them speak or how to give them back speech, even if it is in oneself, in the other, in the other in oneself: they are always *there*, specters, even if they do not exist, even if they are no longer, even if they are not yet. They give us to rethink the "there" as soon as we open our mouths, even at a colloquium and especially when one speaks there in a foreign language:

Thou art a scholar; speak to it, Horatio.

notes

exordium

1 Not very far because "apprendre à vivre" means both to teach how to live and to learn how to live. (Tr.)

2 The expression here is "s'expliquer avec la mort": literally, to explain oneself with death. But the idiomatic French sense here is close to the German expression: *auseinandersetzen*, to have it out with someone, to argue with someone, to come to grips with a problem, and so forth. We will translate the expression in various ways when it recurs, signalling it in brackets when necessary. (Tr.)

3 The distinction being made here is between *justice* and *droit*. The French term *droit* means both a legal system and a right, but it is often correctly translated as simply law. Hence a certain possible confusion. Derrida will return several times below to the distinction he insists upon here between *justice* and *droit*, see note 4 below. (Tr.)

4 On a distinction between justice and law [*droit*], on the strange dissymmetry that affects the difference and the co-implication between these two concepts, on certain consequences that follow from this (notably as concerns a certain "undeconstuctibility" of "justice"—but it could be called by other names), permit me to refer to my "Force of Law: 'The Mystical Foundation of Authority'," in *Deconstruction and the Possibility of Justice*, eds. D. Cornell, M. Rosenfeld, D.G. Carlson, trans. M. Quaintance (New York: Routledge, 1992). The French text will appear in 1994.

5 Derrida writes "l'à-venir," which spaces out the ordinary word for the future, *avenir*, into the components of the infinitive: to come. Wherever this insistence recurs, we will translate "future-to-come," but in general one should remember that even in the ordinary translation as simply "future," *avenir* has the sense of a coming, an advent. (Tr.)

1 *injunctions of marx*

1 A common term for ghost or specter, the *revenant* is literally that which comes back. We leave it in French throughout. (Tr.)

2 The term *hantise*, translated here as "haunting," also has the common sense of an obsession, a constant fear, a fixed idea, or a nagging memory. We will con-

tinue to translate it simply with the gerund "haunting" so as to maintain a clearer link with the ghostly in general. (Tr.)

3 Paul Valéry, "La Crise de l'esprit," in *Oeuvres* (Paris: Gallimard, Bibliothèque de la Pléiade, 1957), vol.I, p. 993. Ought one to have recalled here that in the West, near the end of the European peninsula, Denmark almost became, precisely along with England, the last State of the resistance to a certain Europe, that of Maastricht? No, this corollary on the royal head would be oriented instead toward other places. First of all the places of articulation between these propositions and those of *The Other Heading* (Bloomington, Ind.: Indiana University Press, 1992) which also analyzed a treatment of the *capital* (the chief and the head), in particular by Valéry, so as to reintroduce the question of Europe as the question of *spirit*—which is to say that of the specter. And we will not fail to insist as well, accordingly [*c'est le premier chef*], on a certain figure of the head, if one can put it that way, *der Kopf* and *das Haupt*, on the way it returns, regularly, to impose itself in many places of Marx's corpus, and among those that are most hospitable to the ghost. In a more general and more implicit manner, the present essay pursues earlier paths: around the work of mourning that would be coextensive with all work in general (in particular in *Glas* [Lincoln, Nebraska: University of Nebraska Press, 1986]), on the problematic border between incorporation and introjection, on the effective but limited pertinence of this conceptual opposition, as well as the one that separates failure from success in the work of mourning, the pathology and the normality of mourning (on these points, cf. "Fors," Preface to *The Wolfman's Magic Word*, by N. Abraham and M. Torok [Minneapolis: University of Minnesota Press, 1986], esp. pp. xxi ff., "Shibboleth," in *Midrash and Literature*, eds. Geoffrey Hartman and Sanford Budick [New Haven, Ct.: Yale University Press, 1986], *Cinders* [Lincoln, Nebraska: University of Nebraska Press, 1991), *Of Spirit: Heidegger and the Question* [Chicago: University of Chicago Press, 1989], *Mémoires, for Paul de Man* [New York: Columbia University Press, 1989]), on the surviving of a survival that is reducible neither to living nor dying ("Living On," in *Deconstruction and Criticism*, eds. Geoffrey Hartman et al. [New York: Seabury Press, 1979]), on the economy of debt and gift (*Given Time* [Chicago: University of Chicago Press, 1992]). As for the logic of spectrality, inseparable from the idea of the idea (of the idealization of ideality as effect of iterability), inseparable from the very motif (let us not say the "idea") of deconstruction, it is at work, most often explicitly, in all the essays published over the last twenty years, especially in *Of Spirit*. "Revenant" was also there the first noun ("I will speak of the *revenant...*").

4 Valéry, p. 1025.

5 Valéry, p. 1029.

6 Also it concerns us, it is our concern: "[il] nous regarde."(Tr.)

7 Paul Valéry, *Lettre sur la société des esprits*, op. cit., p. 1139.

8   *La Nouvelle Revue Française* 80, 1 August 1959

9   In *L'Amitié* (Paris: Gallimard, 1971), pp. 109–17; "Marx's Three Voices," trans. Tom Keenan, *New Political Science* 15 (Summer 1986). Page numbers in the text refer to this translation, which has been somewhat modified here in accordance with the emphasis on certain terms. (Tr.)

10 There are three idiomatic expressions here—*ça va, ça marche, par les temps qui courent*—that all speak of movement: going, walking, running. (Tr.)

11 *Hamlet*, trans. Yves Bonnefoy (Paris: Gallimard, Folio, 1992).

12 *Hamlet*, trans. Jean Malaplate (Paris: Corti, 1991).

13 *Hamlet*, trans. Jules Derocquigny (Paris: Les Belles Lettres, 1989).

14 *Hamlet*, trans. André Gide (Paris: Gallimard, Bibliothèque de la Pléïade, 1959).

15 I must here refer to a more systematic approach to these questions of law and the oblique (especially with regard to Kant), notably in my *Du droit à la philosophie* (Paris: Galilée, 1990), p. 80 and *passim*, and in *Passions* (Paris: Galilée, 1993), pp. 33ff.

16 That is, respectively, "to rejoin," "to return to order," "to put right again," "to put back in place." (Tr.)

17 On the manner in which these values are in turn gathered up in those of the title, cf. my "Title (to be specified)," in *Sub-Stance* 31, 1981.

18 Emmanuel Lévinas, *Totalité et infini* (The Hague: Martinus Nijhoff, 1961), p. 62.

19 "*Dikē, aus dem Sein als Anwesen gedacht, ist der fügend-fugende Fug.* Adikia, *die Un-Fuge, ist der Un-Fug*," Martin Heidegger, "Der Spruch des Anaximander," in *Holzwege* (Frankfurt am Main: Klostermann, 1950), p. 329; "*Dikē*, thought on the basis of Being as presencing, is the ordering and enjoining Order. *Adikia*, disjunction, is Disorder," "The Anaximander Fragment," in *Early Greek Thinking: The Dawn of Western Philosophy*, trans. David Farrell Krell and Frank A. Capuzzi (New York: Harper & Row,1975), p. 43.

20 *Holzwege*, pp. 326–27; *Early Greek Thinking*, p. 41.

21 *Holzwege*, p. 323; *Early Greek Thinking*, p. 37.

22 *Holzwege*, p. 330; *Early Greek Thinking*, p. 44.

23 Ibid.

24 "Er sagt es und sagt es nicht," *Holzwege*, p. 328; *Early Greek Thinking*, p. 42.

25 *Holzwege*, p. 327; *Early Greek Thinking*, p. 41.

26 Cf. *Given Time*, p. 2, n. 2 and ff., and pp. 159–60, n. 28, and *Sauf le nom* (Paris: Galilée, 1992), pp. 83 and 112.

27 *Holzwege*, p. 329; *Early Greek Thinking*, p. 43.

28 The term used here is *prévenance*, which ordinarily has the sense of thoughtfulness, consideration, kindness, but is here being taken also in its etymological sense of "coming before."(Tr.)

29 This is perhaps a reference specifically to the "programmes d'agrégation," that is, to the list of works drawn up annually by the French university establish-

ment for the competitive examination that qualifies the successful candidates for advanced teaching positions in each discipline. (Tr.)

30   This point is developed in *Passions,* op. cit.

31   For a novel elaboration, in a "deconstructive" style, of the concept of *hegemony,* I refer to Ernesto Laclau and Chantal Mouffe, *Hegemony and Socialist Strategy: Toward a Radical Democratic Politics* (London: Verso, 1985).

32   Karl Marx and Frederick Engels, *The German Ideology,* in *Collected Works* (New York: International Publishers, 1976), pp. 230–31.

33   *The German Ideology,* p. 230.

34   *A Contribution to the Critique of Political Economy,* chapter 2, part 2 b ("The Circulation of Money") (New York: International Publishers, 1970).

35   *Critique,* p. 109.

36   *Critique,* p. 132.

37   *Critique,* p. 142. This is a semantic chain that we have examined in *Glas* (in Hegel) and in *Of Spirit: Heidegger and the Question.*

38   *Critique,* p. 119 and 140.

39   *Critique,* p. 134.

40   The idiomatic expression here is "(se) fait peur," frightens (itself). Literally, however, it says: to make (itself) fright. Later, the text will exploit this literality when it describes a structure of the self as fear or fright, as that which makes itself into fear. (Tr.)

2   conjuring—marxism

1   This fragmentary outline of Hölderlin's (1800) is quoted by Heidegger in *Hölderlin und das Wesen der Dichtung,* in *Gesamtausgabe* vol. IV (Frankfurt am Main: Klostermann, 1981), p. 35; "Hölderlin and the Essence of Poetry," trans. Douglas Scott, in *Existence and Being,* ed. Werner Brock (Chicago: Henry Regnery Company, 1949).

2   Benjamin does so in a text that interests us here for many reasons, in particular for what it says, at its beginning, about the automaton. We will refer more than once to the figure of the automaton, notably when we get around to what *Capital* has to say about a certain *table*: figure of market value, at once an autonomous and automaton specter, the irreducible origin of capitalizations if not *of* capital. Benjamin begins by evoking the story "of an automaton constructed in such a way that it could play a winning game of chess, answering each move of an opponent with a countermove." This automaton also sits on a "table" that a system of mirrors made appear transparent. Then he looks for a philosophical "counterpart" (*Gegenstück*) to this "device" (*Apparatur*). It is "the puppet called 'historical materialism'": "It can easily be a match for anyone if it enlists the services of theology, which today, as we know, is wizened and has

to keep out of sight." The following paragraph names messianism or, more precisely, messianic without messianism, a "*weak* messianic power" (*eine schwache messianische Kraft*, Benjamin underscores). Let us quote this passage for what is consonant there, despite many differences and keeping relative proportions in mind, with what we are trying to say here about a certain messianic destitution, in a spectral logic of inheritance and generations, but a logic turned toward the future no less than the past, in a heterogeneous and disjointed time. What Benjamin calls *Anspruch* (claim, appeal, interpellation, address) is not far from what we are suggesting with the word *injunction*. "The past carries with it a secret index [*heimlichen Index*] by which it is referred to redemption [*Erlösung*].... There is a secret agreement between past generations and the present one. Our coming was expected on earth. Like every generation that preceded us, we have been endowed with a *weak* messianic power, a power to which the past has a claim [*Anspruch*]. That claim cannot be settled cheaply. Historical materialists are aware of that [*Der historische Materialist weisz darum*]" ("Uber den Begriff der Geschicht," in *Illuminationen* [Frankfurt am Main: Suhrkamp, 1955], pp. 183-84; "Theses on the Philosophy of History," in *Illuminations* [New York: Schocken, 1969], pp. 253-54; trans. modified). We should quote and reread here all these pages—which are dense, enigmatic, burning—up to the final allusion to the "chip" (shard, splinter: *Splitter*) that the messianic inscribes in the body of the at-present (*Jetztzeit*) and up to the "strait gate" for the passage of the Messiah, namely, every "second." For "this does not imply, however, that for the Jews the future turned into homogeneous, empty time" (p. 264).

3 New York: The Free Press, 1992. *La fin de l'histoire et le Dernier Homme*, the French translation by D.A. Canal (Paris: Flammarion), was published *the same year*.

4 I.e., the one who or that which arrives, or simply the arriving. Derrida makes extensive use of the word in another recent text, *Aporias* (trans. Thomas Dutoit [Stanford: Stanford University Press, 1993]). We have left it untranslated throughout. (Tr.)

5 Ibid., p. 203.

6 Ibid., p. 139; the quotation marks around "empirical" disappear when it is a question of "empirical evidence of challenges to democracy," p. 288.

7 There is an allusion here to the fact that not only was Fukuyama's book translated into French (and doubtless into other languages as well) the same year the original appeared (1992), but it was also given a lot of "play" by the French media, including television "reviews." (Tr.)

8 In a work that is remarkable in many respects, and which I became aware of, unfortunately, only after having written this text, Etienne Balibar recalls that the formula "dialectical materialism" was not literally used either by Marx or Engels (*La Philosophie de Marx* [Paris: La Découverte, 1993], p. 4). Among all

the priceless contributions of a book that also interprets and displaces in a very dense fashion a whole history of Marxism (and notably of French Marxism of the last decades), I will pick up schematically those that are most pertinent to me here: (1) The necessity of taking into account the motif of Marx's "injunction" (the word returns frequently, for example, pp. 19, 20, 24, and so forth); (2) the theme of the "spellbound" world as world of market-values (pp. 59 ff.) around the "non-sensuous sensuous" (which we will talk about later); (3) the category of imminence—whether messianic or not, in any case anutopic— (pp. 38, 39, 69, 118), but especially that of "transition," a category "glimpsed by Marx" as "a political figure of 'non-contemporaneity' to itself of historical time, yet which remains inscribed by him in the *provisional*" (p. 104). (On "transition" and non-contemporaneity, cf. above, pp. 24–25). Of course, it is not in a last-minute note that one can initiate a discussion or spell out one's agreement. To begin to do so, I would have to adjust what I am attempting to say here, behind these words, about the *philosophy* or the *ontology* of Marx (that which remains deconstructible in his philosophems) to what Balibar advances in *La Philosophie de Marx*: "there is not and there never will be a Marxist philosophy" (p. 3), which should not prevent one from "seeking...the *philosophies* of Marx" (p. 7). Since what I am calling here Marx's philosophy or ontology does not belong exactly to the space or the level of utterances analyzed by Balibar, the protocols of a discussion, wherever they may lead,would require a long and detailed elaboration. But I hope that such protocols are readable, at least in the implicit state, in an essay that is as schematic and preliminary as this one.

9 Quoted by Michel Surya, "La puissance, les riches et la charité," in *Lignes* 18, 1993, pp. 21 and 29.

10 Alexandre Kojève, *Introduction à la lecture de Hegel: Leçons sur "La Phénoménologie de l'Esprit"* (Paris: Gallimard, 1947), pp. 436-37.

3   *wears and tears*

1 The text cites François-Victor Hugo's translation: "*Le Poète:* Il y a longtemps que je ne vous ai vu. Comment va le monde? *Le Peintre:* Il s'use, Monsieur, à mesure qu'il croît en âge." (Tr.)

2 Allan Bloom, quoted by Michel Surya (op. cit., p. 30) who points out that Bloom was Fukuyama's "master and laudator."

3 Two recent examples, snatched out of the stream of "information," at the moment of rereading this pages. They are two more or less calculated "faux-pas" whose possibility would have been unthinkable without the current medium and rhythms of the press. (1) Two cabinet ministers attempt to influence a governmental policy that is being formulated (under the direction of one of their colleagues) by explaining themselves to the press (essentially the

ect of a letter said to be "private" (secret, "person-
y wrote to the head of the government and which
ed against their will. Despite himself, and without
t, the head of the government nevertheless follows
ernment, followed by the Parliament. (2) While
ike a blunder during a morning radio interview,
e government provokes in a neighboring country a
al bank and a whole politico-diplomatic process.
ne role played by the speed and power of the media
n—individual and international—speculator who,
ores up this or that national currency. His telephone
arks weigh heavily in all the legislative bodies of the
d the political decision of governments.
ld have to add the economic dependency of the U.N.,
king about its major interventions (political, socio-educa-
or military) or simply its administrative management. Now,
cknowledge that the U.N. is going through a serious financial
gest States do not all pay their dues. Solution: a campaign to
attract the support of private capital, constitution of "councils" (associations of
the biggest leaders in industry, commerce, and finance) meant to support, on
certain conditions, either spoken or unspoken, a politics of the U.N. that can
go (often, here or there, here rather than there, precisely) in the direction of
the interests of the market. One must underscore and reflect on the fact that
the principles that are today guiding international institutions often agree
with such interests. Why, how, and within what limits do they do so? What do
these limits signify? This is the only question we can pose here for the
moment.

5 On these points, cf. Etienne Balibar, *Cinq études du matérialisme historique* (Paris:
   Maspero, 1974), notably the chapter on "La rectification du *Manifeste commu-
   niste*" and the pages on "The 'end of politics',", "The new definition of the
   State," and "A new political practice," pp. 83 ff.

6 By specifying "women's and children's rights," the text is not distinguishing
   them from human rights, but rather remarking on the possible exclusion indicated by the French expression: "les droits de l'homme," the rights of man.
   (Tr.)

7 The phrase "en veillant (sur) ses ancêtres" puts in play first of all the sense of
   keeping watch over the bodies of the dead until they are buried, as is the cus-
   tom in France and elsewhere. (Tr.)

8 On this difference between justice and law [*droit*], permit me to refer once
   again to "Force of Law" (op. cit., above p. 177, n. 4). The necessity of this distinction does not entail the least disqualification of the juridical, its specificity,
   and the new approaches it calls for today. Such a distinction appears on the

contrary to be indispensable and prior to any reelaboration. In particular, in all the places where one may remark what is called today, more or less calmly, "juridical voids," as if it were a matter of filling in the blanks without re-doing things from top to bottom. There is nothing surprising in the fact that it is most often a question of *the property and proper nature of life* [la propriété de la vie], of its inheritance, and of its generations (the scientific, juridical, economic, and political problems of the so-called human genome, gene therapy, organ transplants, surrogate mothers, frozen embryos, and so forth). To believe that it is merely a matter of filling in a "juridical void," there where the point is to think the law, the law of the law, right, and justice, to believe that it is enough to produce new "articles of the legal code" to "regulate the problem," would be tantamount to turning over the thinking of ethics to an ethics committee.

9   But what does "to radicalize" mean? It is not, by a long shot, the best word. It does indicate a movement of going further, of course, and of not stopping. But that is the limit of its pertinence. The point would be to do more or less than "radicalize," or rather something other, for the stakes are precisely those of the root and its presumed unity. The point would be not to progress still further into the depths of radicality, of the fundamental, or the originary (cause, principle, *arkhē*), while taking another step in the same direction. One would try instead to go there where the schema of the fundamental, of the originary, or of the radical, in its *ontological* unity and in the form in which it continues to govern the Marxist critique, calls for questions, procedures of formalization, genealogical interpretations that are *not* or *not sufficiently* put to work in what dominates the discourses that call themselves Marxist. Not sufficiently in the thematics and in the consequence. For the questioning unfolding of these formalizations and of these genealogies affects almost the whole discourse, and in a way that is not just "theoretical," as one says. The stake that is serving as our guiding thread here, namely, the concept or the schema of the ghost, was heralded long ago, and in its own name, across the problematics of the work of mourning, idealization, simulacrum, *mimesis*, iterability, the double injunction, the "double bind," and undecidability as condition of responsible decision, and so forth.

This is perhaps the place to underscore the fact that relations between Marxism and deconstruction have called forth, since the beginning of the 1970s, approaches that are various in all respects, often opposed or irreducible the one to the other, but numerous. Too numerous for me to be able to do them justice here and recognize my debt to them. Besides those works which took this as their proper subject (such as that of Michael Ryan, *Marxism and Deconstruction: A Critical Articulation* [Baltimore: Johns Hopkins University Press, 1982], or *Marx est mort*, by Jean-Marie Benoist [Paris: Gallimard, 1970], the first part of which, despite its title, salutes Marx, aims to be deliberately "deconstructive,"and less negative than the death certificate would lead one to think; the title of this present work may be read as a reply to that of J.-M. Benoist, however much time it may have taken or left to time, to the *con-tretemps*—that is to the *revenant*), one would have to recall a great number of essays that it is impossible to list here (those in particular by J.-J. Goux, T. Keenan, T. Lewis, C. Malabou, B. Martin, A. Parker, G. Spivak, M. Sprinker, A. Warminski, S. Weber).

10   It is not clear whether the "foule crimes" that happened "in my dayes of Nature" were his or not. And this is, perhaps, the secret of these "secrets of my Prison-House" which it is "forbid" to the King to reveal. Performatives *en abyme*. The oaths, the calls to swear, the injunctions, and the conjurations that then proliferate—as in all of the plays of Shakespeare, who was a great thinker and great poet of the oath—suppose a secret, to be sure, some impossible testimony, one which cannot and especially must not be exposed in a confession, still less in a proof, a piece of evidence, or a constative utterance of the type S is P. But this secret also keeps the secret of some absolute contradiction between two experiences of the secret: I tell you that I cannot tell you, I swear it, that is my first crime and my first confession, a confession without confession. They do not exclude any other of the kind, believe me.

4   *in the name of the revolution*

1   Sigmund Freud, "Eine Schwierigkeit der Psychoanalyse," *Gesammelte Werke*, Bd. XII, p. 8; Standard Edition, Vol. XVII, p. 141.

2   We will approach this scene below (pp. 147 ff.), around a certain table, regarding fetishization as spectralization of exchange-value. It is the very opening, the first scene, if not the primal scene, of *Capital*.

3   *A Contribution to the Critique of Political Economy* (1859), trans. S. W. Ryazanskaya, ed. Maurice Dobb (New York: International Publishers, 1970), p. 107.

4   On the expression "faire peur," cf. above, p. 180, n. 40. (Tr.)

5   Perverse logic, abyssal perversity of all "revisionisms" that mark the end of this century and will doubtless continue into the next. Of course, there must be no let-up in the opposition to the worst revisionisms and negationisms, those whose figure and interests are now fairly well determined, even if their manifestations continually proliferate and get renewed. The task will therefore always be urgent, always something to be reaffirmed. But here and there one sees advance signs of a symmetrical perversity that is no less threatening. Armed with a good conscience that is imperturbable because often enveloped in ignorance or obscurantism, sheltered from any effective right to reponse in the mass media (I am thinking of a certain recent article by Michiko Kakutani, "When History and Memory Are Casualties: Holocaust Denial," *New York Times*, 30 April 1993), there are those who are not content to profit from the

ghosts that haunt our most painful memory. They also authorize themselves thereby, in the same élan, to *manipulate* with impunity, without any scruple, the very word "revisionism." They are prepared to use it to accuse anyone who poses critical, methodological, epistemological, philosophical questions about history, about the way it is thought, written, or established, about the status of truth, and so forth. Whoever calls for vigilance in the reading of history, whoever complicates a little the schemas accredited by the *doxa*, or demands a reconsideration of the concepts, procedures, and productions of historical truth or the presuppositions of historiography, and so forth, risks being accused today, through amalgamation, contagion, or confusion, of "revisionism" or at least of playing into some "revisionism." This accusation is now at the disposal of the first comer who understands nothing of this critical necessity, who wishes to be protected from it, and wants first of all his or her culture or lack of culture, his or her certainties or beliefs to be left untouched. A very disturbing historical situation which risks imposing an *a priori* censorship on historical research or on historical reflection wherever they touch on sensitive areas of our present existence. It is urgent to point out that entire wings of history, that of this century in particular, in Europe and outside of Europe, will *still* have to be interrogated and brought to light, radical questions will have to be asked and reformulated without there being anything at all "revisionist" about that. Let us even say: on the contrary.

6 *The Eighteenth Brumaire of Louis Bonaparte*, in Karl Marx, Frederick Engels, *Collected Works*, vol. 11 (New York: International Publishers, 1979), pp. 103-04; emphasis added.

7 We are obviously thinking here of the work of Michel Henry (*Marx* in two volumes [Paris: Gallimard, 1976]) who classifies the *Eighteenth Brumaire*, as well as *The Manifesto of the Communist Party* and a few other works, among the "political" or "historico-political" texts. They are, according to Henry, less philosophical, if indeed they are philosophical, because they "do not bear their principle of intelligibility within themselves" (I, p. 10). (What does it mean, strictly speaking, for a text to *bear a principle of intelligibility within itself*? [Patrice Loraux devotes to this strategy of Michel Henry several very lucid pages of his book (*Les Sous-Main de Marx* [Paris: Hachette, 1986], pp. 34–36) in the foreword titled "The Theory of Texts"; in particular, he recalls the tradition of this strategy]; has there ever been an example of it? This is not the place to discuss it—even though the strange and confident belief in such an immanence of intelligibility is not foreign to the concept of life that supports this whole book.) This "historico-political" dimension (either weakly philosophical or non-philosophical) would be manifest, according to Henry, in the "case notably of the *Eighteenth Brumaire of Louis Bonaparte*, written for an American newspaper" (I, p. 11). Now, this latter work does not seem to be at all bounded by the closure of "political" or "historico-political" texts, assum-

ing that one can accept such a problematic distinction, in particular in the case of a work like that of Marx. Notably one finds again his spectral paradoxology, the one that matters to us here, in the most "philosophical" and significant texts in Henry's own view, for example, as we will soon see, in *The German Ideology*. By weighing and thinking this spectrology, we are not directly opposing the philosophy of life or of the "radical subjectivity from which any objectivity is excluded" (I, p. 326), nor its interpretation by Henry (with whom we share at least some concerns, but doubtless from a wholly different point of view, about the way Marx has been read until now). But we are trying to accept the necessity of complicating it in an abyssal fashion, there where the supplement of an internal-external fold forbids simply opposing the living to the non-living. Whoever subscribes, as we would be tempted to do, to the final words of the very last conclusion of Henry's *Marx* ("Marx's thought places us before the abyssal question: what is life?") has indeed to refer to this abyss, which is to say, to re-problematize all the preceding statements of that book which is so wholly about the *living*, the *living* individual, *living* subjectivity, real work as *living* work, and so forth, in other words, the whole critical arsenal of a profoundly polemical work. For it is finally in the name of this univocal reference to the living that it tries, with great violence, to discredit more or less all previous readings of Marx, and especially in their political dimension. One wonders: Why would the question of life be "abyssal," precisely? In other words, why this question? Does it not open onto the unthought non-self-identity of the concept or the being called "life"? Onto the essential obscurity, for both science and philosophy, of what is called life? Does not all of this mark the internal or external limits, the closure or principle of ruin of a philosophy of life? And of subjectivity, however novel its conceptual presentation may be, once it is determined as essentially living? If one integrates into the life of this living subjectivity the work of negativity or of objectivity, the phenomena or rather the non-phenomena of death and so forth, why persist in calling it life? On the other hand, we do not think this interpretation of being or of production as manifestation—or radical immanence—of a living and monadic subjectivity (cf. for example II, pp. 41–42), an interpretation that is found to be widely justified in the letter of numerous texts of Marx, should be opposed by some philosophy of death (which could claim just as many rights and references in the same texts read differently). We are attempting something else. To try to accede to the possibility of this very alternative (life and/or death), we are directing our attention to the effects or the petitions of a survival or of a return of the dead (neither life nor death) on the sole basis of which one is able to speak of "living subjectivity" (in opposition to its death): to speak of it but also to understand that it can, itself, speak and speak of itself, leave traces or legacies beyond the living present of its life, ask (itself) questions regarding its own subject, in short, also address itself to the other or, if one prefers, to other living individuals, to other "monads." For all these questions, and such is the hypothesis of our reading, the work of the specter here weaves, in the shadow of a labyrinth covered with mirrors, a tenuous but indispensable guiding thread.

8   The text introduces this passage by pointing out that "the French translation most often loses these traits." (Tr.)

9   Before I had found this allusion to the "red specter" in *The Eighteenth Brumaire*, Etienne Balibar had alerted me to the existence of a newspaper titled *The Red Specter* ("during the Revolution of '48...apparently after the June massacres...that is, the specter of the dead proletarian revolutionaries"). "'I am announcing the *jacquerie!*' writes Romieu in *The Red Specter.* 'The proletarians are ready, lying in ambush in the least little village, hate and envy in their hearts...'" (cited by J. Bruhat, *Le Socialisme français de 1848 à 1871*, in *Histoire générale du socialisme* [Paris: Presses Universitaires de France, 1972-78], vol. I, p. 507). "One also thinks," adds Balibar, "of 'the specter of the red death' by Villiers de l'Isle-Adam, written, if I am not mistaken, after the Commune, even if the 'red death' is not apparently the same thing as the 'death of the reds'..."

10 Cf. above, p. 186, n. 7.

11 "Stirner discovers that at the end of the ancient world, 'spirit' 'again foamed and frothed over irresistibly because *gases*' (spirits) [*Gase/Geister*] 'developed within it...'" Marx then analyzes the "wonderful play" that Saint Max thus describes (*The German Ideology*, in Marx and Engels, *Collected Works* 5 (New York: International Publishers, 1976), pp. 186–87). Hegel had already been attentive to the affinity *Gas-Geist*: the work of death, the fermentation of the cadaver in decomposition mark the passage from a philosophy of nature to a philosophy of spirit. On these themes, permit me to refer to *Glas* (especially pp. 59, 91, 235) and *Of Spirit* (p. 99).

12 *The German Ideology*, p. 153. As is well known, Marx constantly weaves into his polemical remarks long quotations from *Der Einzige und sein Eigenthum* (1845; translated as *The Ego and His Own*).

13 The word "chaire," pulpit or professorial chair, is a homonym of "chair," flesh. (Tr.)

14 On the tangled and overdetermined history of the relations with Stirner and on the historico-political context of this polemic, cf. Henri Arvon, *Aux sources de l'existentialisme, Max Stirner* (Paris: Presses Universitaires de France, 1954), pp. 128ff.

5   *apparition of the inapparent*

1   The English translation of *The German Ideology* retains "conjuring trick" for

Marx and Engels' term *Eskamotage*. We will do so as well for obvious reasons, although the French word "escamotage" could also be translated by "dodge," "evasion," "filching," "pinching," and so forth. (Tr.)

2 The French term has the sense of a secret conversation, sometimes with conspiratorial overtones. See below, Derrida's own gloss. (Tr.).

3 On the strangely murmured implication of death (not only of an "I am mortal" but of an "I am dead") in the declaration of the "I am," cf. my *Speech and Phenomena* (Evanston, Ill.: Northwestern University Press, 1973), pp. 88 ff.

4 Cf. pp. 157, 449, and especially 229.

5 In French, *ça me regarde*: it is looking at me, but also more idiomatically, that's my concern. (Tr.)

6 Of course, the narrow and strict concept of the phantom or the *phantasma* will never be reduced to the generality of the *phainesthai*. Concerned with the original experience of haunting, a phenomenology of the spectral ought, according to good Husserlian logic, to isolate a very determined and relatively derived field within a regional discipline (for example, a phenomenology of the image, and so forth). Without contesting here the legitimacy, or even the fertility of such a delimitation, we are merely suggesting the following, without being able here to go any further: the radical possibility of all spectrality should be sought in the direction that Husserl identifies, in such a surprising but forceful way, as an intentional but *non-real* [*non-réelle*] component of the phenomenological lived experience, namely, the *noeme*. Unlike the three other terms of the two correlations (noese-noeme, *morphē-hulē*), this non-reality [*non-réellité*], this intentional but *non-real* inclusion of the noematic correlate is neither "in" the world nor "in" consciousness. But it is precisely the condition of any experience, any objectivity, any phenomenality, namely, of any noetico-noematic correlation, whether originary or modified. It is no longer regional. Without the non-real inclusion of this intentional component (therefore inclusive *and* non-inclusive inclusion: the noeme is included without being a part), one could not speak of any manifestation, of any phenomenality in general (that being-for-a-consciousness, that appearing appearance which is neither consciousness nor the being that appears to it). Is not such an "irreality" [*irréellité*], *its independence both* in relation to the world *and* in relation to the *real* stuff of egological subjectivity, the very place of apparition, the essential, general, non-regional possibility of the specter? Is it not also what inscribes the possibility of the other and of mourning right onto the phenomenality of the phenomenon?

7 When *The German Ideology* recalls the Hegelian origin of Stirner's philosophy of history, it insists on another thematics of the Negro, the one for which "'The *Negroid character* [*die Negerhaftigkeit*] represents *antiquity*, dependence on *things*' (*child*)," pp. 163 ff.

8 Cf. *The Republic*, 555e.

9   This precise sense of the word from venery has been glossed over in everyday usage where *acharnement, s'acharner* mean, as we will continue to translate, ferocity, relentless pursuit. But the form of the word retains what is most pertinent here and will be exploited more later: its link to flesh, to the carnal, to *chair*. We will insert it in brackets whenever this link needs to be underscored. (Tr.)

10 The term used here is *voler* ("il a *volé* les spectres de Marx"). The play is on the exact homonyms which mean "to steal" and "to fly," the latter also having a relation to *volerie*, that is, hunting with birds of prey. (Tr.)

11 The phrase is "chasse à l'éloignement" in which "éloignement" could indeed designate either the hunter's prey or the means of the hunt. The other untranslatable feature of this sentence is the link between "longtemps" and "éloignement," which is not repeated in "long time" and "distance." (Tr.)

12 As we are attempting here to reaffirm the heritage of Marx while according it or bending it to a thinking of the spectral that takes into account (in particular in the political apprehension of the *res publica* and its—more or less new— space) an irreducible *virtuality* (virtual space, virtual object, synthetic image, spectral simulacrum, teletechnological differ*a*nce, *idealiterability*, trace beyond presence and absence, and so forth), we must attach great importance to what Patrice Loraux himself says, in a well-chosen formulation, about "Marx's writing" as "synthetic image" and "virtual object." He is talking about a Marxist discourse that "does not, therefore, accede by itself to the threshold of readability." The written does not remain under "Marx's hand," within reach of his body that "takes pleasure in holding on to it" (but also, we should say, in not holding on to it, and everything begins with this other pleasure, which is nevertheless the same). Loraux then comments: "But, with us in mind, publishers fabricate a completely other object: Marx's text, product of a sophistical *manipulation* that must furnish the reader with a *synthetic image* of Marx's writing, for the latter is never but a virtual object, and no one holds it in his *hand*" (*Les Sous-main de Marx*, pp. 21–22; emphasis added).

13 As a necessary and fascinating task, one ought of course to read Stirner beyond the extracts (which are generous, it is true) that *The German Ideology* selects and submits most often to the twist of satire. One ought as well to reconstitute a tradition or genealogy, which traverses Stirner's text, of this thematics of the ghost in the nineteenth century, at least, from Kant (not only the Kant interested in Swedenborg, but the thinker of the transcendental imagination and thus of all the conceptual third terms that the fantastic introduced between the sensible and the intelligible, which are so many propitious places for spectrality), to the Schopenhauer of the *Essay on Ghosts* (*Versuch über Geistersehen und was damit zusammenhängt*, 1851), to Nietzsche—who had indirect knowledge of Stirner's texts and recommended them to Baumgartner in 1874, or to Mallarmé, whose work keeps watch next to a "ghost white as a still

unwritten page" (*Mimique*). As such a reconstitution exceeds the limits of our concerns here, let us cite at least once a few passages from *The Ego and His Own*: "The Romantics felt the attack on the very faith in God represented by the abandonment of belief in spirits and ghosts; they sought to remedy the fatal consequences of this, not only by resuscitating the world of fable but especially by 'opening the gates to a higher world' with their sleep-walkers, Prévorst's clairvoyants, etc. The faithful and the Church Fathers did not realize that by destroying belief in ghosts, they were also taking away the basis of religion, which left it floating, detached from the ground that nourished it. Whoever no longer believes in ghosts has only to pursue his unbelief to its conclusion to realize that there is no being hidden behind things, no ghost or—what comes down to the same thing if one understands the word in its naive sense—no 'spirit'." And under the heading of "specter" or "spook": "With ghosts, We enter into the realm of spirits, of *beings*. What haunts the universe, pursuing there its secret and unfathomable activities, is the mysterious spook We call the Supreme Being. For centuries, men have given themselves the task of knowing its nature, of *conceiving* it, of discovering *reality* there (of proving 'the existence of God'); it is in this frightening, impossible, and endless labor of Danaïdes that they persist, seeking to change the specter into a non-specter, the unreal into the real, the *spirit* into a total person of *flesh* and *blood*." *The Ego and His Own*, trans. Steven T. Byington, ed. John Carroll (New York: Harper & Row, 1971). [This is an abridged edition of Byington's 1907 translation and does not include the passages quoted by Derrida. These may be found in *L'Unique et sa Propriété et autres écrits*, trans. P. Gallissaire et A. Sauge (Paris: Bibliothèque l'Age d'Homme, 1972), pp. 107 and 112 respectively. (Tr.)]

14 Marx thus refuses the mirages of Saint Max's Christian onto-theology as Saint Max had already refused the mirages of Christian onto-theology. Both of them relentlessly pursue [*s'acharnent sur*] ghosts, both of them chase and hunt them, and *they are the same* except that Marx's relentless pursuit chases (those of) the relentless other, Saint Max. But both mean to chase the onto-theological and trinitary specter in the name of a more demanding ontology that not only no longer confuses the *revenant* with the being as living body, in flesh and blood, but especially does not confuse it with that arch-ghost in flesh and blood that is, as Saint Max explains so clearly, Christ, God made Man in the incarnation. Marx and Saint Max seem to put in question, others might say a little quickly "deconstruct," an onto-theological and Christian phenomenology; but it is to the extent that it is occupied, they both say, and thus inhabited, haunted only by ghosts. Their "deconstruction" is limited at the point at which they *both* oppose this spectral onto-theology—each in his own way but regardless of the differences between them—to the hyper-phenomenological principle of the flesh-and-blood presence of the living person, of the being

itself, of its effective and non-phantomatic presence, of presence in flesh and blood.

The program of this disagreement is interesting in itself, to be sure, but it also furnishes us with a virtual model for many debates going on today. It also matters to us for this reason.

15   Let us once again quote Stirner beyond the excerpt that Marx supplies: "The longing to make the spook comprehensible, or to realize *non-sens* [in French in the text], has brought about a *corporeal ghost*, a ghost or spirit with a real body, an embodied ghost. How the strongest and most talented Christians have tortured themselves to get a conception of this ghostly apparition! But there always remained the contradiction of two natures, the divine and human, the ghostly and sensual; there remained the most wondrous spook, a thing that was not a thing. Never yet was a ghost more soul-torturing.… But through Christ the truth of the matter had at the same time come to light, that the veritable spirit or ghost is—man.… Henceforth man no longer, in typical cases, shudders at ghosts *outside* him, but at himself. In the depth of his breast dwells the *spirit of sin*; even the faintest thought (and this is itself a spirit, you know) may be a devil, etc.—The ghost has put on a body, God has become man, but now man is himself the gruesome spook which he seeks to get behind, to exorcize, to fathom, to bring to reality and to speech; man is—spirit" *The Ego and His Own*, pp. 56–57).

16   In the conclusion of a book that has just appeared, *La pénultième est morte, Spectrographies de la modernité* (Paris: Champ Vallon, 1993), Jean-Michel Rabaté underscores forcefully that "Marx and Engels pretend not to understand the critical scope of Stirner's analyses" (p. 223). Even as he denies wanting thus to "rehabilitate 'Saint Max'," Rabaté remarkably reinscribes *The Ego and His Own* in a powerful lineage—which is thus spectrographic—that the anarchist posterity of the book is not even close to exhausting (from Shakespeare to Sade, Mallarmé, Joyce, Beckett).

17   In French, "une table tournante" refers most often to the spiritualist séance. (Tr.)

18   *Capital*, trans. Ben Fowkes (New York: Vintage, 1977), Vol. 1, Ch. 1, sect. 4, pp. 163 ff.

19   The English translation conjures away this difficulty with "a thing which transcends sensuousness." (Tr.)

20   "The form of wood, for instance, is altered if a table is made out of it. Nevertheless the table continues to be wood, an ordinary, sensuous thing. But as soon as it emerges as a commodity, it changes into a thing which transcends sensuousness. It not only stands with its feet on the ground, but, in relation to all other commodities, it stands on its head, and evolves out of its wooden brain grotesque ideas, far more wonderful than if it were to begin dancing of its own free will.

The mystical character of the commodity does not therefore arise from its use-value" (pp. 163–64).

21 As the editor specifies, "A reference to the simultaneous emergence in the 1850s of the Taiping revolt in China and the craze for spiritualism which swept over upper-class German society. The rest of the world was 'standing still' in the period of reaction immediately after the defeat of the 1848 Revolutions." Even though, as we have remarked, every period has its ghosts (and we have ours), its own experience, its own medium, and its proper hauntological media, even though an "epochal" history of haunting poses the same problems, and not by chance, as an "epochal" history of Being, this complication ought not to forbid an historical inquiry on this subject. It should merely cause such an inquiry to be very cautious. It is certain, for example, that the texts of Stirner, Marx, and Engels to which we are referring correspond—and respond—in their own time to a powerful "craze" that could summarily be called "mediumistic." One can find social, philosophical, and literary signs of this (let us recall Stirner's interest in Eugène Sue's *Mysteries of Paris*, the "spiritualist" temptations of Victor Hugo and a few others) and one can try to isolate, or even explain up to a certain point its historical singularity. But one must not fail to reinscribe it in a much larger spectrological sequence.

22 Trans. Alan Bass (Chicago: University of Chicago Press, 1982), p. 45.

23 The term is used in the sense of a mistaken substitution of one thing for another, in particular in the theater when characters reply to each other out of some misunderstanding, and not in the now prevalent sense in English of tit for tat. The English translation of the passage in question from *Capital* substitutes "substitution" for Marx's use of the Latin phrase. (Tr.)

24 Both a word that is whispered, for example by the prompter [*souffleur*], but also a word that is stolen or pinched. "La parole soufflée" is the title of Derrida's first essay on Artaud, in 1965, collected in *Writing and Difference*, trans. Alan Bass (Chicago: University of Chicago Press, 1978). (Tr.)

25 In the course of an admirable reading of *La Peau de chagrin*, Samuel Weber points out this *vampiristic* character of capital, this living monster (*beseeltes Ungeheuer*), and precisely in relation to the spectral logic of the fetish. Cf. *Unwrapping Balzac: A Reading of "La Peau de chagrin"* (Toronto: University of Toronto Press, 1979), p. 86, and especially notes 1–3 devoted to Marx—and to Balzac.

26 Since Marx was also, in a different way than Shakespeare, a thinker of the pact and the oath, one may consult what he ironically says about the oath in *The German Ideology*, p. 162.

27 However one interprets this trajectory, it goes back at least to what the third of the *1844 Manuscripts* says about death and the senses, about the manner in which the senses become "theoreticians" in their very practice, thus insensibi-

lizing, one could say, the sensible and ruining thereby in advance all oppositions between "subjectivism and objectivism, spiritualism and materialism."
Marx is thinking then and, it seems to me, will never cease to think that these
oppositions, deemed insoluble by a philosophy that would only see a theoretical task in them, are and or must be lifted by the state of society and by social
practice. Cf. *Economic and Philosophic Manuscripts of 1844*, trans. Martin Milligan
(Buffalo, N.Y.: Prometheus Books, 1987), pp. 105 ff.

28   *The German Ideology*, p. 161.

29   See *The Critique*, for example p. 93.

30   *Capital*, p. 184.

31   In the French translation cited by the text (ed. Jean-Pierre Lefebvre [Paris:
Presses Universitaires de France, "Quadrige" collection, 1993]), the final sentence of this passage reads: "Si donc nous nous échappons vers d'autres formes
de production, nous verrons disparaître instantanément tout le mysticisme du
monde de la marchandise, tous les sortilèges qui voilent d'une brume fantomatique les produits du travail accompli sur la base de la production
marchande." Derrida then comments in his text: "With the expression 'brume
fantomatique' [ghostly fog], the recent translation we are citing marks very
well the literal reference to the ghost (*Spuk*), there where so many earlier
translations regularly effaced it." (Tr.)

32   The English translation of this passage reads: "The riddle of the money fetish
is therefore the riddle of the commodity fetish, now become visible and dazzling to our eyes" (p. 187). (Tr.)

33   In its general form, I have attempted to approach it elsewhere (cf. in particular
Glas, pp. 42, 130, 206 ff., 222 ff., 237 ff.). On the relation between fetishism and
ideology, cf. Sarah Kofman *Camera obscura—de l'idéologie* (Paris: Galilée, 1973),
in particular what precedes and follows "La table tournante" (p. 21), and
Etienne Balibar, *Cinq études du matérialisme historique*, as concerns the "theory of
fetishism," pp. 206 ff.

34   Cf. Balibar, *Cinq études*, pp. 208 ff.

35   In the figure of its sensuous materiality, the proper body of this phantomatic
objectivity takes form, hardens, erects, or petrifies itself, *crystallizes* out of a
slack and undifferentiated substance, it institutes itself out of an amorphous
residue: "Let us now look at the residue of the products of labour. There is
nothing left of them in each case but the same phantom-like objectivity; they
are merely congealed quantities [*Gallerte*: gelatin, figure of the homogeneous
mass] of homogeneous human labour, i.e., of human labour-power expended
without regard to the form of its expenditure. All these things now tell us [all
that is presented in them: *Diese Dinge stellen nur noch dar*] is that human labour-
power has been expended to produce them, human labour is accumulated in
them. As crystals [*Als Kristalle*] of this social substance, which is common to
them all, they are values—commodity values" (*Capital*, p. 128).

On this "phantomatic objectivity" (*gespenstige Gegenständlichkeit*), cf. Samuel Weber (*Unwrapping Balzac*, p. 75) who, between Balzac and Marx, insists quite rightly on the feminine charater of the commodity-chimera. There is in fact more than one sign of this. But how to stabilize the sex of a fetish? Does it not pass from one sex to the other? Is it not this movement of passage, whatever may be its stases?

In a text that has just appeared, Thomas Keenan also analyzes, among other things, what gets "sublimated" in this "ghostly reality": "In the rigor of the abstraction, only ghosts survive" ("The Point Is To (Ex)change It," in *Fetishism as Cultural Discourse*, E. Apter and W. Pietz, eds. [Ithaca: Cornell University Press, 1993], p. 168).

36 For all these motifs, we refer obviously to the work of Paul Virilio, as well as to Bernard Stiegler, *La technique et le temps, La faute d'Épiméthée*, (Paris: Galilée, 1994).

37 The palindromic syntax here is: "tout autre est tout autre, "both "every other is altogether other," and "altogether other is every other." (Tr.)

38 Why does Freud consider haunting to be "perhaps the most striking of all [examples]," a kind of prototype, in the experience of *Unheimlichkeit*? Because many people experience "in the highest degree" (*im allerhöchsten Grade*) the sense of the "unheimlich" "in relation to death and dead bodies, to the return of the dead, and to spirits and ghosts" (*Geistern und Gespenstern*). But to the great chagrin of translators, Freud wants to illustrate this assertion by remarking not that "es spukt" is so difficult to translate (for the reasons we indicated above), but that "some languages in use to-day can only render the German expression '*ein unheimliches Haus*' by a house in which '*es spukt*' [*manche moderne Sprachen unseren Ausdruck: ein unheimliches Haus gar nicht anders wiedergeben können als durch dies Umschreibung: ein Haus, in dem es spukt*]" ("Das Unheimliche," *Gesammelte Werke*, XII, pp. 254–55). In truth, "unheimliche" is just as untranslatable as "es spukt." And this yields awkward and in fact incomprehensible translations. For example: "plusieurs langues modernes ne peuvent rendre notre expression 'une maison *unheimlich*' autrement que par cette circonlocution: une maison hantée" ("L'Inquiétante étrangeté," trans. M. Bonaparte et E. Marty, in *Essais de psychanalyse appliquée* [Paris: Gallimard, 1933], pp. 194–95); or again: "some languages in use to-day can only render the German expression 'an *unheimlich* house' by 'a *haunted* house' (*Standard Edition*, vol. XVII, p. 241). As for what Freud then puts forward concerning death itself, we return to it elsewhere in order to relate it to the discourses of Heidegger and Lévinas on this subject (cf. *Aporias*). Another period, another modality, another mode for ghosts: Freud remarks, on the same page, that distinguished lectures on communication with spirits were showing a tendency to proliferate. Subtle minds, he notes, among men of science and especially at the end of their lives, give into the telepathic or mediumistic temptation. He knew what he was

talking about. And since *Hamlet* will have been our subjet, let us specify that Freud deemed its apparitions wholly devoid of any power of *Unheimlichkeit* (*GW*, p. 265; *SE*, p. 251). Like those of Macbeth or Julius Caesar, like those in Dante's Inferno. They may be terrifying (*schreckhaft*) or lugubrious (*düster*), to be sure, but no more *unheimlich* than the world of Homeric gods. Explanation: literature, theatrical fiction. According to Freud, we adapt our judgment to the conditions of *fictive* reality, such as they are established by the poet, and treat "souls, spirits, and specters" like grounded, normal, legitimate existences (*vollberechtige Existenzen*). A remark that is all the more surprising in that all the examples of *Unheimlichkeit* in this essay are borrowed from literature!

39 Freud and Heidegger. In *The Post Card* (Chicago: Chicago University Press, 1987), the signatory of *Envois* couples them like two specters: "Here Freud and Heidegger, I conjoin them within me like the two great ghosts of the 'great epoch.' The two surviving grandfathers. They did not know each other, but according to me they form a couple, and in fact just because of that, this singular anachrony" (p. 191).

Given that a *revenant* is always called upon to come and to come back, the thinking of the specter, contrary to what good sense leads us to believe, signals toward the future. It is a thinking of the past, a legacy that can come only from that which has not yet arrived—from the *arrivant* itself.

index of names